# Instructor's Resource Manual

*for*

# The Longwood Guide to Writing

Ronald F. Lunsford
*University of North Carolina - Charlotte*

Bill Bridges
*Sam Houston State University*

Allyn and Bacon
Boston  London  Toronto  Sydney  Tokyo  Singapore

Copyright © 2000 by Allyn & Bacon
A Pearson Education Company
160 Gould Street
Needham Heights, Massachusetts 02494

Internet: www.abacon.com

All rights reserved. The contents, or parts thereof, may be reproduced for use with *The Longwood Guide to Writing*, by Ronald F. Lunsford and Bill Bridges, provided such reproductions bear copyright notice, but may not be reproduced in any form for any other purpose without written permission from the copyright owner.

ISBN 0-205-31092-3

Printed in the United States of America

10 9 8 7 6 5 4 3 2 1   03 02 01 00

**Acknowledgments:**

Page 199. Lunsford, Ronald F. "Planning for Spontaneity in the Writing Classroom and a Passel of Other Paradoxes." *Training the New Teacher of College Composition*. Ed. Charles W. Bridges with Ronald F. Lunsford and Toni A. Lopez. Urbana, IL: National Council of Teachers of English, 1986. Reprinted with permission of NCTE.

# Table of Contents

## Preface

## Syllabus Construction

    Sample Syllabi ................................................................. 1

## Chapter Guides

    Teaching Chapter 1 ........................................................... 21
        Invention: Finding Something to Say

    Teaching Chapter 2 ........................................................... 43
        Shaping an Essay

    Teaching Chapter 3 ........................................................... 50
        Revising

    Teaching Chapter 4 ........................................................... 56
        Responding to Readings

    Teaching Chapter 5 ........................................................... 62
        Personal Essays

    Teaching Chapter 6 ........................................................... 70
        Informative Essays

    Teaching Chapter 7 ........................................................... 78
        Evaluation Essays

    Teaching Chapter 8 ........................................................... 86
        Essays *About* and *From* Literature

    Teaching Chapter 9 ........................................................... 92
        Position Essays

    Teaching Chapter 10 ......................................................... 108
        Persuasion Essays

    Teaching Chapter 11 ......................................................... 117
        Problem/Solution Essays

    Teaching Chapter 12 ......................................................... 125
        Researching and Writing

Teaching Chapter 13 .................................................... 135
      Essay Examinations

Teaching Chapter 14 .................................................... 143
      Portfolio

Teaching Style (Chapters 15 and 16) ...................................... 145
      Working with Words
      Shaping Sentences

# *Theory and Practice*

"Logology and *The Longwood Guide to Writing*: What We Owe to Kenneth Burke" ........... 168

"Teaching Writing as Process" ............................................ 178

"Giving Feedback to Student Writers: Marking, Evaluating, and Responding" ................ 188

"Planning for Spontaneity in the Writing Classroom and a Passel of Other Paradoxes" ......... 199

"Newcomers in First-Year Composition: Teaching Writing to ESL Students" ................ 209

# *Preface*

## *How We Write*

*The Longwood Guide to Writing* is truly a collaborative effort, and we thought we'd give you an idea of how we write, or rather, how we wrote both our text and this manual. We'll take Chapter 5 as an example. Bill assumed primary responsibility for this chapter and wrote it, seeking help and answers to questions from Ron as needed throughout the thinking through, prewriting, shaping, drafting, and revising that chapter. Upon its completion, Bill shipped the chapter via e-mail to Ron, who then revised it and returned it to Bill, who then revised that revision and shipped that back to Ron, who made whatever comments he felt necessary and returned the chapter to Bill–we came to label this the ping-pong approach to composing. This back and forth movement of chapters continued till we were both satisfied that the chapter at hand said what it needed to. At times, we revised while working on new chapters all but simultaneously, realigning the order of the various sections until we felt we had the text in its proper order. Our text, then, is the result of a long process that was steeped in collaboration, so much so that, at times, it is difficult for us to know who wrote a particular section of a given chapter.

We have taken care not to enter *The Longwood Guide to Writing* as individual authors, but that's not the case in this manual. Even though we used the same process for writing the chapters in this guide that we used in writing the text, we elected to use first person where we thought it appropriate and less awkward to do so. (Self-referencing yourself via pronouns can indeed prove awkward.) To help you identify the principal author for each of the chapters, we've listed the name of that author (i.e., Ron or Bill or, in a couple of instances, both) at the end of the chapter so that you may identify which of us is speaking of our own classroom and teaching practice. In the case of co-authored chapters, we've listed the principal author first.

## *Pronoun Reference*

Throughout *The Longwood Guide to Writing* and this manual, we use third person singular pronouns when talking about individual student writers and individual teachers. To avoid the appearance of sexist use of language, we alternate between feminine and masculine pronouns, maintaining one or the other to fit the context of the passage in which it's at work. We did this because we think using such pronoun phrases as "he or she" and "her or him" and using third person plural in places where a singular pronoun makes more sense can make for awkward writing.

## *Structure of the Instructor's Resource Manual*

We've divided this manual into three parts:

First, *Syllabus Construction*, a section presenting sample syllabi for the various writing courses in which *The Longwood Guide to Writing* may be used. In this section, you'll find a syllabus for a one-semester course, a two-semester sequence with the second semester taking argumentation as its primary focus, and a two-semester course with the second semester taking literature as its primary focus. These syllabi are fairly detailed approximations of a day-by-day guide to using the text, and we present them to aid you in preparing your own syllabus.

Second, *Chapter Guides*, a section comprising guides to teaching each of the text's chapters. Each of these guides presents an overview of the chapter at hand, teaching tips, and responses to the chapter's exercises. Many of these responses were completed by Elizabeth Aragon, a graduate assistant in the Department of English at New Mexico State University, while other exercises one or both of us completed. We offer them not as the right answers but to suggest how student writers might respond. You may use the teaching tips and exercise responses as you see fit to support your work in the classroom.

Third, *Theory and Practice*, a section containing five essays discussing some of the theories that inform our text and some of the practices we employ in our own writing classrooms. "Logology and *The Longwood Guide to Writing*: What We Owe to Kenneth Burke" discusses several of the theoretical underpinnings of our text which are grounded in the writings of Kenneth Burke. "Teaching Writing as Process" offers our consideration of what it means to employ a process approach to composing. The third essay, "Giving Feedback to Student Writers: Marking, Evaluating, and Responding," discusses the teacher's role as a reader of student writing. "Planning for Spontaneity in the Writing Classroom and a Passel of Other Paradoxes," the fourth essay, originally appeared in *Training the New Teacher of College Composition* (1986); it is reprinted here with the permission of the National Council of Teachers of English. And the fifth, "Newcomers in First-year Composition: Teaching Writing to ESL Students," by Nancy Pfingstag, Lecturer in the English Language Training Institute at the University of North Carolina at Charlotte, discusses ways in which writing teachers may attend to the special needs of students for whom English is a second language.

# *Acknowledgments*

We wish to acknowledge the invaluable support of Paul D. Ruffin, Professor of English and Director of *Texas Review* Press, in preparing camera-ready copy of this guide. *Texas Review* Press is sponsored by Sam Houston State University's Department of English and Foreign Languages. We wish also to thank Melissa Morphew, Visiting Assistant Professor of English (Sam Houston State University) for her proofreading expertise and Christie McWillliams, a staff member of *Texas Review* Press, who helped prepare several of the graphics in the chapter guides section. Finally, we also wish to thank Eben W. Ludlow, Vice President (Allyn and Bacon), for his continuing patience as we worked to complete this manual.

Bill and Ron

# Sample Syllabi

We have designed *The Longwood Guide to Writing* as a flexible rhetoric that can be useful in several different teaching situations. In this section, we present syllabi that may be used as guides for:

1. a one-semester writing course that gives students practice in a full range of writing occasions.

2. a two-semester sequence in which the first course is dedicated to personal and expository writing and the second course to persuasive writing and research.

3. a two-semester sequence that combines the course outlined in #1 above with a course that focuses on writing about literature and research writing.

The syllabi presented below are designed for courses that would guide students in the writing of the following types of papers:

1. One-semester course (or first of two, in which the second focuses on writing about literature)

   Personal, Informative, Evaluation, Writing *From* Literature, Position, Portfolio

2. Two-course sequence:

   a. first course focusing on personal and expository writing:

   Personal, Informative, Evaluation, Writing *From* Literature, Writing *About* Literature, Essay Examination, Portfolio

   b. second course focusing on persuasive writing and research writing:

   Writer's Choice, Position, Persuasion, Research (Problem/Solution), Portfolio

3. Second course on literary writing (with a first course as outlined in #1 above).

   Writer's Choice, Writing *About* Literature, Writing *From* Literature, Essay Examination, Research (on literary topic), Portfolio

We devote the rest of this section to day-by-day syllabi for each of these courses and some discussion of key concepts and activities contained in these syllabi. Asterisks in the syllabi indicate items discussed in more detail after the syllabus, and numbers in parentheses represent page numbers in *The Longwood Guide to Writing*.

## 1. One-Semester Course (or first of two, with literature the focus of the second)

This one-semester course is designed to introduce students to several different types of writing–personal, informative, evaluative, literary, and argumentative. It does not treat persuasive writing (as distinguished from argumentative writing), problem solving, or research writing. There is also relatively little treatment of the process elements in Part 1 of *The Longwood Guide to Writing*. However, the concepts having to do with writing process are all present in the Writing Occasions chapters, since each of the these chapters contains a section entitled "Assignment and Guidelines for Writing" (that takes students through a writing process) and a section entitled "Sample Student Writing Process" (that shows the development of a piece of writing from beginning to end).

| Meeting | Readings Due | Other Work Due | Class Activities |
|---|---|---|---|
| **Week 1** Day 1 | | None | *Read Strategies for the Writing Process (1-6) in class and discuss |
| 2 *Getting Started: Personal Essay* | Ch 1 (7-14) | *Interest Inventory (8, 9) | Discuss Interest Inventory; do Exercise 1.2, p. 13; do Exercise 1.3, p.15; discuss. |
| 3 *Prewriting Activities* | Ch 1 (15-21); Occasions (125-129); Ch 5 (131-143) | Exercise 1.5, #1 (18); *selected Questions for Review | Discuss their prewriting; discuss sample stories and Questions for Review |
| **Week 2** 1 *Organizational Strategies* | Ch 2 (33-45 ); Ch 5 (144-150) | Focus Statement (151) for Personal Essay | Discuss readings; *discuss some of their focus statements |
| 2 *Peer Review Strategies* | Ch 5 (151-164); Ch 3 (75-78) | Selected exercises | *Fish Bowl |
| 3 *Peer Review* | | Discovery Draft of Personal Essay | *Group Peer Reviews |
| **Week 3** 1 *Revise for Diction* | *Style (535-541); Ch 15 (547-549; 556-564) | Selected exercises | Discuss exercises; if time, *let students work on revising their papers |
| 2 *Revise for Sentences* | Ch 3 (65-75); Ch 16 (571-573; 582-590) | Exercise 16.8 (589) | Discuss revision |
| 3 *Peer Review* | | Second Draft of Personal Essay | *Peer Critiques |
| **Week 4** 1 *Read-around* | | Final Draft of Personal Essay | *Read-around; introduce Informative Essay |
| 2 *Getting Started: Informative Essay* | Ch 6 (165-185) | Selected Questions for Review | Discuss readings |
| 3 *Prewriting* | Ch 6 (185-192); Ch 1 (22-29) | Selected exercises | Discuss exercises; do freewriting (192); then work with one or two of their topics, using the Questions for Analysis |

| | | | |
|---|---|---|---|
| **Week 5** 1 *Thesis Sentence* | Ch 6 (192-203); Ch 2 (46, 47) | Selected exercises; thesis for Informative Essay | Discuss readings; be sure their theses work; allow time for drafting |
| 2 *Revise for Diction* | Style (541-545); Ch 15 (549-555) | Selected exercises | Discuss readings and exercises; allow time for work on second draft |
| 3 *Peer Review* | | *Draft of Informative Essay | Group Peer Reviews |
| **Week 6** 1 *Revise for Sentences* | Ch 16 (573-582) | Selected exercises | Discuss readings and exercises |
| 2 *Read-around* | Ch 6 (203-210) | Final Draft of Informative Essay | Read-around; begin Evaluation Essay |
| 3 *Getting Started: Evaluation Essay* | Ch 7 (211-232) | Selected Questions for Review | Discuss readings |
| **Week 7** 1 *Prewriting* | Ch 7 (232-237) | Selected prewriting exercises | Discuss prewriting techniques |
| 2 *Peer Review* | | Discovery Draft of Evaluation Essay | *Peer Letter Reviews |
| 3 *Introductions, Conclusions* | Ch 2 (47-51; 58-61) | Exercise 2.1 | Discuss readings; allow time for work on papers |
| **Week 8** 1 *Read-around* | Ch 7 (238-244) | Final Draft of Evaluation Essays | Read-around; begin Writing From Literature Essay (WFL) |
| 2 *Getting Started: Writing From Literature* | Ch 8 (245-262) | Selected Questions for Review | Discuss readings |
| 3 *Reading Literature* | Ch 8 (262-281) | Selected Questions for Review | Discuss readings |
| **Week 9** 1 *Prewriting* | Ch 8 (281-292) | Selected exercises | Discuss readings; allow time for prewriting about literature topic |

| 2<br>*Drafting* | Ch 8 (296-300) | Focus Statement for WFL paper | Discuss; continue drafting WFL paper |
|---|---|---|---|
| 3<br>*Peer Review* | Ch 8 (300-308) | Draft of WFL paper | Group Peer Reviews |
| **Week 10**<br>1<br>*Read-around* | | Final Draft of WFL paper | Read-around; begin Position Essay |
| 2<br>*Getting Started: Position Essay* | Ch 9 (309-323) | Selected Questions for Review | Discuss readings |
| 3<br>*Supports for Arguments* | Ch 9 (324-334) | Selected exercises | Discuss readings and exercises |
| **Week 11**<br>1<br>*Prewriting* | Ch 9 (334-339) | Dialogue (337-339) | Do sample causal and value statements for a few students' topics |
| 2<br>*Structuring Arguments* | Ch 9 (339-346) | Outline of Formal (or Informal) structure for argument | Discuss argument structures |
| 3<br>*Logical Arguments* | Ch 9 (346-354) | Selected exercises | Discuss fallacies |
| **Week 12**<br>1<br>*Peer Review* | | Draft of Position Essay | Peer Critiques |
| 2<br>*Revise for Diction* | Style (545, 546); Ch 15 (564-570) | Selected exercises | Discuss readings and exercises |
| 3<br>*Revise for Sentences* | Ch 16 (590-594) | Selected exercises | Discuss readings and exercises |
| **Week 13**<br>1<br>*Read-around* | Ch 9 (354-363) | Final Draft of Position Essay | Read-around; begin work on Portfolio |
| 2<br>*Introduce Portfolio Assignment* | Ch 14 (525-534) | | Discuss readings |

| | | | |
|---|---|---|---|
| 3<br>*Portfolio Workshops* | | | *In-class work on choosing essays for Portfolio and drafting Reflective Essay |
| **Week 14**<br>1<br>*Peer Review* | | Draft of Reflective Essay Due | Peer Letter Reviews |
| 2<br>*Portfolio Workshops* | | | Continue work on portfolios |
| 3<br>*Read-around* | | Portfolio Due | Read-around; celebrate the semester |
| **Week 15**<br>*Make-up* | | | |

*\*Read Strategies for the Writing Process*

Reading and discussing this introduction to Part I in class is a good way to send the message that yours is a writing class, with an emphasis on that adjective *writing*. Talk through the two scenarios about writing, and ask your students to talk about what they do when they have a writing assignment to fulfill. And having them complete the two exercises at the end of this short section offers a way of getting them to locate potentially valuable support for their work as writers.

*\*Interest Inventory*

The Interest Inventory proves useful to many of our students. We suggest that you emphasize its importance to your students by asking them to prepare two copies of their responses, one for you and one for them. They should refer to it at any time they are directed to do so by our text or by you. Ask them to be sure to bring their completed Interest Inventory to all conferences with you. And if you're teaching the first of a two-sequence course, remind them to keep their Inventory, so that they'll have it for the next course.

*\*Selected Questions for Review*

Depending on your assessment of class time available for particular activities, you may wish to have your students read all the essays in a given chapter but to answer, either in class discussion or in writing, only some of the Questions for Review following each reading or all of the questions for only two of the essays.

*\*Discuss Focus Statements*

The issue of discussing students' work in class is a tricky one. Some students are very timid about having anything they have done looked at by other members of the class. We attempt to create an atmosphere of sharing so that students become more and more comfortable with these types of activities. We do so, in part, by focusing first on the positive aspects of a piece of writing, then on ways to strengthen it. We suggest that you discuss this issue with your class early on and ask anyone who objects to this kind of sharing to let you know.

*\*Fish Bowl*

The Fish Bowl is an exercise I have borrowed from Beverly Varnado, a teacher at Wando High School in Charleston, S.C. It is designed to help students prepare to work with each other in group critique situations. Early in the semester, I dedicate a day to a practice critique of a student paper, usually one from my files. On that day, I ask for three or four volunteers to be in the "Fish Bowl." The volunteers come to the front of the room, or if possible, I arrange chairs so that the critique group sits surrounded by the class. One member of the group takes on the role of the writer of the paper, though she has never seen the paper before. She then reads the paper to the other members of the group. While she reads, the other members listen silently. Then, she slowly reads the paper a second time. This time, the members of the writing group take notes about issues that catch their attention in the paper. [Note: they may or may not have copies of the paper themselves.] When the second reading is completed, the person playing the role of the writer allows some time (a couple of minutes) to pass while members of the group continue their thinking and note taking. Then the student playing the role of writer opens by saying what she likes best about the paper at this point. She then points to any issue in the paper that is particularly in need of work. [Note: it is very important to have an imaginative student playing the role of this writer. Be ready to help your "writer" if you need to.] After she makes these comments, other members of the group may speak. But the words of the first speaker must be words of encouragement. What works in the paper? What does this reviewer particularly like in the paper? Then the members of the group will continue to critique the paper, following the general rule that every comment must be intended to help the "writer" make her paper better and no comment may be intended to hurt or demean the writer.

If you are fortunate, you will have to muzzle the rest of your class while this is going on to keep them from entering the discussion too soon. Watching from the sidelines, they will probably want very much to get in on the discussion. Hold them off until the critique session has run its course. Then, open the discussion up to the class with this general question: what did you learn about critiquing from this exercise? You should find that they learned a great deal. At the end of the period, wrap up the discussion by drawing their attention to principal characteristics of successful group critique sessions.

*Group Peer Review*

In this session, students will do group peer reviews in the fashion illustrated in the "Fish Bowl." As you think about group work, you'll need to settle two key issues:

> *How large should your groups be?* In most cases groups should contain either three or four members. Three is probably the optimal number, but if you are working with established groups and you expect absences, you may want to have groups of four so that you will usually have at least three members present.

> *Should groups continue to function for the entire semester?* There are pluses and minuses both ways. The longer we use groups (and the more we use them), the more fluid we tend to like them, so we may form new groups for each occasion. However, if you do have established groups, you may find that group members meet with each other out of class and begin to depend upon each other for help when one has missed class and so forth.

*Style*

It should be obvious that we do not envision a course in which one works her way through our textbook from start to finish. However, the book does provide a basic structure for the syllabi we have constructed here. The basic progression follows the units in Part 2: Writing Occasions. Within that framework, we weave readings from other sections of the text. Here, we are including materials from Part 5 on style. As you will remember, each of the two chapters in Part 5 has major headings that correspond to the divisions in Part 2. Thus, in working on Personal Writing (as in the case here), you can direct your students to the sections having to do with "strategies that focus on the writer" in Chapters 15 and 16.

*Let them work on revising their papers*

It's interesting to note how little in-class writing often gets done in writing classes. Teachers tend to feel that when students are writing, they aren't teaching. Surely we should expect our students to work out of class, and we should allow them time for a piece of writing to develop, but there is no substitute for having students write in your presence. If you make an assignment and leave 15 to 20 minutes at the end of the class for students to begin that assignment, most will get a start that will be very helpful to them when they come back to the assignment out of class–getting started is half the battle. And if they are undertaking this difficult part of the process with you present, they may ask you questions that will move the process forward.

*Peer Critiques*

Peer critique sessions can be very useful. Rather than having them respond to each other's papers in a group setting, have students exchange papers (or you arrange the exchange) and then respond to questions on a critique sheet that you provide them. [Note: for more information on critique sheets and on ways to make peer review an integral part of the writing process, see the essay "Teaching Writing As Process" in this guide.]

*Read-around*

Read-around is an activity I use to celebrate the completion of an assignment and to continue the sense of community already at work. It works like this. At the beginning of the period, I ask students to take out a blank sheet of paper and write their names in the upper right-hand corner. I then take up final drafts of the papers that are due and redistribute them so that everyone has someone else's paper. I then tell class members that they have a set time to look over a paper, usually three or four minutes. This enforces a fast reading. After that reading, I call time and ask students to write the name of the student whose paper they have just read on the blank paper in front of them. They then write reflections on what they've read: questions about the paper, things they like in it, things they think need strengthening, an informal assessment about how it has developed (if they have seen it in draft form). These reflections come to me at the end of the exercise, not to the writers of the essays, so the reviewers can and should be frank. I keep time when these reflections are being written, allowing only a minute or two. When the time is up, students are instructed to draw a line under the last sentence they have written. Then papers are exchanged and the process is repeated. I usually allow students to read three papers in this process, but the number can vary. After the last reflection is written, I usually open up the floor for any comments students want to make about the process. This usually leads to some good discussion of the writing that is taking place in the class. When the session is over, I take up the reflections, read them, give them a check mark for having completed the assignment (and sometimes a comment about the effectiveness of the reaction), and then return them at the next class meeting. Students see only the reflections they've written; they don't see the reflections about their writing written by other class members.

Read-around provides an apt conclusion to an essay assignment. My students have seen various drafts of each other's papers, and they're often interested to see final drafts, to see the kinds of final changes a writer may have made. Because I want my students to develop their critical reading skills, I am the audience for their read-around responses; I want them to feel free to say that a given paper works but that another one doesn't.

*Draft of Informative Essay*

Note that we do not call this a discovery draft; in fact, there is no formal discovery draft stage for this paper. This is consistent with the practice in *The Longwood Guide to Writing*. Sometimes we present discovery drafts, but sometimes we don't because many times our students don't write such drafts. As we say early in the text, THE Writing Process, one consisting of an unvarying number of steps or stages, simply doesn't exist. Our practice is to begin by asking students to go through a very detailed process including at a minimum prewriting, discovery draft, second draft, and final draft. After that, we vary the formal steps that we ask for, being sure to emphasize to students that they may well find it helpful to include steps that we are not requiring. Our goal is for students to develop process strategies that work for them.

*Peer Letter Reviews*

The peer letter is another type of peer critique. In this activity, you assume that your students have the sophistication to respond without prompts; thus, these usually come later in the semester. Students exchange papers and write each other letters in which they suggest ways for improving the next draft of a paper.

*In-class work on choosing essays*

By the time you reach this point, your students should be accustomed to the workshop atmosphere. Devote as much time as you can to students' workshopping their papers, making them ready for their portfolios. While this is going on, you can serve as a resource, perhaps stopping the class from time to time to talk about issues that come up as you work with individual students.

## 2.a. First Course in a Two-Semester Sequence (with persuasion and research the focus of the second)

The two courses in this sequence make full use of the materials in *The Longwood Guide to Writing*. This first course introduces students to writing assignments with the following aims: personal, informative, evaluative, and literary. In addition, students learn the fundamentals of writing for essay examinations

| Meeting | Readings Due | Other Work Due | Class Activities |
|---|---|---|---|
| **Week 1**<br>1<br>*Introduction* | | None | Read Strategies for the Writing Process (1-6) in class and discuss |
| 2<br>*Writing Process* | Ch 1 (7-14) | Interest Inventory (8,9) | Discuss Interest Inventory; do Exercise 1.2 (13); do Exercise 1.3, (15) |
| 3<br>*Reading Strategies* | Ch 1 (15-21);<br>Ch 4 (89-105) | Exercise 1.5, no.1 (18); Exercise 4.1 (97) | Discuss their prewriting; discuss readings in Ch 4 |
| **Week 2**<br>1<br>*Reading Strategies* | Ch 4 (105-124) | Selected exercises | Discuss reading strategies |
| 2<br>*Getting Started: Personal Essay* | Writing Occasions (125-129); Ch 5 (131-148) | Selected exercises | Discuss characteristics of personal writing; go over assigned exercises; do others in class if time permits |
| 3<br>*Organizational Strategies* | Ch 2 (33-45);<br>Ch 5 (149-164) | Focus Statement (151) for Personal Essay | Discuss some of their focus statements; allow time to refine them in class |

| Week 3<br>1<br>*Peer Review Strategies* | Ch 3 (65-88) | | Fish Bowl |
|---|---|---|---|
| 2<br>*Peer Review* | | Discovery Draft of Personal Essay | Group Peer Reviews |
| 3<br>*Revise for Diction* | Style (535-541); Ch 15 (547-549; 556-564) | Selected exercises | Discuss exercises; if time, let them work on revising their papers |
| Week 4<br>1<br>*Revise for Sentences* | Ch 16 (571-573; 582-590) | Exercise 16.8 (p. 589) | Discuss revision |
| 2<br>*Peer Review* | | Second Draft of Personal Essay | Peer Critiques |
| 3<br>*Read-around* | | Final Draft of Personal Essay | Read-around; introduce Informative Essay |
| Week 5<br>1<br>*Getting Started: Informative Essay* | Ch 6 (165-192) | Selected exercises and Questions for Review | Discuss readings |
| 2<br>*Prewriting* | Ch 1 (22-31) | Selected exercises | Discuss exercises; do freewriting (p. 192); then work with one or two of their topics using the Questions for Analysis |
| 3<br>*Thesis Sentence* | Ch 6 (192-203); Ch 2 (46, 47) | Selected exercises; thesis for Informative Essay | Discuss readings; be sure their theses work; allow time for drafting |
| Week 6<br>1<br>*Revise for Diction* | Style (541-545); Ch 15 (549-555) | Selected exercises | Discuss readings and exercises; allow time for work on second draft in class |
| 2<br>*Peer Work* | | Second Draft of Informative Essay | Group Peer Reviews |
| 3<br>*Revise for Sentence Structure* | Ch 16 (573-582) | Selected exercises | Discuss readings and exercises |

| | | | |
|---|---|---|---|
| **Week 7**<br>1<br>*Read-around* | Ch 6 (203-210) | Final Draft of Informative Essay | Read-around; begin Evaluation Essay |
| 2<br>*Getting Started: Evaluation Essay* | Ch 7 (211-232) | Selected Questions for Review | Discuss readings and Questions for Review |
| 3<br>*Introductions, Conclusions* | Ch 2 (47-64);<br>Ch 7 (232-237) | Selected exercises | Discuss readings; allow time for work on papers in class |
| **Week 8**<br>1<br>*Peer Review* | | Draft of Evaluative Essay | Group Peer Reviews |
| 2<br>*Read-around* | Ch 7 (237-244) | Final Draft of Evaluation Essay | Read-around; introduce Writing *From* Literature Essay (WFL) |
| 3<br>*Getting Started: Writing From Literature* | Ch 8 (245-281, selected readings) | | Discuss readings |
| **Week 9**<br>1<br>*Literary Analysis* | Ch 8 (281-292) | Selected exercises | Discuss elements of literature |
| 2<br>*Literary Analysis* | Ch 8 (245-281, selected readings) | | Continue to discuss elements of literature |
| 3<br>*Prewriting and Drafting* | Ch 8 (296, 297) | | Discuss readings; allow time for drafting in class |
| **Week 10**<br>1<br>*Peer Review* | | Draft of WFL Essay | Peer Letter Reviews |
| 2<br>*Read-around* | | Final Draft of WFL Essay | Read-around; introduce Writing *About* Literature (WAL) |
| 3<br>*Getting Started: Writing About Literature* | Ch 8 (245-281, selected readings; 293-295) | | Discuss readings |

| | | | |
|---|---|---|---|
| **Week 11**<br>1<br>*Structuring Essay* | Ch 8 (297-308) | | Discuss structure of literary essay |
| 2<br>*Peer Review* | | Draft of WAL Essay | Peer Critiques |
| 3<br>*Read-around* | | Final Draft of WAL Essay | Read-around; introduce Essay Examination |
| **Week 12**<br>1<br>*Essay Examination* | Special Writing Tasks (497-499); Ch 13 (501-518) | Selected examples (518) | Discuss essay exam |
| 2<br>*Essay Examination* | Ch 13 (519-523) | | Continue to discuss (and give examples of) essay examinations |
| 3<br>*In-Class Essay Examination* | | | Essay Exam |
| **Week 13**<br>1<br>*Introduce Portfolio* | Ch 14 (525-534) | | Discuss readings |
| 2<br>*Portfolio Workshops* | | | In-class work on choosing essays for portfolio and drafting reflective essay |
| 3<br>*Peer Review* | | Draft of of Reflective Essay | Peer Letter Reviews |
| **Week 14**<br>1<br>*Portfolios* | | | Continue work on portfolios |
| 2<br>*Portfolios* | | | Continue work on portfolios |
| 3<br>*Read-around* | | | Read-around; celebrate semester |
| **Week 15**<br>*Make-up* | | | |

## 2.b. Second Course in a Two-Semester Sequence (focus on persuasion and research)

This course introduces students to assignments in argumentation, persuasion, and problem/solution (with research).

| Meeting | Readings Due | Other Work Due | Class Activities |
|---|---|---|---|
| **Week 1** <br> 1 <br> *Introduction* | | | *Introductory Activities |
| 2 <br> *Interest Inventory* | *Ch 1 (7-14) | *Interest Inventory (8,9) | Discuss Interest Inventory |
| 3 <br> *Reading Strategies* | Ch 1 (15-21); Ch 4 (89-105) | Exercise 1.5, #1 (18); Exercise 4.1 (97) | Discuss their prewriting; discuss readings in Ch 4 |
| **Week 2** <br> 1 <br> *Reading Strategies* | Ch 4 (105-124) | Selected exercises | *Discuss reading strategies, drawing particular attention to summary |
| 2 <br> *Getting Started: *Writer's Choice Essay* | Ch 1 (22-31) | Selected exercises | Discuss exercises; do freewriting (192); then work with one or two of their topics using the Questions for Analysis |
| 3 <br> *Peer Review Strategies* | Ch 3 (65-88) | | Fish Bowl |
| **Week 3** <br> 1 <br> *Peer Review* | | Draft of Writer's Choice Essay | Group Peer Reviews |
| 2 <br> *Read-around* | | Final Draft of Writer's Choice Essay | Read-around; introduce Position Essay |
| 3 <br> *Getting Started: Position Essay* | Ch 9 (309-323) | Selected Questions for Review | Discuss readings |
| **Week 4** <br> 1 <br> *Supports for Arguments* | Ch 9 (324-334) | Selected exercises | Discuss readings and exercises |

| | | | |
|---|---|---|---|
| 2<br>*Prewriting* | Ch 9 (334-339) | Choose topic and do a dialogue in which you take both sides (337-339) | Do sample causal and value statements for a few students' topics |
| 3<br>*Structuring Arguments* | Ch 9 (339-346) | Outline of argument | Discuss argument structures |
| **Week 5**<br>1<br>*Logical Arguments* | Ch 9 (346-354) | Selected exercises | Discuss fallacies |
| 2<br>*Drafting* | | Draft of Position Essay | Group Peer Reviews |
| 3<br>*Revise for Diction* | Style (545, 546); Ch 15 (564-570) | Selected exercises | Discuss readings and exercises |
| **Week 6**<br>1<br>*Revise for Sentences* | Ch 16 (590-594) | Selected exercises | Discuss readings and exercises |
| 2<br>*Read-around* | Ch 9 (354-362) | Final Draft of Position Essay | Read-around; introduce *Research Writing and Problem/Solution Essay |
| 3<br>*Getting Started: Problem/ Solution Essay* | Ch 11 (409-430) | Selected exercises | Discuss readings and exercises |
| **Week 7**<br>1<br>*Getting Started: Research Writing* | Ch 11 (430-433); Part Three (447, 448); Ch 12 (449-452) | Selected exercises | Discuss topics for Problem/Solution essay; go over assigned exercises; do freewriting in class |
| 2<br>*Library Search* | Ch 12 (452-457) | Selected exercises | Discuss library search. If your library has a tour, assign that at this point. |
| 3<br>*Other Types of Search* | Ch 12 (457-470) | Selected exercises | Discuss various ways of searching for information |

| | | | |
|---|---|---|---|
| **Week 8** 1 *Organizing Problem/ Solution Essay* | Ch 11 (433-446) | | Discuss readings |
| 2 *Getting Started: Persuasion Essay* | Ch 10 (363-387) | | Discuss readings |
| 3 *Features of Persuasion* | | | Read Ch 10 (387-395) in class; discuss |
| **Week 9** 1 *Sourcing* | | Note Cards for Research Paper | Check cards in class; allow time for working on research paper |
| 2 *Research Issues* | | | Continue working on research papers; workshop specific problems |
| 3 *Drafting Persuasion Essay* | | | *Allow time for drafting of Persuasion Essay in class |
| **Week 10** 1 *Revise Diction* | | | Read and discuss Ch 15 (564-570) |
| 2 *Revise Sentences* | | | Read and discuss Ch 16 (590-594) |
| 3 *Peer Review* | | | Peer Letter Reviews |
| **Week 11** 1 *Read-around* | | Final Draft of Persuasion Essay | Read-around; allow time to work on Research Paper |
| 2 *Incorporating Sources* | Ch 12 (470-483) | | Discuss readings; *apply to their research papers |
| 3 *Research Paper as a Whole* | Ch 12 (483-496) | | Discuss readings; apply to their research papers |

| | | | |
|---|---|---|---|
| **Week 12**<br>1<br>*Research Issues* | | | Continue working on research papers; workshop specific problems |
| 2<br>*Peer Review* | | Draft of Research Paper | Peer Critiques |
| 3<br>*Workshopping Research Paper* | | | Allow time for final questions about Research Paper |
| **Week 13**<br>1<br>*Read-around* | | Final Draft of Research Paper | Read-around; introduce Portfolio |
| 2<br>*Getting Started: Portfolios* | Ch 14 (525-534) | | Discuss readings |
| 3<br>*Portfolio Workshops* | | | In-class work on choosing essays for Portfolio and drafting Reflective Essay |
| **Week 14**<br>1<br>*Portfolio Workshops* | | | Portfolio continued |
| 2<br>*Peer Review* | | | Peer Letter Reviews |
| 3<br>*Read-around* | | Portfolios Due | Read-around; celebrate semester |
| **Week 15**<br>*Make-up* | | | |

\*Introductory Activities

If your students have not used *The Longwood Guide to Writing*, have them read and discuss pp. 1-6.

\*Ch 1

If your students have used *The Longwood Guide to Writing*, there will be some repetition in the first few reading assignments. Tell your students that this is just to ensure that everyone has the basic information on process and that the repetition will not continue.

\*Interest Inventory

Students may well have written an Interest Inventory in an earlier writing course. If they have a copy of that inventory, suggest that they look back to see if they can develop any answers more fully. In particular, draw their attention to the questions in item #6 that may be most relevant to the writing they will be doing in your course.

*Discuss reading strategies, drawing particular attention to summary*

Since you will be dealing with research later in this term, this is a good place to give attention to summary. Develop additional summary exercises to give students more practice in the skills they will need for the research paper.

*Writer's Choice Essay*

You may want to choose a particular aim for this essay, or, since your students will have had a previous writing course in which they practiced several aims, you may want to leave the essay's aim open. This would work well with the review of materials in Part 1, because the sample essays in this section illustrate a variety of writing aims.

*Research Writing and Problem/Solution Essay*

We suggest that you combine research and the problem/solution essay, since there is not time to do both assignments separately and since problem/solution lends itself so well to research. However, you could certainly combine research with various other writing aims.

*Allow time for drafting of Persuasion Essay in class*

Note that our syllabus calls for much of the work on the persuasion essay to be done in class. While this work is progressing, students are also engaged in the research paper; thus, they need their out-of-class time for that process. You may want to take some in-class time to touch base with them on a regular basis about the progress of their research papers. In the meantime, by having students work on the persuasion paper in class, you allow them to work on their writing while you are available to consult with them.

*Apply to their research papers*

Ask students to discuss problems or issues they are having in working with sources for their research paper; then use the materials in the text as a guide for dealing with them.

## 3. Second Course in a Two-Semester Sequence (focus on literature)

This course offers students the opportunity to write an essay that responds to literature, one that analyzes literature, and one that researches a literary topic. In addition, students practice writing essay examinations.

| Meeting | Readings Due | Other Work Due | Class Activities |
|---|---|---|---|
| **Week 1**<br>1<br>*Introduction* | | | *Introductory Activities |
| 2<br>*Interest Inventory* | Ch 1 (7-14) | Interest Inventory | Discuss Interest Inventory |
| 3<br>*Reading Strategies* | Ch 1 (15-21);<br>Ch 4 (89-105) | Exercise 1.5, no. 1 (18); Exercise 4.1 (97) | Discuss their prewriting; discuss readings in Ch 4. |

| | | | |
|---|---|---|---|
| **Week 2** 1 *Reading Strategies* | Ch 4 (105-124) | Selected exercises | Discuss reading strategies |
| 2 *Getting Started: *Writer's Choice Essay* | Ch 1 (22-31) | Selected exercises | Discuss exercises; do freewriting (192); then work with one or two of their topics using the Questions for Analysis |
| 3 *Peer Review Strategies* | Ch 3 (65-88) | | Fish Bowl |
| **Week 3** 1 *Peer Review* | | Draft of Writer's Choice Essay | Group Peer Reviews |
| 2 *Read-around* | | Final Draft of Writer's Choice Essay | Read-around; introduce Writing *About* Literature (WAL) |
| 3 *Getting Started: Writing About Literature* | Ch 8 (245-281, selected readings) | | Discuss readings |
| **Week 4** 1 *Elements of Literature* | Ch 8 (281-292) | Selected exercises | Discuss readings and exercises |
| 2 *Prewriting* | Ch 8 (292-295) | Focus Statement for WAL | Discuss readings and focus statements |
| 3 *Drafting* | Ch 8 (297-308) | | In-class work on drafting WAL |
| **Week 5** 1 *Peer Review* | | Draft of WAL | Peer Letter Reviews |
| 2 *Revise Diction* | Ch 15 (549-556) | Selected exercises | Discuss exercises |
| 3 *Revise Sentences* | Ch 16 (573-582) | Selected exercises | Discuss exercises |
| **Week 6** 1 *Read-around* | | Final Draft of WAL Essay | Read-around; introduce Research Paper |

| | | | |
|---|---|---|---|
| 2<br>*Getting Started: Research Writing* | Ch 12 (449-452);<br>Ch 8 (245-281, selected readings) | | Discuss literature and possible literary research topics |
| 3<br>*Library Search* | Ch 12 (452-457) | Selected exercises | Discuss library search. If your library has a tour, assign that at this point. |
| **Week 7**<br>1<br>*Other Types of Search* | Ch 12 (457-470) | Selected exercises | Discuss various ways of searching for information |
| 2<br>*Getting Started: Writing From Literature* | Ch 8 (245-281, selected readings; 296, 297) | | Discuss readings; discuss possible topics for Writing *From* Literature (WFL) |
| 3<br>*\*Analyzing and Interpreting Literature* | Selected readings | | Discuss readings |
| **Week 8**<br>1<br>*Analyzing and Interpreting Literature* | Selected readings | | Discuss readings |
| 2<br>*Drafting* | | | *Drafting WFL Essay in class |
| 3<br>*Peer Review* | | | Peer Letter Reviews |
| **Week 9**<br>1<br>*Workshopping* | | | Workshopping WFL papers in class |
| 2<br>*Read-around* | | Final Draft of WFL Essay | Read-around; continue work with Research Paper |
| 3<br>*Sourcing* | | Note Cards for Research Paper | Check cards in class; allow time to work on Research Paper in class |
| **Week 10**<br>1<br>*Essay Examination* | Ch 13 (501-518) | | Discuss Essay Examination |

| 2<br>*Essay Examination* | Ch 13 (519-523) | | Continue to discuss (and give examples of) essay exams |
| --- | --- | --- | --- |
| 3<br>*Essay Examination* | | | Continue to analyze essay exams in class |
| **Week 11**<br>1<br>*In-class Essay Examination* | | | Essay Examination |
| 2<br>*Incorporating Sources* | Ch 12 (470-483) | | Discuss readings; *apply to Research Paper |
| 3<br>*Research Paper as a Whole* | Ch 12 (483-496) | | Discuss readings; apply to Research Paper |
| **Week 12**<br>1<br>*Research Issues* | | | Continue working on research papers; workshop specific problems |
| 2<br>*Peer Review* | | Draft of Research Paper | Peer Letter Reviews |
| 3<br>*Workshopping Research Paper* | | | Allow time for final questions about research paper |
| **Week 13**<br>1<br>*Read-around* | | Final Draft of Research Paper | Read-around; introduce Portfolio |
| 2<br>*Getting Started: Portfolios* | Ch 14 (525-534) | | Discuss readings |
| 3<br>*Portfolio Workshops* | | | In-class work on choosing essays for Portfolio and drafting Reflective Essay |
| **Week 14**<br>1<br>*Portfolio Workshops* | | | Portfolio continued |

| 2<br>*Peer Review* | | Draft of Reflective Essay | Peer Letter Reviews |
|---|---|---|---|
| 3<br>*Read-around* | | Portfolios Due | Read-around; celebrate semester |
| **Week 15**<br>*Make-up* | | | |

*Introductory Activities*

If your students have not used *The Longwood Guide to Writing*, have them read and discuss pp. 1-6. If they have used the text, there will be some repetition in the first few reading assignments. Tell your students that this is just to ensure that everyone has the basic information on process and that the repetition will not continue.

*Writer's Choice Essay*

Because your students should have experience in a previous course, you may want to allow them the freedom to choose the aim of their first piece of writing.

*Analyzing/Interpreting Literature*

Even though this unit concerns itself with Writing *From* Literature, you will want to spend a good bit of time analyzing literature. Students must be able to interpret a piece of literature in order to use it successfully as a springboard for a WFL essay.

*Drafting WFL Essay in class*

Note that our syllabus calls for much of the work on the WFL essay to be done in class. While this work is progressing, students are also engaged in the research paper; thus, they need their out-of-class time for that process. You may want to take some in-class time to touch base with them on a regular basis about the progress of their research papers. In the meantime, by having students work on the WFL paper in class, you allow them to work on their writing while you are available to consult with them.

*Apply to their research papers*

Ask students to discuss problems or issues they are having in working with sources for their research paper; then use the materials in the text as a guide for dealing with them.

Ron

# Teaching Chapter 1
# Invention: Finding Something to Say

## OVERVIEW

Oftentimes, students begin a writing assignment by flailing around. They're convinced they have absolutely nothing to write about. Or if they have something to write about (a topic), they're convinced that they don't have anything of substance to say. Either way, they're very often blocked from the outset. The purpose of Chapter 1 is to offer the student writer a number of invention strategies that can help make her flailing around more productive and easier.

Invention involves the writer in generating ideas, in shaping them for a particular audience, in developing a structure for them, in revising them. While some rhetoricians may see invention as synonymous with prewriting, it actually stretches across the entire writing process. As she struggles to define her topic at the beginning of her writing, the writer invents. As she works to find the right order for her ideas, she invents. As she changes a single word or perhaps the language in an entire paragraph, she invents. Every decision the writer makes will, to a greater or lesser extent, engage her in creating meaning. This creation is precisely what invention is about. And the writer may use any invention strategy she needs at any point in her writing process.

The invention strategies we present in *The Longwood Guide to Writing* are not limited to those in Chapter 1. But we begin by labeling them as invention strategies because they are immediately applicable to prewriting. These strategies range in complexity from informal brainstorming and freewriting to the formal heuristic search represented by the Questions for Analysis. As you work through Chapter 1, have your students try out each strategy in turn, both in class and out.

**Significance in Writing**

Significance is an elusive quality, but it is the primary trait or characteristic of good writing. To help your students understand this, work through this exercise on the first or second day of class:

> Define good writing: In a paragraph or a list, identify the traits or markers or characteristics of good writing. Think about the last piece of writing you read that you thought good. What made it good? After you've completed this paragraph or list, rank your responses from most to least important, and be prepared to defend your ranking.

As your students write, you should also write your own definition. Then, using the blackboard or an overhead, create a definition of good writing based on the class' consensus. Take your students' responses as they come; that is, simply write on the board the things they say. As you record their responses, focus on those you think most important, being sure to comment on such aspects of their definitions as these:

> the need for the writing to say something of interest and importance for the writer
> the importance of audience
> the need for the writing to say something of interest and importance for the reader
> a strong sense of purpose in the writing

clarity of language
sufficient detail
a structure that's appropriate for the writer's purpose and audience
spelling, grammar, and mechanics

If your students don't talk about spelling, grammar, and mechanics, then you should broach the subject of correctness and talk about when it's most appropriate to consider correctness in the writing process. That time: at the end of but not during the process. This is not to say that correctness is unimportant; clearly, it is. Rather, it is to point out that too much concern with correctness before the writer nears the end of the process can stifle creativity and the flow of ideas.

When I work this exercise, I invite my students to consider correctness this way:

Assume that you've just gotten a letter from one of your dearest friends, one you haven't seen for a long time. Here's the gist of that letter:

Dear Old Friend,

On Sat. nite, we're gonna come thru Las Cruces, & we'd just luv to see ya!

What would your response be? Would you reach into your backpack for a red pen, mark every error, and send it back with a note like this:

Dear Old Friend,

I am in receipt of your letter, and I am appalled at its abject lack of correctness. Please be advised that if you cannot write more literate prose than this piece, I fear that our friendship will be at an end.

Or would you write something like this:

Awwwwright!! Come on down!!!!

In all likelihood, your response would be the latter, not the former. You wouldn't be concerned by the errors because they wouldn't matter for either you or the writer.

Now picture a different scenario. Let's assume that I, a Professor of English, wrote Dr. Marks [President of Sam Houston State University] a memorandum with this text:

Next Sat. nite, a company of Shakespearean actors are gonna come thru Las Cruces, & we'd just luv to see ya in the audience.

Dr. Marks's response to this memorandum could take this form: "Who is this guy? We hired him to teach writing? Get the hook!" And he would be right, for I would have committed a major error in judgment; I would have written a piece of writing totally inappropriate for my purpose and my reader.

The point to make with your students is that good writing is appropriate for its rhetorical situation, one that requires the writer to consider her purpose, her audience, and her language. Each of these aspects must be in balance with the others, if the writing is to be as effective as it can be.

**Interest Inventory**

To help students uncover potential topics for their writing, have them complete the Interest Inventory. It's designed to help them focus on their background and experiences and to speculate about issues that concern them. Have them follow the directions given in the text. It's especially important that you have them make two copies, one for them, the other for you. Place the inventories in a notebook so that you may refer to a given student's response readily, should he tell you he has nothing to write about. My response to such statements as "I don't know what to write about" or "I don't have anything interesting or important to use as a topic" is to pull out the student's inventory, peruse it briefly, point to one of the entries, and tell the student to write about it. Either the student does so or, far more likely, decides to write on something else.

## The Role of Invention throughout the Writing Process

Invention is a term that has been reduced in scope. Many writing teachers and students alike see invention and prewriting as synonymous. But they aren't. Invention embraces anything the writer does to generate ideas, to consider his reader, to shape or arrange or structure those ideas, and then to revisit them so that he makes his ideas available to his audience. Invention actually overlays the writing process from start to finish, with every aspect, every part of an essay only tentative until the writer decides he's finished.

Admittedly, student writers attempt to make most of their discoveries during prewriting, wanting them to be firm, hard and fast. They don't want to change anything; they want to make all their decisions up front and then just proceed. Given this propensity, we need to find ways to make our students' prewriting as fruitful as possible. One of the best ways is the application of heuristic search.

A heuristic procedure (sometimes called simply a heuristic) is a device that structures the writer's search for significance. In *Rhetoric: Discovery and Change* (Harcourt, Brace, and World, 1970), Richard Young, Alton Becker, and Kenneth Pike define a heuristic procedure as a process whereby "a person can systematically ask questions or perform operations that speed up the process [of discovery] and encourage the intuition of [ . . . ] hypotheses" (120). While this definition stresses the systematic nature of heuristic search, you could infer that heuristic procedures (or devices or models) are designed to be applied mechanically to the subject under investigation. But the function of a heuristic device is not to elicit stock or mechanical responses from the student; rather, the device serves only to guide the students in exploring a subject. Young, Becker, and Pike offer a concise statement of the function of a heuristic procedure:

(1) It aids the investigator in retrieving information that he has stored in his mind. (When we have a problem we generally know more that is relevant to it than we think we do, but we often have difficulty in retrieving the relevant information and bringing it to bear on the problem.)

(2) It draws attention to important information that the investigator does not posses but can acquire by direct observation, reading, experimentation, and so on.

(3) It prepares the investigator's mind for the intuition of an ordering principle, or hypothesis. (120)

We'd call your attention especially to the third of these traits. Note that Young, Becker, and Pike say that heuristic search "*prepares* the investigator's mind for the intuition of an ordering principle, or hypothesis" (emphasis added). We can't will significance to visit us, but we can entice it to come. Heuristic search provides a way of enticement.

The heuristic procedure–the Questions for Analysis–that we have developed provides a comprehensive approach to inventing material. If we look at the questions, we can see that they meet Young, Becker, and Pike's three criteria for the well-wrought heuristic model.

First, they enable the writer to range far over his topic. They help the writer probe the topic in depth, to amass a great deal of information if he answers each question in turn. In probing his topic deeply, the writer may well come to remember or discover things about his topic he didn't realize he knew. And by offering a systematic approach or guide through the topic, the questions may ease the difficulty Young, Becker, and Pike note we often have in retrieving or uncovering information.

Second, if the writer applies each question in turn but finds he has no response for one or more, he'll readily see blank spaces instead of ideas. He'll be pointed to those areas he knows little or nothing about. Once he finds these gaps in his knowledge, he then may decide whether they are important enough to warrant his filling them in.

Third, the questions lead the writer toward realizing significance or purpose for his writing, particularly as the writer applies the fourth set of questions, those based on consequence. This fourth set asks the writer to make value judgments, to decide whether something should or shouldn't be, whether it's ethical or unethical, necessary or unnecessary, harmful or not harmful, harmful but necessary, and so on. As the writer responds to questions which lie in the realm of "should versus should not," he may more nearly realize the significance his topic holds for him .

A well-designed heuristic procedure should help provide a route or even series of routes the writer may take as he investigates his topic. While the writer may flounder or wander through the realm of his topic, heuristic search can make that floundering or wandering more fruitful than it might otherwise be. Thus, heuristic search can help the student writer effect at least some control over his subject.

# TEACHING TIPS

*Unpacking an Assignment*. Students may need help learning how to read assignments so that they understand what the assignment calls for. "Unpacking an assignment" means examining the key terms of the assignment to see precisely what it calls for. In Chapter 5, we suggest the following:

> Describe an event from which you learned something. Your job is to use your language to recreate the scene so that your reader feels that he's been at least an observer if not a participant in the event.

The key terms here are "describe," "event," "learned something," "recreate the scene," "reader as observer or participant." Given that good writing presents something the writer thinks significant, let's focus on "learned something" as the term that drives the assignment.

Students are sometimes mystified by what we mean by "significance." They think we want them to discover the answer to those mysterious questions that have plagued philosophers for hundreds of years. But that's not what we're after at all. As I tell my students, they don't have to capture "deep, blue-green, shimmering insights into life"; instead, they just need to find something they think important and then decide why it's important. The something that they learned from their chosen event may well be of lifelong importance; then again, it may be of only fleeting importance, something that helped them through a particular moment but not so important that they'll keep it as a touchstone. But such moments of epiphany can be valuable nonetheless.

Have your students begin by brainstorming, listing, or freewriting for ten to fifteen minutes every event they can remember. The event's relative importance doesn't matter; what does matter is that they write without stopping for the specified time. Have them read back over their response, marking events that interest them or that stand out against the others for whatever reasons. Next, have them select one of these and write again for ten to fifteen minutes, longer if they're motivated to do so. Repeating this process should eventually yield a topic for the personal essay required. For an example of this kind of writing, see the two freewrites in Chapter 1 by Arlene Yusnukis and then the essay in Chapter 5 that she wrote based on them.

We also tell our students the kinds of topics we're really not interested in seeing. These are the predictable ones: the time a bunch of us went nightclubbing and I got absolutely drunk and threw up and I learned not to do that again; the time I slept through a major exam and learned not to rely on my roommate to wake me up. While such events may well have taught the student something, they're too obvious to yield writing that carries significance of the kind we're talking about.

Other key terms come into play as well. Because the writer is asked to "describe" and "recreate the event" vividly for the reader, descriptive detail will figure prominently. And because the paper will be about an event, narrative structures will be important. That is, the paper will tell a story, so chronology will likely be the ordering principle.

Help your students by unpacking each assignment you make, especially early in the semester. As your students gain experience in reading assignments and unpacking them for themselves, you may not need to provide as much direction later in the semester.

***Exploring Topics and Correctness.*** Invention is all about exploration and discovery, neither of which suggests much neatness. Stress to your students that the prewriting they'll do will be messy, that it's all right for them to wander all over a topic as they write to decide what it holds for them. Stress especially that they should not be concerned with correctness at this point in their writing process. Prewriting, being messy, sanctions misspelling and ungrammatical sentences. The time for correctness is much later in the process, not in the initial stages.

***Using Invention Strategies.*** Writers need a number of strategies available to them so that if a particular strategy doesn't work, they may use a different one. But if they're to switch from one strategy to another, they have to become familiar enough with other strategies. Have your students work with each of the strategies we present, both in and out of class. For example, have them complete a freewrite in class and then a follow-up freewrite as homework. Do the same with clustering. Lead them through a clustering exercise on a more concrete topic (e.g., see the gardens cluster); then assign a cluster on a more abstract topic as homework, using one or two of the possibilities listed in Exercise 1.5.

***Visualization.*** Lead your students through the visualization exercise with a favorite place as the subject. After they've written a paragraph describing this place, turn your class into an editing/response session. Ask your students what the role of an editor is. They'll probably tell you at first that the editor's job is to correct a piece of writing, to tell the writer what's wrong. You may need to steer them to more positive responses. We tell our students that as writers we want to hear from our editor what worked and then what needs strengthening. Note that "strengthening" doesn't mean what's wrong; instead, it means what needs more work. Having established this dual focus for response, we follow this procedure:

1. Each student divides a sheet of paper in half by drawing a line from top to bottom. The lefthand column is for notes about what worked, the righthand column for notes about what needs work.

2. A student volunteers to read her paragraph. As she reads, the other students take notes, listing on their note sheet those aspects of the paragraph (e.g., images or phrases) that struck them as effective and those that need strengthening. It's a good idea to have the writer read her paragraph a second time.

3. We ask the students to comment on what they marked as effective, to identify an image, for example, and tell why they found it effective. Once these comments are exhausted, we ask this question: "What advice do you have for this writer now to help her make the paragraph better?" Again, note that the focus is not on what's wrong but what can be done to improve the paragraph.

4. When students are finished (when they run out of comments), we move to another student, repeating this procedure as many times as a class period allows.

We also take our own notes and comment as an editor as well, though we're careful not to dominate the conversation. Primarily, we enter the conversation when it lags and to reinforce comments that our students make.

The benefits of this activity? First, students read their work aloud and come to understand that we want to hear their voices in this class. They become active participants from the outset. Second, by focusing on what works and what needs work instead of what's good and what's bad, we begin to set a positive tone for group response. This becomes especially important when we assign students to peer review groups. We are very clear about the kinds of comments that are inappropriate, reinforcing that remarks like "It's really good; I wouldn't change anything" and "This really stinks" won't fly in our class. Third, because we participate in rather than simply monitor this activity, our students begin to see us as members of their class, which helps to create a good climate.

Once you've done one whole-class response, take your students through a second visualization. Then divide them into review groups, and have them use the method above to hear and respond to each writer in their particular group.

*Questions for Analysis*. We've given a fair amount of space to the Questions for Analysis, which we discuss in "Logology and *The Longwood Guide to Writing*: What We Owe to Kenneth Burke." These questions are extensive, and we doubt that students will take the time to apply every question to every writing topic. You should, however, spend some time with these questions because of their potential to generate a substantial amount of information and to help the writer discover his topic's significance.

To begin, talk about the logic of the four divisions. We think in terms of association, opposition, sequence, and consequence. That is, when we confront a new experience, we compare and contrast it to other similar experiences; we examine it in terms of "first" and "second," and we then make a value judgment about it. Many times, we're not even aware that we're thinking in these ways; we perform these operations subconsciously and all but instantaneously. Once students understand the key terms of the Questions–association, opposition, sequence, and consequence–they can either use the sample questions we've listed or frame their own questions to ask.

Given our definition of good writing as carrying significance, asking questions of consequence will be especially important for the student writer. These questions can lead the writer to discern the meaning in her topic, for they require her to make a value judgment about that topic.

# SAMPLE STUDENT PROCESS

In Chapter 1, we introduce the writing of Marisol Vargas, a first-year writing student at New Mexico State University. The writing we present takes students through Marisol's response to the personal essay assignment in Chapter 5, so that they may gain a sense of a writer at work from start to finish. Specifically, we present Marisol's prewriting in Chapter 1, her drafting in Chapter 2, and then her rewriting in Chapter 3.

Point out to your students that Marisol decided not to write an essay based on her first freewrite. While some students may view such writing as wasted motion, point out that she had to write that piece to realize that she didn't want to spend any more time with it, so the writing was hardly wasted. Far better to find out early on that you don't have enough interest in a topic to sustain a whole paper than to find that out after you've struggled through more prewriting and two drafts of an essay.

Note also the numerous grammatical and mechanical errors in both of Marisol's freewrites. Have your students identify these and ask if they're problematical. Be sure to point out that freewriting is messy and probably won't be free of error, that it is, in fact, good to see some errors because that means the writer is engaged with the topic, not with correctness too early in the writing process. You may reinforce this idea by revisiting Arlene Yusnukis's two freewrites, noting especially the number of sentence fragments and punctuation errors they hold.

# RESPONSES TO EXERCISES

## *Interest Inventory*

Although the Interest Inventory wasn't required as an exercise, we suggested instead that the student open a file and create it on a diskette. Below, we present a sample response to the Interest Inventory:

*Interest Inventory*

*1. Community*

*a. Where do I live?*

*Las Cruces, New Mexico*

*b. What type of a community is my community or neighborhood?*

*This town used to be a big retirement community and a college town, but it is changing so much. It used to be that the town emptied when the students left for vacations or summer, and then it would boom again in August, but in the last two years, even that has changed. Las Cruces is making the local contractors rich because people are moving here, as well as many new businesses, restaurants, and other economies.*

*c. What especially disturbs you about your community? Why?*

*The gangs are expanding and becoming more obvious, and there is also much more violence. Kids are taking weapons to school and little kids are talking about knives and killing and things like that. Even though I know this is happening all over the country, it disturbs me because I never really thought about how violent everyone is becoming. I don't want my son to grow up like that, and I don't know where we can go to keep him from being exposed to violence.*

*d. What particular places or events in your community do you enjoy? Why?*

*We have a new movie theater that I love to visit, because I love to go to the movies, there is also a lot of historic value to this area, and the downtown mall and the old town of Mesilla offer lot of freedom to move and explore. It is nice to think about the distant past. These places also offer a diverse crowd of people to meet and talk to. The high school basketball, football and baseball games are fun to go to also because they are very competitive, and so are the city league softball games for both men and women. The university offers some excitement, but anymore that is such a political arena, it isn't nearly as much fun.*

*e. What things about your community would you like to see changed? Why?*

*I hope to see the kids maturing and looking around to say, "Hey, this is a great place. Why do we have to keep screwing it up like this?"*

2. *Family, Friends, and Acquaintances*

*a. What about your family is unique?*

*We are a large family of seven kids, and most of us are married and either have kids or are expecting. My sister and my sister in law are both pregnant, and I and my other sister-in-law have little boys who were born within two weeks of each other. We aren't just a large family anymore, now we are a huge family!*

*b. Which of my relatives are especially interesting or important to me? Why?*

*My sister Rebekah is very important to me because she always listens to what I have to say, and she thinks I am very smart, funny, and independent. She gives me a lot of advice on my son, what to do for diaper rash, ear infections, the whole works. She is a lot more like me than I ever realized while I was growing up, even though she is eight years older.*

*My brother Pete is really great, he is so incredibly smart, and he has never lost his sense of humor. He is the oldest, and he and I are even more alike than I ever thought also. My family is kind of broken into two generations, and I am the oldest of the second generation. We are both the most educated, having gone to universities, and he is the most driven to accomplish great things, aside from me. He is a surgeon in Los Angeles, so I rarely get to visit or talk to him, but when I do, it is wonderful, because he just is a really great guy.*

*This is really hard, because I want to do a paragraph for each sibling, both of my parents, and my grandparents. Everyone in my family is so awesome, and it is really hard to narrow it down. For instance, my dad and I never got along when I was growing up, and now I want to always be with him. I miss him a lot, and he has already had three heart attacks, as well as surgery, so I don't know how much time I have with him. My mom is just awesome. She is so even tempered and calm, and I only remember seeing her cry three times when I was growing up. She cries more now; I think she misses having her kids around her, and life has been hard on her. She has never had any money, so she has financial stress; she works hard all the time, and her husband doesn't take care of himself. My dad still smokes, and he just retired, so he collects social security, but that certainly isn't enough to take care of mortgage and other bills. I always want to go home and take her on a vacation, but she is really good at giving herself the opportunities to go see her kids or whatever. One time she came all the way down to Las Cruces, for five minutes, just because she was in TorC for the day, and wanted to say hi.* [Note: TorC is a local abbreviation for Truth or Consequences, a town in New Mexico.]

*My grandma is great. She is old anymore, but she is still so vibrant. My grandfather died when I was a junior in high school, and yet grandma still wears a ring on her finger. She always signs her cards (which she sends for every single occasion, including Halloween) G-ma. I hope Aidan (my son) gets to know her before it is too late.*

*c. What special customs does your family have?*

*We used to always get together at one person's house for Thanksgiving and Christmas, but as we all grow older and become more involved with our own families, that doesn't happen nearly as much anymore. I miss that. We also used to go on vacation together, the whole family, but we don't do that anymore either. I guess as you choose your paths, things change.*

*d. Which of your friends are especially interesting or important to you? Why?*

*I don't really have many friends anymore, I have more acquaintances than anything. I guess that is what marriage did to me, unfortunately. I think my friends that I gained in college are the most important to me, aside from the friends I gained from childhood. I still keep in touch with my best friends from back east, and also my best friend Craig, but he is in love now, so I never talk to him. My friends who are married and have kids are vital to me now because it is nice to reaffirm my feelings. My husband could be my best friend, but he chooses not to be, so his sister is probably the closest to me right now. My son is by far my greatest friend, although he doesn't really offer too much in the way of conversation, because although he understands my language, he doesn't speak it, and I don't speak his.*

e. *Do you know any unusual people? If so, what makes them unusual?*

*Unusual is hard to define, because I know so many different types of people. I think I could talk about people who are trying to redefine the norm, people who don't believe in the way modern society is being perpetuated, but then I can talk about people who are trying to make changes in society. Or, I could talk about those rare couples who have been married twenty five years, and just renewed their wedding vows, and are as giddy as the first time. I could talk about kids who have kids, or kids who don't. Unusual, anymore, is such an obscure term.*

f. *Which of your neighbors is especially interesting or important to you? Why?*

*I don't really know my neighbors, except that the ones directly next door are the parents of a kid who killed a young college student last year. I wanted to be angry at them, but they are very nice. I think their kid was just screwed up, but I am not defending the criminal. I think he should suffer, in fact, but these people just seem to be sad. I don't think I can blame them. My son would break my heart if he did something like that.*

3. Education

a. *What type of educational background do you have?*

*When I was in elementary school, I went to a central school, where kindergarten through senior high met. I was always somebody's little sister, and while I didn't mind that, it was nice to move to a whole other state and be me. Instead, my brother and sister, and even my oldest sister, when she moved out here, had to deal with being my sister. School was great. I loved being in high school, I was smart, and it came easy to me. I was in National Honor Society, Student Council, Volleyball, Basketball, Softball and Track. I lettered seven times, and played Varsity Volleyball as a freshman. I don't think popularity was important to me after awhile, but if I really think about it, of course it was. When I first moved to New Mexico, it was all I could think about, because I had never been popular when I lived in New York.*

*When I got to college, I realized just how much I had to learn. I wasn't as smart as I thought I was, and I screwed up–a lot. I had to repeat several courses; I was a terrible student. When I turned 21, I started to take things more seriously. I was working in a bar, and although I still wasn't a great college student, I realized that I wanted to get out sometime soon, and I started to focus more. When I got married a year later, I really started to think about my future and push to finish.*

b. *What type of courses have you taken? Are you taking? Which are your favorites?*

*I have taken just about every type of course. I still don't like math, but I love literature, and I love to write. I have been having a lot of fun over the last year working on a degree in English. My degree in education, while it is nice to have, just doesn't fire me up like English literature does.*

*c. If you could change anything about any of the schools you have attended, what would you change? Why?*

*The high school I attended has a bad reputation, although I always felt it was a good school, and I learned a lot from being there. I think, however, that I was one of the lucky ones, because I had really good teachers because I was in the honors program. All of my teachers had fun teaching what they did, and they were there because they loved it. I know that many of the other teachers in the school were there primarily for a paycheck, which often accounts for poor teaching, and low learning. I would change the attitudes and the reputation that sticks to my old alma mater.*

*c. What informal (not strictly related to school) educational experiences have you had? How were they educational?*

*I think my whole life has been one big educational experience, and it is difficult to pinpoint one area outside of actual education that has been beneficial. I think my mother in law is one of the people who has really impacted my life and taught me so much–primarily about religion.*

*4. Jobs*

*a. What types of jobs have you had? What about them interested or disturbed you? Why?*

*I have worked in many different areas–but the main one is service to paying customers. I worked for a long time during high school at the local McDonald's, and then when I went to college, I broadened my experiences. I was a resident assistant on campus, I tutored high school and elementary kids, I substituted at the local high schools, I bartended for awhile, and now I am teaching a class in writing. I think all of them have taught me a lot about life and people, and about society, but I think one that has really impacted a lot of my beliefs, and made me stronger in many of them, is the bartending job. Particularly the second time around, after I had gained my own family, a husband and a son.*

*The one thing that really disturbs me about bartending is that I get to see so many different people screwing up their lives. I've watched a woman go from being just a regular unhappy housewife/barfly to becoming an adulteress, even though she has three kids and a job, and could just as easily have gotten a divorce before she chose to cheat on her husband. I know she was very unhappy, but I don't believe it is any excuse to cheat on the man you marry.*

*I love teaching. I can't wait until I finish this degree and get a job. I am really looking forward to the whole thing–even getting involved, or at least knowing about all of the bureaucratic baloney that happens in the workplace. I feel that being in college is definitely being in the real world, but I am ready to be in the world that goes to work, comes home and makes dinner. I don't have time for that lifestyle right now, and in fact, I don't even clean anymore because I am always so busy. It causes a lot of stress on my marriage, but I am willing to deal with it, because I know the benefits of finally getting the job are going to outweigh the others.*

*b. What career do you hope to have? Why have you chosen this particular field?*

*I want to teach high school English for awhile, and then I hope to move into the university setting. I am thinking about getting my doctorate in both English and Education, and then perhaps either teaching how to teach English at a university, or teaching education majors. I haven't decided, but for now, I definitely want to teach high school. I think that one of the most amazing things is to watch a kid who hates to read learn to love it. One kid in particular stands out in my mind, because he rejected my teaching so much, until we opened <u>Bless Me, Ultima,</u> and I told him I would help him as much as he needed. He was the first done with the book, and for a kid who never opened his mouth* *except to spout 2Pac rap songs, and talk about gangsters and gangster music, it was a miracle. Every day he had something to talk about from the book, and I was floored. It was incredible. To see such a brilliant mind sitting dormant for so long was such a shame, but I was so pleased to watch him open up. That is why I want to teach. Kids like that are a dime a dozen, but they are so closed up by so many different reasons, that it makes them much more valuable when they open up.*

6. Attitudes and Issues

a. Have you experienced a change in your attitude toward such things as politics, religion, school, family or friends? If so, what was the change and what caused it?

*I have experienced so many different attitude changes and shifts, and I think that a lot of what caused them has to do with my marriage. I used to be very nice and naive, and now I have become very jaded in many things. I am not always happy in my marriage, and it has made me very cynical about a lot of things. I do not like to cook and clean, especially when I have a huge house with tile floors, and I have always hated to mop. (I can't wait to move!)*

*All of this has really changed my attitude toward marriage, the role of a wife, to a certain extent, it has changed my views on school, and family, friends and religion. I don't have very much time for politics. I reject the traditional role of wife, and I don't agree with a lot of values that many men are still brought up with. I don't know if I have changed to believe these things, or if they have just been brought out by my own marriage. I think the latter is more true. I value my family and his family much more now than I ever did before, and part of that is because he does not value either.*

b. What events in the past year or so have interested you or disturbed you most? Why?

*Everything disturbs me anymore. I have no idea how much time we have left here on Earth, but it makes it seem as if God is going to be taking us very soon. I have mixed feelings about that, but for awhile there, I thought for sure that Hussein was going to cause the end for us all. It seems that guy just can't get enough of scaring everybody. I was also very bothered when I realized that smaller and smaller countries are testing and stockpiling nuclear weapons. What do we need them for? Why can't everyone just get along? I think so much of this war talk really bothers me because my son isn't even two years old, and I don't want him to have to live his life in fear of who is going to push which button. I want him to grow up like I did, with no worries or cares in the world.*

a. What types of issues interest you? Why?

*Well, for one thing, this computer is driving me crazy. I have never been able to format the screen correctly, and I have always depended on a lab assistant, or on the computer itself to know what was going on. I finally have my own computer, and I can't even figure all of this stuff out! Things like this are what really interest me. I have been so busy with school and with my son, that current events, unless they are really big, get passed by. I don't have time to watch tv, and if I do, it is always a junk show, just to pass the minutes mindlessly. I spend most of my time with Aidan, and if I am on my computer, it is to do work. I don't get any time to just watch the news, or browse on the web, so the issues that get me are usually quite domestic. Like, for example, when I forget to take out the garbage in time for the truck. Or when I forget to get the meat out of the freezer for dinner, or when I don't have a chance to do the dishes, etc.*

b. Have the technological advances or changes you've seen been for the best? Why? What technological developments would you like to see take place?

*I had a student this summer who was very interested in nanotechnology, and he introduced the entire class to this topic. It is very interesting. Scientists are developing machines the size of atoms to take place of many different things in the sphere of human life. For example, these machines conceivably will be able to patrol the bloodstream and fix sick cells, or whatever. I think that is great, but this leads to cloning, robots taking over, government conspiracies, the whole bit. I think that some science is fantastic, and really will make the quality of life better, but when is it too much? When will science start to take over human life, and make us obsolete?*

*I think I would like to see sick organs fixed, and cancer cured, but at the same time, I think we all must die at one point, and immortality should only be achieved after death. We must earn it during life, not make it during life.*

*c. Have the societal changes or advances you've seen been for the best? What changes in society would you like to see take place?*

*I think that a lot of changes have been good–a broader social conscience has started to develop, there is a lot more acceptance for people who are different from the norm, but I think that with that come dangers, the people who are resistant often become even more so, and then we have high school shootings, more gang violence, more violence against minorities, etc. Of course, I think that a lot of this stuff would still occur, it is tough to tell what causes what, and why things occur the way they do.*

*d. What particular social customs interest or disturb you? Why?*

*I think the rising tide of awareness is fascinating. It is okay to be different for the most part, but people recognize that there are dangers associated with a lot of differences. The glass ceiling is still there, and it needs to be broken by a lot more women, but it is probably still going to be there fifty years from now.*

## *Exercise 1.1*

Brainstorm about potential topics for an assignment. If your instructor has already made an assignment, then use this brainstorming to begin work on it. If you do not have an assignment yet, then brainstorm about significant events or about problems you have encountered since enrolling at your university. List every idea that comes to mind, whether you think it a good one or not. Do not censor any idea. Write for 10 minutes or until you fill at least a page from top to bottom.

*Scissors*
*Nanotechnology--a bunch of bullschtuffff?*
*I keep looking at the words I've already typed, and they are closing up my brain*
*Aidan loves his new big wheel*
*Nick and I just got in a fight about my schooling again.*
*I need to clean the kitchen*
*My new dryer is not drying, so it takes forever to get my laundry done.*
*FOREVER FOREVER FOREVER I keep thinking of the kid from the <u>Sandlot</u> with the glasses when he tells the story of the junkyard dog*
*I can't type, especially when I am in a hurry, this is making me crazy*
*I need to think, but all that comes out is crap*
*Photography--I wonder how they do the photos at Target*
*I spent too much money yesterday, I need to make sure I can pay my bills this month*
*I worry too much about money.*
*I can't wait to get a job and move away from here*
*I remember Aidan's first words, but I can't remember when he started talking.*

*I wish he was here right now, but I wouldn't get any work done.*

*He has an ear infection. I keep forgetting to give him his medicine, because he sure isn't acting like he's sick.*

*Angie is a great babysitter. She gets him to eat all kinds of different things. Good thing, he doesn't eat at home.*

*My stomach is very soft. I eat too much at McDonald's.*

*I wish I was a better cook. I wish Nick would cook, he can really go to town on a pork chop.*

*My office is atrocious. I need to clean!!!*

*I wonder where I'll get a job? I hope I get one in April, I need to be able to plan to move away. Gosh, I want to move away.*

*I am looking forward to school starting in the next few weeks. I am scared about my thesis. I still haven't nailed down a topic, and it is fast approaching, especially with Aidan running the show in this house.*

*I only have two more minutes. SO much is on my mind, but nothing wants to come out. I wonder if my brain does that on purpose. I wonder if it wants to mull over all of this stuff before I write it out and can see it on paper.*

*It's been a great weekend. We went to a Diablos game. Right fielder seemed nervous, the people behind us kept ragging on him, and that got Nick started. Too bad. He really was good, just screwed up a couple of times.*

> *I think doing this on the computer was a lot harder than doing it by hand, for one, I couldn't keep up with my fingers. When I type or write, I am very visual, and if I screw up a word, I have to fix it before I can go on, but I knew that if I did that with this, then it would break my train of thought. I kept catching myself trying to fix my spelling and vocabulary. Doing it by hand would have at least kept me thinking in stronger lines.*

## Exercise 1.2

Pick an entry from your Interest Inventory or one of the topics you listed in your brainstorming and freewrite about it for 10 minutes. Once you get started, don't stop until this time is up. Don't worry about grammar or spelling. Don't lift your pen or pencil off the page; don't stop typing–just write. When you finish, let the freewrite sit a few minutes; then read back over it. How many potential topics can you identify? Did any of what you wrote surprise you? If so, why? Did you uncover something you didn't think you would? If so, what?

> *My interest inventory was a great way to learn a lot about myself. I really had to think quite a bit about how I worked, what interested me and why, and it was a good adventure, even though it took forever. This freewrite is going to be hard to do, merely because I have such a hard time letting errors go by, especially when I have the delete button right at my fingertips. I really want to talk about Aidan, because he means everything to me, and everything I do is because of him. It is kind of like that Brian Adams' song from <u>Robin Hood</u>, that movie made years ago. My kid is the best. We bought him a big wheel this weekend, and he lives on it. He figured out the seat before I even put it on the bike. He is so smart. He says so many words. I just took him to the doctor the other day for his shots and she asked me how many words he is saying. I told her five, but she didn't believe me. She was right, it is more like 35. He has a huge vocabulary, I just don't pay attention to it well enough. She told me that too, and she is right. I have noticed many more words just in the last few days. He said bird perfectly when I pointed at a picture of a bird on the wall at the doctor's and today I put his Elmo slippers on him and he called Elmo Melmo. He is so sweet. He hugs me and squeezes me, and makes me love him so much. We play a game and I squeeze him and then he squeezes me, and we show each other how much we love each other. Then he slimes me with his kisses and makes me laugh. He wakes*

*me up with his kisses, which make my day. Man, that kid kills me. I love him so much. It is unbelievable how much you can love someone. He brings tears to my eyes at least once a day. The other day because he threw a tube of Vaseline at me and gave me a fat lip, but usually it is because I love him so unbelievably much.*

*I have three more minutes, so I am not sure I want to start another idea about Aidan, otherwise I will be typing for thirty more minutes. Man I am a horrible typer. I can't believe all of the mistakes I have made. Usually I take the extra second to fix them, and I keep catching myself still doing that, but some of these words would be so unintelligible like that one if I ding didn't fix them. Gosh I am having a hard time. I type fast, but my pinky works almost as fast to fix them, however, I know that is not he point of this exercise, and so I am trying to do what the exercise asks me to. Man this is hard. I think harder because I am concentrating on it so much. Whoa, a whole sentence with no errors!!! I can't believe it! I keep thinking of Adam Sandler and the movie <u>The Water Boy</u> for some reason, the line "you can do it" I guess you had to see it. DONE!*

*I'm not sure if many of these ideas would work for a research topic, but I definitely could write a personal reflection paper on my son and I. I think that is a major topic in my life itself, and everything else pretty much pales in comparison. He would definitely be what I would want to focus on.*

*Other potential topics could be: perfectionism, a mother's love (of course), current movies, how music works in movies, how kids learn, how kids develop vocabulary.*

## *Exercise 1.3*

From your initial freewrite identify a particular topic or idea that interests you. Then do a second freewrite about it, this time taking 20 to 30 minutes to write.

*It isn't difficult to determine what topic interests me. I am going to say Aidan every time. I think I might have helped myself type better by switching the font size to 12 point. I don't know how that helps, but maybe the bigger size just works better on my eyes. Anyway, I think Aidan is definitely someone/thing that I can write about for a whole hour or day if I had to .. He is the best because he just does something amazing about every other second. He loves balloons, so the other day I spent 20 bucks on balloons just to surprise him when he woke up. At three in the morning, I was blowing up these crazy balloons with Happy Birthday on them, even though his birthday is in March, and tying knots in them. One popped, and I thought for sure he would wake up, but he didn't , and the next morning he was so happy. He loved them so much, and two weeks later, they are still all over the living room, but he still plays with them, so I don't mind. I just pick up the ones that are fading and throw them away. I am stuck, I am listening to Trisha Yearwood, and I think I am focusing on her song, which is a particularly sad one, instead of paying attention to what I am trying to do here. I am also eating a fruit rollup, and it is stuck to my teeth, so I keep wanting to take my fingers off the keyboard and get it out, but I am going to finish this first, and then I am going to brush my teeth for about ten minutes. Nothing but a fairy tale, never come true, see, there are lyrics from the next song, and I am not focusing on my topic. Aidan is at the babysitter's. Gosh, she is so good. She really loves him, and I think that makes it all the better. I was really nervous to be sending him to a daycare, and then I found her, and even though she has four other kids that she watches, he gets so much individual attention because the others usually come later than he does. He also gets to hang out with a little baby, a 10 week old, and so he is really good with her, and he is really good with his little cousin now, who is only four weeks old also. He is learning a lot from being at the sitter's. He still doesn't pick his toys up at home, although I have seen him do it at her house, and at his grandma's. He needs to learn to do it wherever he goes, but he thinks he can get away with so much just because I love him so much. Little does he know he is going to have some serious boundaries, and he might as well get used to it right now, while he is still young.*

*We took him to a Diablos' game the other day, and he had a blast. He was such a good boy, although a bit restless. We sat right behind home plate and he kept trying to put Nick's keys through the fence and then he almost put his fire truck through! Luckily we caught him, or the poor catcher would have been surprised when he went to catch a foul ball at the fence!*

*I am discovering that this is really hard to do on the computer. I think I would be more effective on paper, because the misspellings are really throwing me off, and my thoughts are not coming nearly as quickly because I am so wrapped up in all of the red squiggly lines that are drawing my attention to the mistakes. I hate those and the green ones, I don't think I am following the assignment very well, but these are where my thoughts are going. Why can't I type!!??? I usually am so much more effective, and it is driving me crazy. I think it is because I am trying to focus so much on this that I am forgetting where my fingers are going.*

*Blash balch blah there, I finally typed that silly word correctly. I have only been typing for 15 minutes, and I still haven't even gotten to Aidan. I think it is because I can't focus. I need to turn off this music, but I can't stop typing, so I am very distracted. That will teach me. Next time I try to do this, I need to chill out and just type.*

*Aidan was very restless the other night when he first started getting sick, so at three in the morning, he and I were watching <u>Ghostbusters</u>. He even said busters. It was kind of weird, because I had just been thinking about wanting to watch that movie when I noticed it was on tv. SO, that wasn't a hard decision about what we would watch at that hour. HMMMMMMMMMMMMMMMMMMM Well, I took that hmmmbreak to push the cd button on the computer so music is gone. Aidan is sixteen months and two days, no three days old. It is amazing how time flies. He is running all over the place, no longer walking, and he always wants to climb on the couch or on the bed, or on his tricycle, and he always wants to be into things he shouldn't be. This morning I let him take all of the stuff out of the cupboard, and when he was done he put it all back, I didn't even tell him too. Good kid. He just needs to start doing that with all of his cars and toys. I am going to have a yard sale and get rid of a lot of stuff, I am already getting ready to move, and I still have a year! I want to so badly, because I think it will make Nick and me much more reliant on each other, instead of everyone around.*

*I just took my fingers off the key board, and it felt good, this is harder than it seems. I hope this is what I am supposed to be doing, if it isn't, then I don't have a clue. Mexico, Mexico, adios mi corazon. That is a good line. I'd like to go to Mexico. I want to learn to scuba dive, and that has been a dream of mine since I was a kid. I even wanted to be a marine archaeologist, but in New Mexico, it is hard to go to school for that kind of thing. We live in the desert, for crying out loud.*

*Okay, twenty minutes are almost up. This was hard. I think it would have been much easier to do by hand. Most definitely.*

## *Exercise 1.4*

Compare your two freewrites. How detailed is the second? How does it relate to the first? Did any of what you wrote surprise you? If so, why? Did you uncover something you did not remember? If so, what? Did you discover any gaps in your knowledge, anything you either need or want to know more about? If so, what will you need to do to fill them? Does any of this second freewrite point toward the significance of the topic? If so, identify it.

> *Both freewrites are a lot more about Aidan than I thought they were as I was writing. I gave them a lot of time before I went back to them, and I was amazed. At one point in my second one, I thought I hadn't even talked about my son, but I had spent a good ten minutes on just him without even realizing it. I don't know if that is because I felt so distracted, or if it is because I was just writing and letting my thoughts flow. The second freewrite is not necessarily more detailed, but definitely full of more things. I had more time to work out some ideas and thoughts, and instead of focusing as much on my spelling, as I thought I did, I kind of let that go. I was surprised as I reread, because I felt that I had spent the entire 30 minutes lamenting the fact that I couldn't freetype very well, and the red and green squigglies were killing me. Any gaps that I noticed I think were because I knew I was typing to myself and so I could easily fill them in later whenever I went to rereading the document, and not even necessarily with words, but with my thoughts as I went. My topic would definitely have to be the joy that my son brings to my life.*

## Exercise 1.5

This exercise asks the student to write as many as five clusters. So as to avoid repetition, we present only three sample clusters below, with one written in response to 1.5.A., one response to 1.5.B., and one in response to 1.5.D. Prepared by Matt Bridges, the first (1.5.A.) is an example of a personal event cluster, that is, a cluster given to exploring a significant event. The second (1.5.B.) offers an example of a less-focused cluster and takes "winner" (from the suggested list) as its topic. Finally, the third (1.5.D.) is an example of a cluster that explores a controversial topic, in this instance, smoking. And so that you may see them, we reproduce these three clusters at the end of this chapter.

A. Pick an event that was important in your life. If you cannot think of a specific event immediately, look again at your Interest Inventory or at the events you listed in brainstorming. Then cluster that event, following the directions given above. What major clusters or idea groups emerge? How do these point toward the significance of the event for you? Does your clustering point toward any gaps in your knowledge of the topic? If so, what do you need to do to fill them?

> *This summer (1999) we moved from Las Cruces, NM, to Huntsville, TX, and I did that event as my topic. Four major idea groups are there: dislikes, a new world, adapting, and leaving behind a familiar world. I think that "dislikes" contrasts with "adapting" and that "a new world" contrasts with "leaving behind a familiar world." I don't think there are any gaps in my knowledge because I lived it pretty intensely. I didn't like the move because it took me out of my comfort zone, but I'm getting used to being here and liking it more every day.*

B. Cluster at least three of these topic ideas: fear, happiness, fifth grade, winner, pain, family, college, backyard, the future, today, the past, flying, running, racing. What major clusters or idea groups emerge? How do these point toward the significance in these terms for you? Does your clustering point toward any gaps in your knowledge of the topic? If so, what do you need to do to fill them?

> *I took "winner" as the cluster topic. The first thing that came to mind was Bobby Bare's song "The Winner," about a grizzled, beaten-down bar fighter. He talks to a young challenger about what it means to win the kind of battles and "prizes" he's won. They're hardly prizes: lost teeth, scars, broken bones, a woman he didn't and doesn't love ("But I got her, boy, and that makes me The Winner"). Most of the cluster is about the win-at-all-costs attitude in society today and so points out a major trend in society that I don't like. I think I'd need to research the quote attributed to Vince Lombardi (legendary coach of the Green Bay Packers), because I've heard that he really didn't say, "Winning isn't everything; it's the only thing." I don't know what he did say, but I've heard this attributed to him, and I've since heard (on various sports newscasts) that Lombardi was misquoted.*

*I'd also want to research just how much money is involved in the "big money college sports" cluster. Megabucks, I suppose, because television rights (and so advertising and endorsements) are involved.*

C. Use your major as the key term for a cluster. If you haven't declared a major, then pick some topic you're interested in, and use it as the key term for a cluster. What major clusters or idea groups emerge? How do these point toward significance in the term you selected? Does your clustering point toward any gaps in your knowledge of the topic? If so, what do you need to do to fill them?

Not presented

D. Select a topic that has at least some controversy in it, e.g., a campus issue or a community or political issue, and use it as the key term for a cluster. What do you learn about the topic and your interest in it from completing this cluster?

*"Smoking" is the topic I picked. I despise smoking. I don't like being around it or anyone who smokes, even if they're not smoking. Maybe I'm just sensitive to secondhand smoke, but I think it's seeing the waste of money and (potentially) lives. Why do young people smoke? They know the dangers and risks, but they don't believe they'll get cancer or heart disease. I guess they do believe that smoking makes them look cool, and that it's a way of making some kind of rebellious statement. But it's just dumb as a hammer for kids (or anyone else, for that matter) to smoke. Since I did the cluster, I've seen a story in the Huntsville newspaper about a campaign to declare the city a smoke-free zone. I hope it succeeds. Oh, people will complain about that it's their "right" to smoke, but where's that one in the Constitution? Businesses (mostly restaurants) will complain that they'll lose business. Las Cruces passed a no-smoking ordinance, and businesses didn't suffer at all. There was a lot of smoke but very little fire to planned boycotts and other protests. Sorry–I couldn't resist. I'll stop ranting now and just say that my interest in the issue will continue as things move or don't move toward Huntsville becoming smoke-free.*

## *Exercise 1.6*

We invite you to travel in your mind to your favorite place. First, find a quiet spot, one in which you can relax as completely as possible. Throughout this exercise be as still and as attentive as possible to the detail you will generate. Below is a set of directions for you to follow. Do not respond out loud to any of them–visualize first, then respond in writing. You may need to have a friend work through this with you the first couple of times that you try it, reading the directions to you so that you work through the exercise completely:

1. Close your eyes, and take several deep breaths. Sit very still and calm in as comfortable a position as possible.

2. Identify the place, naming it in your mind.

3. Bring this place to life by creating a scene for it in your mind. Recreate the place in your mind's eye.

4. Stand in the center of the scene you have created. Turn very slowly in a complete circle, letting your eyes pan up and down like a camera taking in scenery. What do you see? What particular features dominate the scene? What colors stand out? When you have completed one turn, stop. And stand absolutely still.

5. Let your senses other than sight come into play:

   a. Is there a dominant odor in or to this place? Is it pleasant, sweet, acrid, faint, strong, pungent, foul? Identify its source.

   b. Is there a dominant sound? Is it loud, soft, pleasant, harsh, unpleasant, bright, muted? Identify its source.

c. Is there anything that stands out that you can touch? What is it? Touch it. Is its texture smooth, cold, hot, rough, wet, dry?

d. Does this place have a dominant taste to it, perhaps something on the air? Is this taste pleasant or unpleasant? Identify its source.

6. Is anyone with you in this place? If so, who? Name the person(s) there. What are you (both or all of you) doing? What kind of conversation is taking place–small talk, argument, important discussion? Try to capture as much of the conversation and action as possible.

7. What is the dominant mood of this place? Why is this place important to you? Why is it your favorite place?

8. Slowly, take one last look around, stopping to examine dominant or important aspects of this place in as much detail as you think necessary. When you are ready, leave this place and come back to where you are now.

Write a paragraph in which you detail this place. Your task is to write so that a reader can see that this place is meaningful to you without your having to say that. Do not use words like "favorite" and "meaningful"; instead, let the detail you give the reader carry this message.

*First paragraph: I see trees. Tall long branched pine trees, most of them with tons of green needles, most of them with brown needles ready to drop to the ground. The "floor" is covered with a thick rug of these brown ones that have already dropped, and these mute the sound of my footsteps. The noise is incredible–that sound of silent nature building its cacophony with the sound of birds, squirrels, silence, and the trees growing. The trees dominate every sense as I turn to see more and more. I am in a tiny clearing, just enough space to sit and look at the gaps in the blue sky as the pines fill my eyes. The smell of earth permeates my knowing and I realize that the smell of growing things is what makes the smell of earth so pungent. The rotting layer of pine needles underneath the fresh soft ones lends to this smell of rebirth and I can see the remains of a small campfire–probably from my older brothers and sisters when they last camped up here. I can imagine their laughter and the ghost stories and wish they would let me camp out with them, but I think I would be scared late at night–even without the ghost stories.*

*What surprises me about this paragraph, is that there is really so much more to the area in the woods where we used to camp out than just the trees. I remember little saplings, and a meadow just off to the right, and a huge ravine a little bit farther north than where we always camped out. Off to the left, or the west, was a fence and then a huge cornfield that went down a hill and to the road. That wasn't part of our land, but the ravine and the meadow were, but I think they got cut in half by the property line. I remember some kids trying to claim our forest thinking it was on their land, but they were wrong, because our 60 acres was mostly long instead of wide.*

*Second paragraph: I see so many trees. Tall pine trees that overtake everything in sight, except some tiny patches of sky that fight to be noticed by pushing some spectacular clouds in and out of the way, jockeying for time in my eyes. The trees tend to make me forget about the sky and the clouds though, they are everywhere, and full of both brown and green needles that prickle to the touch and cover the floor of the woods, silencing my steps, except for the scrunching together of the needles under my shoes. These needles must also be what mute the ever present booming of nature, making the sound of the birds and other animals seem so far off, making the sound of growing things, and dying things the main noise. I can almost hear the needles sucking the water out of the air, and the dead ones pushing the last of the water out of their tiny ends into the ground, rotting the ones underneath. If I search long enough, I can make out the hip high grasses of the meadow off to the east, and if I go over there, I bet I can see deer on the other side just shy of the tree line further north. If I walk through the grass, I know I will find a bed for a momma and a baby deer. I think I will walk a little farther into the woods though, I know there is a ravine up ahead, and I may see a fox if I am lucky. I don't think I will go down it though, the soil is too soft, and there is poison ivy in there, but I am not entirely sure of what it looks like. It smells so wonderful here. The noise is more like silence. I am glad Pete and Tom aren't here. They always are laughing and screwing around. They would probably be hiding behind that tree waiting for me to walk past it.*

*This one has so much more detail. I could keep going on, too, it is amazing how much I can remember, especially after I really think about it. I want to say how amazing this place is, but I don't think that would be as effective as trying to show it.*

### Exercise 1.7

Repeat the steps listed above for visualizing two or three of these topics, and write a paragraph detailing your visualization: your school's orientation and/or registration sessions, friendship (or a friend), patriotism (or a patriot), racism (or a racist), sexism (or a sexist).

*Patriotism:*

*The flag wavers in the wind and the stripes become waves as I watch. All down the street, there are flags on porches, doorsteps and in yards. Such is the way of patriotism–in some places. Too many people don't respect our country anymore. I was at a baseball game the other day, and it was cool to listen to the rising voices sing the national anthem along with the music, but I noticed that no one starts singing until the song is half over. Or else everyone is too shy to be noticed singing until others are singing too. I was annoyed when the guy next to me started talking halfway through the song. At least he took off his hat for it. I feel that everyone should have enough respect to just keep their mouths shut unless they are singing. My kid even had the idea and just watched through the song, wondering what everyone was looking at. I always get chills when the song is sung, especially by a woman with a beautiful voice at the major baseball games.*

*Racism:*

*He called the person on the tv a gook, and I sat back and just looked at him in disbelief. My sister-in-law is Korean, and I took offense immediately, and it didn't take me long to let him know how I felt about that. He smiled and apologized and hugged me and said he would never say something like that again. He did. He does. Many times. I think it is to get a rise out of me, because he knows I feel that all people deserve respect until they deserve disrespect, but it doesn't make it ok. No one is spared, particularly Arabs and blacks. I can understand where he is coming from–to a certain degree when it comes to Saddam Hussein, and the idiots testing the nuclear weapons, but for the most part talking in such a manner is stupid–the world is getting much too small for hate.*

Bill

40  The Longwood Guide to Writing Instructor's Resource Manual

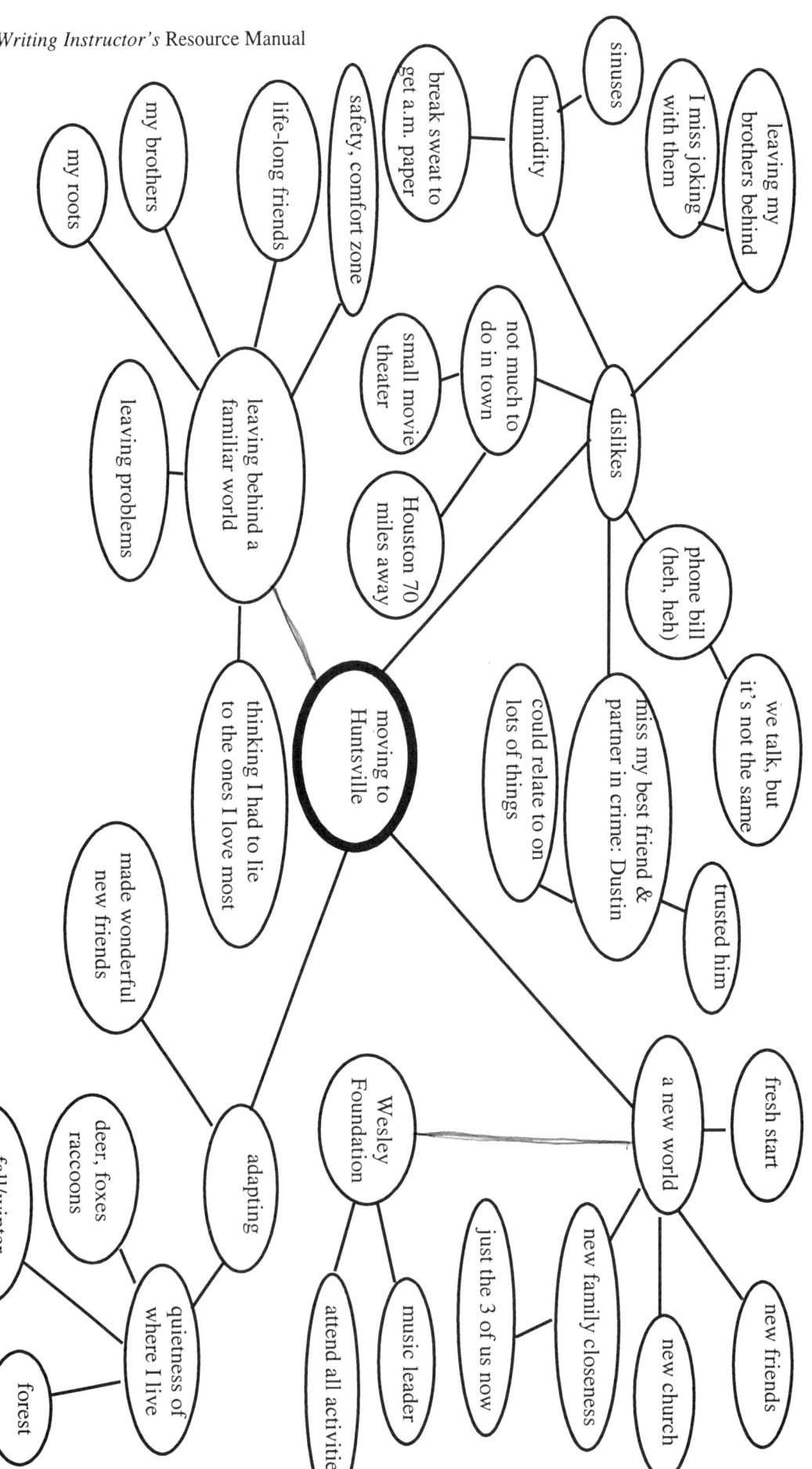

Figure 1.5.A. Important Event Cluster

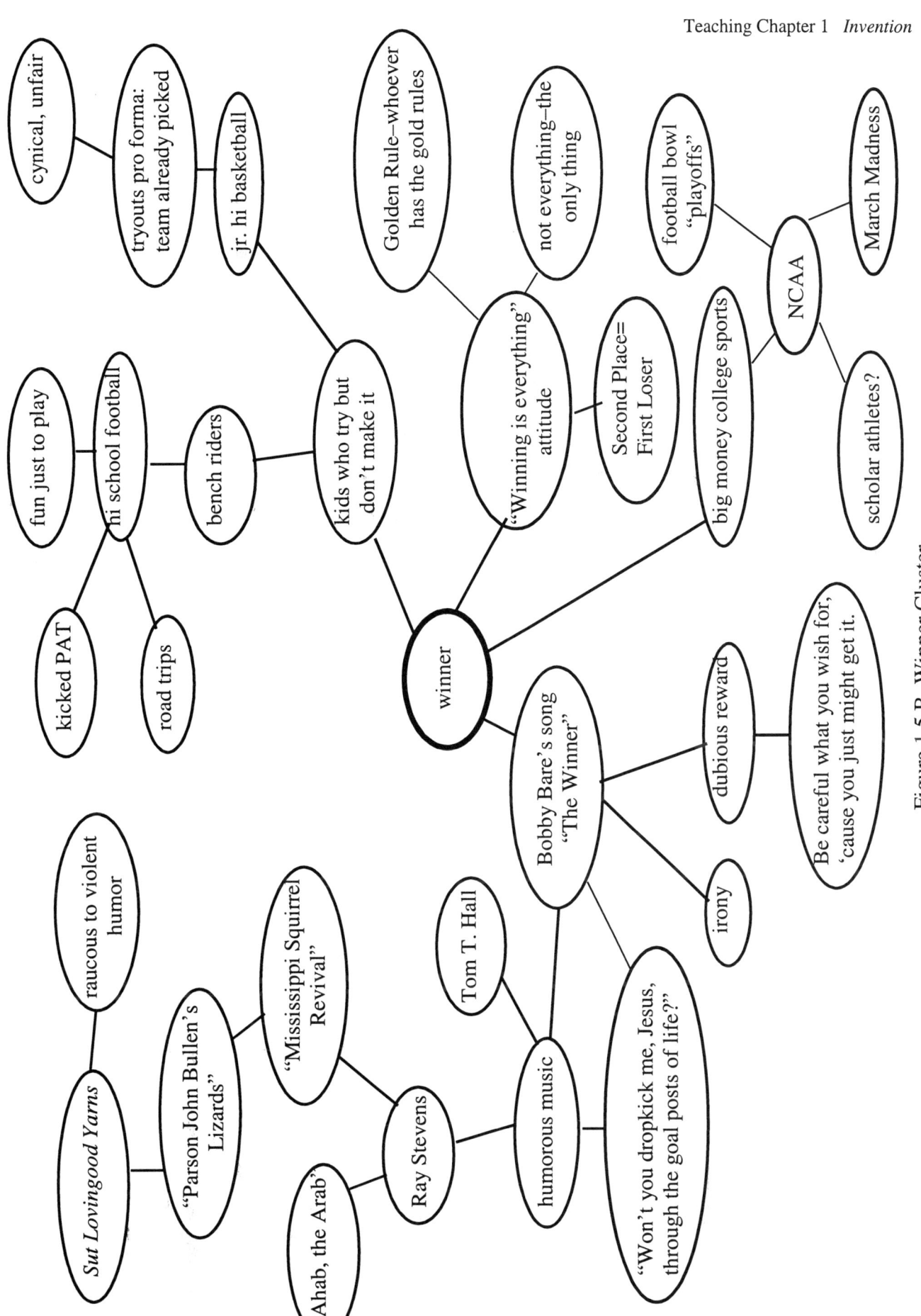

Figure 1.5.B. Winner Cluster

42  *The Longwood Guide to Writing Instructor's* Resource Manual

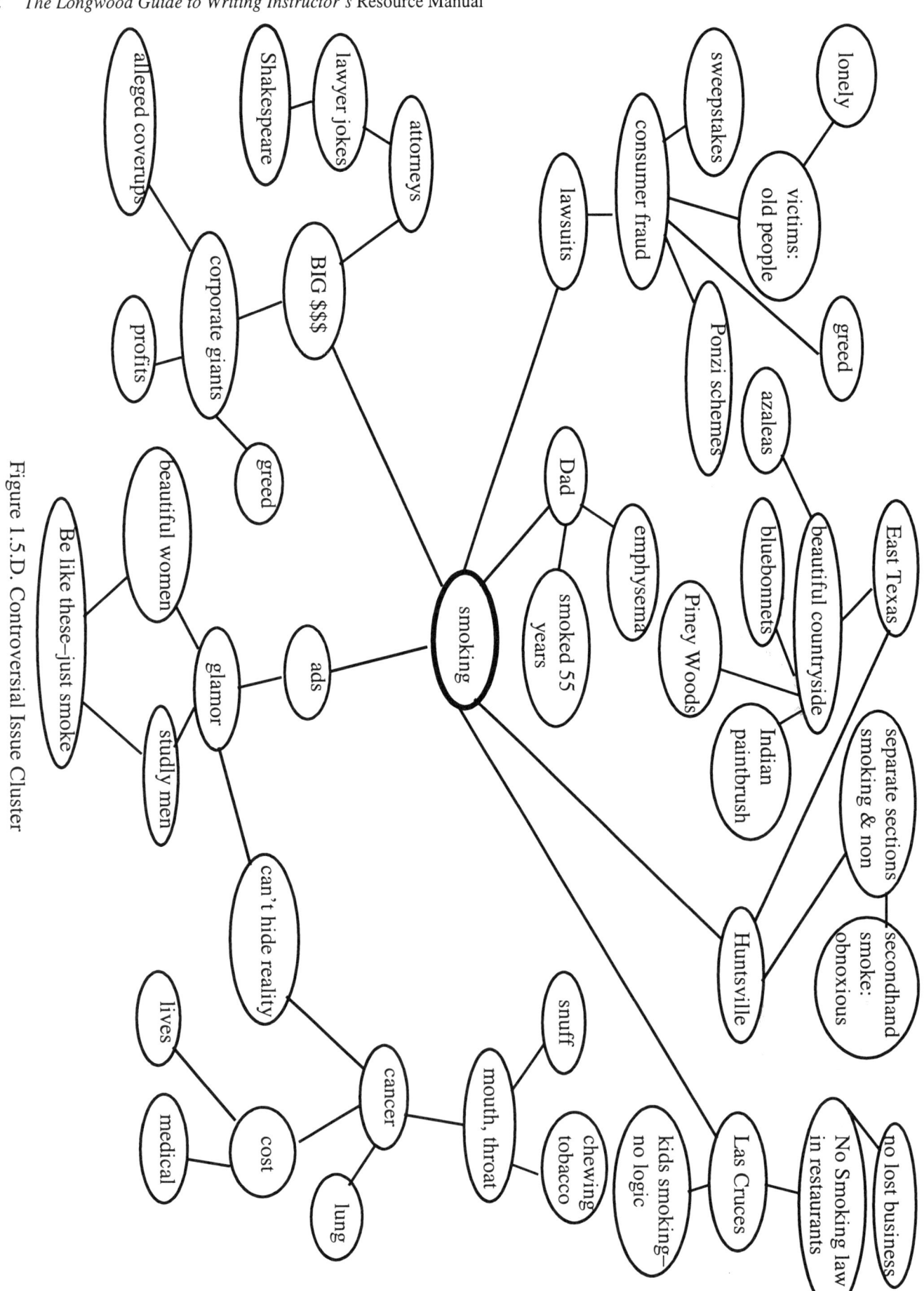

Figure 1.5.D. Controversial Issue Cluster

# *Teaching Chapter 2*
# *Shaping an Essay*

## OVERVIEW

We can readily speak of shaping an essay in terms of *papier-mache* sculpture. The artist begins with a framework, an idea of the overall shape of the sculpture, and then develops the sculpture by layering strips of paper and shaping them into a discernible piece of art. Similarly, prewriting offers many, though certainly not all, of the details the writer may choose from to create layers of text that ultimately form the essay. Shaping an essay focuses on the framework that the writer uses as a guide in incorporating, deleting, and placing details. The purpose of this chapter is to offer advice about developing at least an initial or tentative overall shape for an essay and then using it as a guide for writing.

Visual aids are one of the key features of Chapter 2. Many students are visually-oriented; they are visual learners who need to see a concept in order to grasp it. We've incorporated several visual structures as aids for such students. While some of these may seem elementary at first, we ask that you and your students suspend disbelief until you've tried to use any or all of them.

## TEACHING TIPS

*Audience.* Audience plays a key role in shaping an essay from the beginning of the writing process, which we emphasize at the outset of this chapter by offering these three initial questions involving writer, reader, and topic:

1. What do my readers already know about this topic?

2. What do I want them to know, understand, or learn from reading my writing?

3. Why do I want them to know this?

These questions point toward purpose, so that the writer has this key element of a piece of writing in mind from the start. Be sure to point out to your students the tentative nature of audience early on in the process; later (in Chapter 3) we'll work more extensively with audience analysis.

*Focus Statements*. A focus statement is a tentative, speculative statement about the writer's initial thoughts about purpose; it derives from the three initial questions about audience. Have your students write a focus statement for an essay; then, in their writing groups, have them circulate these statements for their group members' consideration. Each member should write two to three questions evoked by the focus statement or topic. The writer may then use these questions as generative; that is, looking at the questions potential readers want answered can help the writer develop details that will answer them.

*Discovery Draft*. In this chapter, we continue working with Marisol Vargas's writing process. To develop her freewriting (see Chapter 1) into an essay, Marisol wrote brief responses to the initial audience questions, developed a focus statement, and then wrote a discovery draft with her responses and statement as guides.

Having students write a discovery draft emphasizes that writing is a complex process that is far more than a one-shot-draft enterprise. You may well find that they'll be resistant at first, but as they come to see their writing improve by working through several drafts, they'll be more inclined to take the time necessary for good writing to develop. Our way of dealing with resistant students is to require submission of all materials, including a Discovery Draft, a draft for peer review, and then a final draft. Students who do not engage multiple drafting do not get credit for having completed the essay, and we have them rewrite, using a different topic. While this may seem Draconian, we think it necessary to elicit our students' best writing.

As you work through Marisol's writing in this chapter, stress the tentative, exploratory nature. Have your students consider these elements of the essay:

*Introduction.* How has Marisol opened her essay? How engaging is the introduction; that is, how effectively does it catch the reader's attention?

*Paragraphing.* How complex is Marisol's paragraph structure? How effectively does each paragraph support or develop her purpose?

*Detail.* What is the depth of detail in this draft?

*Conclusion.* How does Marisol conclude her essay? How effectively does she prepare the reader for the statement she makes in the last paragraph?

As you work with Marisol's essay, have your students point to one or two aspects of each question that work well and others that need strengthening. Ask for specific advice from your students on strengthening the paper. If your students don't make this point, be sure to point out the lack of descriptive detail in this draft. Marisol tells the reader a lot, but she doesn't use enough detail to make the event come alive. Bill uses the analogy of pop-up books to make this point. Most students have read pop-up books, either as children or, for example, as babysitters keeping their young charges entertained. When you turn the page on one of these books, a scene literally pops up off the page to provide a three-dimensional representation of the text. The writer's words are all that he has to make a scene come to life; the detail he presents makes his writing "pop up" for the reader.

**Visual Aids.** Why use such visual aids as those we present in Chapter 2? Gilbert Highet offers an answer in the short passage we quote from *Explorations* (Oxford U Press, 1971): "Every article ought to have a shape." Student writing many times seems shapeless, a collection of details without a discernible structure. Visual aids can help students see such structure.

Because some students are visual learners, using drawings can help them see the whole of an essay and how it's constituted by its parts. Drawings can also help make the task of writing less formidable by helping students see it as a series of components that can be addressed one at a time instead of a whole to be addressed all at once.

Have your students draw structures for several of the sample essays we provide. In our discussion of chapter 5, we've drawn a structure for Datus Proper's "Dark Hollow" that you may use as an example. Proper weaves a story back and forth, detailing a day's fishing but interjecting at key points a second narrative, that by Betty Cave. It's in the retelling of Cave's story that Proper develops the significance of the situation he comes to understand from encountering her. Have your students draw a structure for other sample readings, either using the templates we've provided in Chapter 2 or developing their own.

**Elements of an Essay.** In our discussion of the elements of an essay, we've used parts of several of the professional and student essays that we provide throughout the text. It may be helpful for your students to read these essays to see the excerpted parts in context, though you may want to have your students read not every essay for this discussion but one or two that you think to be particularly effective.

> ***Thesis sentences.*** Be sure to note that a thesis statement may appear just about anywhere in an essay (at the beginning, near or in the middle, at the end) depending on the writer's purpose and that it may be written at any point in the writing process. Stress also that the thesis may change as the essay develops. Throughout the semester, ask your students to identify the thesis statement for each sample reading, remarking its placement in the essay and how effectively it seems to have guided the writer. Note especially the writer's stance on the topic or attitude toward it and her reader as reflected by the thesis.

> ***Introductions.*** In our discussion of introductions, we've given a brief analysis of the openings from five of the sample essays we present in other chapters of our text. As you work with these, focus on the job the introduction does: identifying the topic and (in many cases) the writer's particular stance on or attitude toward both topic and reader. Ask your students how effective each introduction is and why. Note also that, like the thesis statement, the introduction may be written at any point in the process, that in fact it is often written near the last of the process.

> ***Paragraphs.*** Have your students discuss the role of a paragraph in an essay, stressing that each paragraph is like a brick that joins with other bricks to form a whole wall or building. Note that each paragraph develops some aspect of the writer's purpose as expressed in the thesis sentence.

> In working with the concept of cohesion, present your students with scrambled paragraphs. Either as a handout or on an overhead, write the sentences of a paragraph as a list, scrambling the original order. Have your students unscramble the sentences so that they create a logical order for them. Have them defend their ordering, focusing on the clues inherent in the sentences that tell them how the sentences relate to each other.

> ***Conclusions.*** In our section on conclusions, we return to the five sample essays we selected for discussion of introductions. Have your students respond to the questions we list early in this section, focusing on how effective each conclusion seems and why.

***Writer's Block.*** All writers get stuck at one time or another. To help your students understand writer's block as something to expect but not necessarily to fear, talk about how and why you get stuck when you write. Then talk about how you get unstuck. Have your students add to the list of ways to beat writer's block offered in the text block at the end of the chapter.

# RESPONSES TO EXERCISES

### Exercise 2.1

Select an essay in another chapter in this text, and look especially at its introduction. How effective is that introduction? What does that introduction do for the reader? How well does it establish a context for the essay it introduces?

> *I read the introduction in chapter three to an essay about Homer Simpson, and although I don't think it is the greatest introduction I've ever read, I do think that it would set a context for the paper. It also would let the readers know exactly what the author is going to write about and discuss in detail. I think this type of introduction is one of those that takes the reader by the hand and says "this is what I am going to do, and then I am going to do this, and then this" . . . etc. The author is also going to attempt to alter the reader's point of view to match his point of view. The introduction*

*fits what the author is trying to do, so yes, it is effective.*

## Exercise 2.2

Select an essay in another chapter of this text and examine each paragraph of the body for its topic sentence. What idea does the topic sentence imply that the paragraph will develop? How well does the paragraph develop this idea? Where does the topic sentence appear? Is it where it should be? If a given paragraph does not have a topic sentence, does it develop a topic idea expressed in a preceding paragraph? If not, should it have its own topic sentence? Why or why not?

> *I used the essay "Mirror Image" to analyze the topic sentences. In the first paragraph, Marisol is relating an argument effectively through the use of conversation, and she develops it into the second paragraph, both through her description of body language and lack of conversation. She also includes the thoughts she was having at the time which back up the entire scenario. In the third paragraph, she presents the images so that we can see them as she remembers them, and then she introduces one of the main ideas of the essay, the food. In the fifth paragraph, the author develops her stereotypes and prejudices, and in fact relates to the readers by relaying many of our own. The sixth paragraph shows how Marisol has to take fruit out to the people, and in so doing, she has to learn that they don't deserve to be treated any differently from anyone else, or feared, but instead treated as people. The topic sentences in the next three paragraphs all work together to explain the one idea at hand, Marisol observing the people as people, and sharing her food with them. This leads her to her final paragraphs, which detail Marisol's change of heart, her realization that these people are no different from her, except that they live under different circumstances. They are still people and deserve respect.*
>
> *I think Marisol's use of topic sentences is very obscure throughout much of her essay, but this works to make her essay much more effective. Several areas of the essay work together, and the topic sentence for one paragraph leads into several others as she develops her ideas. In the ninth paragraph, the author puts her topic sentence as the first, but in the tenth, it comes as the second sentence in the paragraph. The first few sets of paragraphs come with a topic sentence that leads into several other paragraphs.*

## Exercise 2.3

Select an essay in another chapter of this text and examine its paragraphs for unity and coherence. Does each paragraph follow the direction established by its topic sentence? If a particular paragraph does not contain a topic sentence, does it develop a topic idea, perhaps an idea stated in a preceding paragraph? If so, how well does it develop that idea? Mark any transitional words and phrases you have used. Are these appropriate? Why or why not? Mark any repetition of key words and phrases. Are these appropriate? Why or why not?

*"How Exhausting it is to Keep Up Appearances" (Kristina Geray, Ch. 8)*

> *The final revision of this essay seems to follow a good sense of topic sentence/idea and then development. I underlined each topic sentence in each paragraph, and a good majority of them come at the beginning of each paragraph. There are some that come later in the paragraph, but as in the paragraph on appearances, the main idea of being miserable and hopelessly alone leads into the next paragraph on each of the characters as being miserable. Sometimes the author uses the topic sentence as the second sentence in the paragraph, instead of as the first, but it seems to work. She spends a lot of time transitioning the readers to her new ideas. The third to last paragraph does not seem to hold a topic sentence that continues the idea throughout the paragraph, but the last sentence in the paragraph serves to delineate the topic idea, that of Nola's ultimate concern to not stand out in a crowd.*

*Some transitional words and phrases Kristina uses:*

| | |
|---|---|
| On the other hand | This |
| Finally | But |
| Is shown time and time again | What does show |
| Despite | The most glaring example |
| At this point | However |

*Several of these are repeated at different points throughout the essay, and they do seem to work, although at times, the term "despite" gets a little repetitious. Each example of transition works, because Kristina uses a style that allows her to work on the idea throughout a couple of different paragraphs, developing her ideas to compare and contrast between the mother and the girl.*

*Some terms are repeated, such as the "woman in black," which gets a little overused, but then again, the author does not allow herself any opportunity to use much else, because she spends so little time developing this character. She instead spends the time working on the response the two main characters have to the bag lady. The other repetition I noticed is the use of "despite," which works, because it isn't overused, but I do think the author could have found another term at least once within the text.*

## Exercise 2.4

Read the essays by Datus Proper and Steven Barboza in Chapter Five, Personal Essays, and draw a structure for each. What did you draw? How effectively does your drawing represent the structure for each? What do your drawings suggest to you about potential structures for your own writing?

*[NOTE: See "Teaching Chapter 5" for a drawing of Proper's essay. Represent the structure of Barboza's as a loop. That is, the essay starts in the present, then loops back into the past and comes forward to the present. After having your students present their drawings of the structure of these two essays, offer them either of these representations, and discuss why an essay needs a shape.]*

## Exercise 2.5

1. What is Kirkendall's point in this essay? How effectively does she present and support it?

   *Kirkendall's point is that we consistently oversimplify and misunderstand rural culture, and this causes damage through stereotyping. She's effective in presenting and supporting it through a number of detailed examples and a conclusion that stresses commonalities and positive aspects of rural life.*

2. Does this essay have a thesis? If so, identify it and comment on its effectiveness. If not, do you think it needs one? Why or why not?

   *I think Kirkendall does have a thesis, and it comes at the end of the fourth paragraph when she states, "These negative stereotypes are as unmerciful as they are unfounded." I think this is a good way to sum up her entire argument, and I do think it is effective.*

3. How cohesive are its various paragraphs? Select any two paragraphs and comment specifically on how Kirkendall works to achieve cohesion. Pay particular attention to topic sentences.

   *Each paragraph in this essay works well with the others to form a very cohesive piece of writing. Kirkendall discusses many examples of derision and ridicule that she personally witnessed, and she also discusses how tourists love to do this sort of thing, and they flock to the Ozarks to take advantage of the backwoods people.*

*Two paragraphs and cohesion:*

*¶5 is a narrative about Kirkendall's working in "a nearby city." There's no topic sentence, so she builds cohesion through chronology, working from leaving home through her co-workers responses to her wanting to return home. She also uses transition and repetition of key words to achieve cohesion. E.g., "There" in the second sentence repeats "nearby city," so the first and second sentences are joined. The third sentence uses "also" to continue the idea that Kirkendall was ridiculed, which she first mentioned in the second sentence, so the second and third sentences are joined.*

*¶7 is informative in nature. The first sentence is the paragraph's topic sentence, and the rest of the paragraph develops its primary idea, that of the juxtaposition and stylization of rural culture. Kirkendall supports this assertion by talking about country and western bars being "chic," then gives a personal example of city meeting (and sneering at) country in "the trendiest country bars." Kirkendall connects the first of the paragraph with the last by returning to the theme of juxtaposition, so the paragraph is cohesive.*

4. Block the essay; identify the paragraphs that constitute the introduction, body (its supporting paragraphs), and conclusion. Further, divide the body into mini-blocks; that is, identify the major sections of the essay's body. Justify your divisions.

*Introduction: first 4 paragraphs. Thesis comes at the end of ¶4: "These negative stereotypes are as unmerciful as they are unfounded."*

*Body: ¶s 5-8. These present specific details about the negative stereotypes Kirkendall notes in the thesis sentence. ¶5 presents personal narrative (no topic sentence). ¶s 6 & 7 talk about the chicness of country: it's chic to be (stylized) hick. ¶8 is another narrative (no topic sentence).*

*Conclusion: last 3 paragraphs. ¶9 moves beyond specific examples to begin drawing a significant conclusion (the first sentence of this paragraph). ¶s 10 & 11 work to counter stereotypes and to show the resilience of Ozarkians and so of all rural people.*

5. How effective is the introduction? What does the introduction reveal of Kirkendall's attitude toward the topic? How does Kirkendall show this to her readers?

*The introduction presents some of the implications of the term <u>hillbilly</u>. Kirkendall shows some of the humorous but negative stereotypes from tv and movies. She then leads into her discussion of the American ideals and attitudes that allow this sort of attitude toward a people who are not pushing themselves into the forefront and instead are content with their way of life. We can see her attitude in many of the comments she makes, including her admission of resentment and of being offended. Despite her resentment, she doesn't write in anger, and her tone isn't shrill or strident. She demonstrates her own intelligence and admits that she too is a "hillbilly" and proud of her lifestyle. She wants to educate her readers so that the prejudices can be eliminated.*

6. How effective is the conclusion? How does it work to bring the essay to an end?

*The conclusion works to illustrate many examples of successful people who live in rural areas, working the land, and also the reasons they feel it is important to stay in the hills. She says "through it all, we Ozarkians remind ourselves how fortunate we are to live in a region admired for its blue spring, rolling hills and geological wonders." This sentence alone is designed to make readers recognize that living in populated , "civilized" areas doesn't make anyone smarter or better adjusted than anyone else. It simply means that they have chosen a different lifestyle.*

7. Beginning with the first paragraph, identify this essay's key terms. How do they work to create a cohesive essay?

*Key terms are at work in every paragraph: 1st paragraph, hillbilly, insult, implications. 2nd, belittled, tolerance and discrimination, stereotypes unexamined; 3rd, exaggerated accents and dress, nonsense; 4th, commitment to egalitarianism, oversimplify and misunderstand rural culture, hillbilly stigma; 5th, wisecracks, ribbing, scorn, bewilderment, concern; 6th, hillbilly's marketable, packaged legacy; 7th, authentic elements juxtaposed and stylized, trendiest country bars; 8th, freeways clogged, clear rivers, condescension, insults, tolerated derision; 9th, America's ambivalent, urban culture, urbanites imitate sanitized country lifestyle, embarrassment; 10th, fortunate, not stereotypical, unique sense of community, family ties, beautiful environment; 11th, "bad guys" exception (not the rule), successful, lower standard of living, occasional gibe*

*These terms help to create a cohesive essay because they show the tension between city and country people. These terms show the depth of the ridicule and derision and so the damage that stereotyping does. But they also show resilience, especially in the last three paragraphs.*

Bill

# Teaching Chapter 3
# Revising

## OVERVIEW

How to begin discussion of revision? Revising is crucial to writing well, but far too many of our students don't revise, don't really know how to revise, think it's too difficult, don't give themselves enough time for it, put the whole writing enterprise off till it's too late to do any more than bang out a one-shot draft and pray for the best. So how to get students to realize the importance of revision? Well, we could begin by saying something like this: Writing is revising. But that just doesn't have the right ring to it, doesn't sound quite important enough; somehow, it doesn't seem to give revision its due. Maybe we could pick up on Epictetus's statement about writing: "If you wish to be a good writer, write." Applied to revision, that would become: "If you wish to be a good writer, revise." Nope, that sounds a tad pretentious. Some others:

> If one wishes to write, then one must revise. (too stuffy)
> If you're going to write, then you have to revise. (too conditional, too iffy)
> To write is to revise. (too many infinitives)
> We have ways of making you revise. (too Draconian, too punitive)
> Revision is a necessary part of the writing process. (too understated)
> Rewriting is . . . (nope, we're back to understatement)
> Writers revise. (too pithy; besides, students may not see themselves as writers)

So where does all this leave us, all this flailing around trying to find the right way into discussion of revision? It points to this simple fact: Writing is revising. Each of these statements is but a revision of "writing is revising." Each is different from the others and so carries different connotations about revision, which we can readily use to at least imply the power of revision: when the writer changes a single word or moves a single adjective or adverb around in a sentence, she revises and at the same time creates a new meaning, however slight the difference between the original and revised versions may be. And that's the job of the writer as rewriter: to make those changes in her writing that move it nearer to what she wants it to say than it is when she sits down to revise.

Still, there's another aspect to revising that sometimes gets lost in the rush to champion a process approach: editing. As we say repeatedly in *The Longwood Guide to Writing* and elsewhere in this Instructor's Resource Manual, students should not pay attention to error too early in the process. But at the end of the process, when the writer is preparing the essay for submission to his instructor (a form of publication, hence the title of the handbook section of our text), he must pay attention to correctness; he must become concerned with the conventions of Standard American English. When a reader notices an error, that error has in some way, large or small, diminished the overall effectiveness of the essay. Too many errors can cause the writer's message to be lost in a haze or fogbank of error-induced dissonance, no matter how strongly or clearly or eloquently worded that message may be. Surface errors (i.e., errors in spelling and punctuation) can especially be damaging, particularly when the reader expects an error-free paper. It is not enough, then, for the writer just to revise; he must also edit his work.

# TEACHING TIPS

*Global v. Local Revision*–to revise comprehensively means to consider both global and local matters. The writer engaged in global revision considers larger issues of purpose, audience, and overall essay structure–does the essay reveal a purpose shaped for a particular audience and then structured to reveal that purpose effectively? The writer who engages in local revision attends to smaller (though not especially less important) matters such as individual sentence structure and word choice–how effectively does each sentence work to develop the purpose; does each word convey the writer's intended meaning as effectively as possible? To help your students understand that revision is not merely editing, you'll need to help them understand the need to engage global and local revision.

*Seven Revising Strategies.* In Chapter 3 we present seven strategies for revision:

*Strategy #1, Getting Distance.* One way to help students get some distance between themselves and their writing is to actually create a physical separation. That is, have them write a short piece, perhaps a paragraph or two in response to the favorite place visualization exercise. Take these up; then assign them to rewrite their paragraphs for homework. But don't return the original. When your students return with the revised versions in hand, hand back their originals and ask them to compare the writing done in class with that done out of class. Move from this to stress the need for discipline, for the writer to establish and keep deadlines that will require her to finish an essay assignment at least two days before its due date, so that she can get some distance.

*Strategy #2, Revising for Meaning.* This global strategy requires the student to take an overview of what he intended to say and how effectively he developed his intention. Point out that the seven questions listed under this strategy focus on purpose and the major points supporting or developing this purpose. Discuss Steve Duran's sample assessment of his own essay. It's especially important to point out that Steve remembered an example he wanted to include and so revised once again, even after he thought he had prepared a final draft.

*Strategy #3, Revising for Audience.* This global strategy asks the writer to write a short initial definition of her audience and then to write a more detailed analysis of her readers and what she wants them to understand or gain from having read her writing. Stress the role of audience and the questions we present for analyzing audience as at once generative and evaluative. For example, thinking through what she'll have to do to reach her readers can be generative; it can help the writer generate or find or invent ideas to use in her essay. The evaluative part comes in after the writer's prepared a draft, with the writer considering how effectively she's written for her audience.

*Strategy #4, Revising for Structure.* This global strategy asks the writer to bring the planning he gave to shaping his essay to bear on revising it. How effectively did he use one of the strategies given in Chapter 2? Did he block his essay? Draw it? Write from a list? Have him hold the essay against his planning to see if he developed the paper he thought he would. If there are differences, have him reconcile them.

*Strategy #5, Revising for Sentences.* This local strategy asks the writer to move into her paragraphs to consider the effectiveness of each sentence. Our concern with our own students is that they not write pedestrian sentences, that is, sentences that plod along, all about the same length, all with about the same structure, all lacking sufficient transition between and among them to make them hang together. Here you may want to work through some sentence combining exercises, and you may ground your discussion in any of William Strong's books on sentence combining, including *Sentence Combining: A Composing Book* (3rd ed., 1994), *Sentence Combining and Paragraph Building* (1981), and *Writer's Toolbox: A Sentence-Combining Workshop* (1996). (Note: all three of these books are published by McGraw-Hill.)

**Strategy #6, Revising for Words.** This local strategy asks the writer to look at the words he's chosen to carry his meaning. Is each word correct? Are there any malapropisms? Does each word contribute to the overall effectiveness of the essay? One way to help your students understand the difference between the word that's right and the one that's almost but not quite right involves dictionary work. Find several places in a good collegiate dictionary where synonyms are given for a particular term. Have your students read these and discuss in which context such terms as *approbation*, *attention*, and *regard* might be used.

**Strategy #7, Peer Review.** We've labeled this strategy as both global and local, for effective peer group work involves a thorough, complete reading of an essay. Oftentimes, students gathering in groups for peer review need considerable direction, and we encourage you to provide them with guidelines for their review. At the end of each of our writing occasions chapters (Chapters 5-11) and the end of Chapter 12, we provide a checklist for the essay at hand, and you may use a checklists as review sheets, so that students respond in writing to each of the entries on a given list, or you may use them as a starting point for developing your own review sheets.

One point that is critical involves what we label the Golden Rule of Peer Criticism: Nobody says or does anything wilfully mean. By this we mean that reviewers must work hard to ensure that they don't say or do anything designed to denigrate either the writer or her work. At times, this happens when the reviewers don't understand what it means to critique an essay instead of to criticize it. They take their job seriously, and that job is, after all, to rip the paper at hand to shreds–isn't that how you make it better? Well, no, not exactly. We tell our students that the writer most often needs first to understand what worked in her paper and then how to make it better. We're not suggesting that reviewers ignore the essay's faults; instead, we're saying that every comment a reviewer makes should be as constructive as possible. Another potential problem with peer response is the comment that says, "I liked your paper. It's good. I wouldn't change a thing." Such comments as these suggest that the reviewer either didn't take the review session or the essay seriously or isn't skilled enough in what to look for in a review session to offer genuine help. Whichever is the case, your job will be to ensure the effectiveness of group sessions. As to the former problem (lack of seriousness), give your students an assessment of just how helpful you think their comments were; you may even wish to give some sort of grade on their reviews, perhaps a check, check plus, or check minus, with these to figure at semester's end as part of an overall participation grade. (For more discussion on evaluating student writing, see "Giving Feedback to Student Writers: Marking, Evaluating, and Responding," which appears later in this manual.)

How to handle dysfunctional groups? It's your prerogative to structure groups as you see fit, though one thing to avoid is structuring groups in which friends are members. We've found that students who are friends or who know each other are less likely to give honest critiques of each others' writing; we've also found that these friends are likely to sit together in class. So one way to structure a group is by counting off. If you have 20 students and want to have 5 groups of 4 members each, then have your students number off from 1 to 4, then start again, and so on, till everyone has a number. Then have them assemble in their groups by number, so that you have a random mix of students in each group. Should you have a group that simply isn't working, you'll need to learn why. If one member is particularly disruptive, you may have to move him to another group. If you have a student who isn't participating fully, you may have to put him "on contract." That is, write a contract stipulating your expectations for his participation, and have him sign it. If he violates the terms of this contract, then you may remove him from his group, and he'll have to be on his own to find outside readers for his essays. You should require this student to have his work reviewed, but put the onus on him to find his own readers.

For more discussion of group work, see Ron's essay "Planning for Spontaneity in the Writing Classroom and a Passel of Other Paradoxes," which we present later in this manual.

*Self-assessment*. Have your students write a self-assessment to cover each of their essays. This piece of writing requires the writer to take a step back from the paper and to consider just how effectively it fulfills the assignment. Exercise 3.1 directs the writer to develop such an assessment for "a given paper," but we encourage you to require it, as we do, for every paper. Having experience in writing self-assessments will be important for your students, especially if you require that they submit a portfolio with a reflective assessment of the extent to which their writing has improved over the course of the semester. (For more discussion of this reflective essay assignment, see "Teaching Writing as a Process" below.)

*Name the Game*. Ask students to discuss what they do to revise, to name their revision strategies and tell how effective they think they are. Have them work to make distinctions between revising and editing. We won't belabor the differences between revising and editing, but we will say once again that it's crucial that your students understand these differences. The strategies we present in this section are hardly exhaustive, so you should ask your students what they do to edit. Discuss your own editing strategies with them as well. Work through your own writing experiences with them, naming your own strategies and talking about how you do different things when you edit your work. In particular, talk about the choices available to you and why you chose to revise as you did. Show students your marked up rough drafts. Show them the paragraphs you had to cut, the sentences you moved around in a paragraph, the single word you changed that made a difference in meaning.

## SAMPLE STUDENT PROCESS

In Chapter 3, we present three drafts of Marisol Vargas's "Mirror Image." You'll remember that this is the draft we started working with in Chapter 1 by presenting Marisol's prewriting and then continued with in Chapter 2, where we presented her focus statement and discovery draft. As you work through the three drafts in Chapter 3, have your students comment on whether each subsequent draft is an improvement over the previous one, and why. Focus on both global and local revisions, noting particularly when Marisol seemed to revise and then seemed to edit. Your students may be surprised at all the revising that Marisol did to complete the assignment, but stress to them that that's what writing is: revising.

## RESPONSES TO EXERCISES

*Exercise 3.1*

After you've written your final draft to submit to your instructor of a given paper, let it sit a day or two, and then apply the questions below to it. Based on this application, write a self-assessment paragraph in which you identify the essay's strengths and weaknesses. What will you do differently the next time you write?

1. What is the purpose of this essay? To what extent does your draft fulfill that purpose? What revisions do you think will be necessary?

> *The purpose of my essay was to compare and relate the two novels <u>Beloved</u>, by Toni Morrison, and <u>As I Lay Dying</u>, by William Faulkner. There were several ideas that I thought really related to each other between the two novels. I think my draft only touches on these ideas, and the revision will come in developing my ideas to really show how certain things relate, instead of expecting the reader to simply understand that they relate. I think I am thinking they know what I mean by certain things, and so I haven't fully developed any one of the three areas of comparison.*

2. How well does the introduction work? What did you intend the introduction to do, specifically? Is it appropriate for your audience? If not, what will you need to do to make it appropriate for your audience?

> *My introduction doesn't work. It's weak, boring, short, insignificant. I wanted the introduction to set up my ideas and get me going, but it doesn't even start to do that. It is not nearly appropriate for my audience, particularly if that audience hasn't read the two novels. I am relying much too much on my audience to know exactly what I am talking about, and since I haven't developed my ideas well enough, even a person who has recently read both of them wouldn't know what I am talking about.*

3. How well does the conclusion work? What did you intend the conclusion to do, specifically? Is it appropriate for your audience? If not, what will you need to do to make it appropriate for your audience?

> *My conclusion is weak also. It is much like the intro, I don't have enough flesh, instead I am trying to get out of the paper. It looks like I am bored (which to a certain extent I am, but I don't want my reader to know that). I think I am also just unsure of how to close all of my ideas up, because I haven't developed them. I wanted my conclusion to tie everything together and show how everything works as it does in my mind. I need to develop the body to make a strong conclusion that will work.*

4. How appropriate is the language you have used in the paper? To what extent does it meet the needs of your audience? Is it appropriate for your audience? For your purpose? Why or why not?

> *The language is appropriate. I've tried to retain a professional attitude and exhibit knowledge, but language is only one facet of doing this. I think the language I use is relative to the topic and works for the paper.*

5. What sentence strategies have you used? Are your sentences primarily all of one type (e.g., short or long, loose or periodic)? Is there enough variety in your sentences to keep your writing from being choppy?

> *There is quite a bit of variety of sentence length and texture, but I am trying to make too many paragraphs out of too few sentences. I need to do some combinations and developments. I don't feel that the writing is altogether choppy, but it can definitely use some polishing.*

6. Are your paragraphs unified and coherent? Does each paragraph develop some aspect of your thesis sentence?

> *The paragraphs are trying to be coherent, and the organization is symmetrical, but they need to be developed. I will have many more paragraphs before I am through with the paper, and then the unity will be much stronger, because I will have developed the topic fully.*

7. What grammatical or mechanical problems do you see?

> *I have a couple of comma splices and dash problems, as well as some citation problems. I don't think I have many, but I need to have someone else look at it to make sure I am catching all of those.*

8. What title will you give your paper? What word, phrase, or sentence do you think will best represent your paper to your reader and so serve you well as a title?

*Title . . . I think I will use a little bit of both books and put something together. I am tossing around the idea of "Beloved: My Mother is a Fish," but I am not sure yet.*

## Exercise 3.2

Revisit each draft of Marisol's essay. How effectively does the revised final draft fulfill the promises Marisol makes in her discovery draft? In her freewriting? Point to at least two places in the revised final draft that you think are particularly strong. Why do you think these to be effective? Point to at least two places in this draft that you think need revising. What advice would you offer Marisol about revising them?

*Marisol's first freewrite had nothing to do with her final topic, which is interesting, but her second freewrite was all about feeding the homeless, and her feelings, as well as what she saw, what impacted her, how she didn't want to really get involved in the whole thing. Some of the things she discussed in her freewrite wound up in her paper, which shows how valuable that freewrite was for her in discovering where she was going with the idea.*

*It seems that Marisol fulfills most of the promises she makes with her discovery draft, except for the eagerness that I began to feel in that first draft. At one point, she says she "raced back into the kitchen to refill it [the fruit dish] and hurried back out." Throughout the final draft, I constantly get the feeling of sluggishness, even after she realizes that what she is doing is not such a bad thing. The pace remains very slow and unhurried. I think other than that one thing, though, Marisol does a good job of developing her discovery draft.*

*I think the first strong part of Marisol's final draft is the introduction. I think she really developed the idea of reluctance, and she showed how easy it would have been to just roll over, and how hard it was to actually get up, eat breakfast and get in the car. I think part of why I like that part so much is because I would have behaved in the same manner. I wouldn't have even wanted to talk to my mom, much less look at her, even though she hadn't done anything wrong. My own convictions would make me react that way, just as it seems Marisol's did. She does a really good job of relating to me, and she really didn't even have to explain every single thing. I got a good picture from what I read.*

*The second part that I think is the most effective is the part about the man who looked like Santa Claus. I think that she really portrayed him as someone all of us know, someone who we don't want to feel sorry for, but at the same time, he was someone strong. His behavior, looking at her like she was kind of crazy and then juggling his food so he could take the fruit, seemed so real. The fact that he spilled hot coffee on his hand makes it much more vivid, too. This is one part of the essay that just really sticks out in my mind, and I think that is why I find it so effective. It's memorable.*

*One part that I think needs development is the part about the dogs and their owners. I don't feel that it is that important, because it hasn't been developed to show why it is so important. She should either make it more vital to the paper or take it out. The other part that needs revision, although these parts are hard to find in the final draft, is the part about the little girls whose dresses are loose from starvation. That idea sticks out in my mind so clearly, but I want more. I don't know if I really want to know more, but it just seems to be such a large detail that was brushed over by the rest of the paper. I don't think this idea should be taken out, but I do think this one needs to be expanded on.*

Bill

# Teaching Chapter 4
# Responding to Readings

## OVERVIEW

One of the biggest problems students have is reading. This is not to say that students don't know how to decode words or that they're illiterate. Instead, our assertion is that students generally don't know how to read critically or productively. Nor do the majority of them know how to study productively. Students tend to be passive readers. They'll open a book, hurry through the assigned pages without marking anything or taking any notes, close the book, and think they've read; they think they're prepared for their next class. Chapter 4 derives from our belief that students can make their reading and studying far more productive than they do at present. To this end, we offer a number of reading strategies and illustrate throughout the chapter the connections between writing and reading.

To begin, ask your students how many of them know how to study. Not just read through a text, but really how to study. You may get a few hands, but if your students are like ours, you won't get very many. When you ask how many have had any kind of instruction about studying or even talked about it at some point earlier in their academic careers, you'll get even fewer hands. At this point, you can talk with your students about the time that studying takes (see text box in Chapter 4). Our students are always amazed that we recommend a 1 to 3 ratio of hours taken to hours spent studying. This recommendation translates thus:

| Hours taken | Hours in class and studying (per week) |
| --- | --- |
| 12 | 36 |
| 13 | 39 |
| 14 | 42 |
| 15 | 45 |
| 16 | 48 |

Ask your students to keep a study log in which they record for a one- to two-week period the time they give to studying and the kinds of things they do to study. Then have them compare the time they spend to the chart above. They may well be surprised at the differences. But the biggest chore will be developing effective study skills, so that the time they spend will be productive.

Clearly, going to school is a full-time job. Many students have obligations beyond their studies: family, job(s), extracurricular activities. It's no wonder that many of our students seem frazzled or overwhelmed by the loads they labor under. Helping them to become more proficient at studying can help them succeed and make their load a little lighter. Be sure to point out that this chapter offers far more reading strategies than anyone ought to employ while reading. We offer them as options, as strategies to try out and then use as students find most helpful.

## TEACHING TIPS

***Owning a Book***. The passage we quote by Mortimer Adler provides a good starting point for this chapter. Ask your students to discuss how someone can own a book other than paying for it or having received it as a gift. Have them talk about their favorite book, poem, or quote and why they value it. Discuss the pleasures of reading and the intensity of reading deeply.

*Sample Readings.* Early in Chapter 4, we present three readings: a persuasive essay, a personal essay, and a poem. Have your students speculate about how they usually read a work from each of these genres. Are there things they do differently in preparing to read and then in thinking about an essay as opposed to a poem? If so, what? And why? Have your students write a one- to two-sentence response to the questions that follow each. How well do they know each text? How well have they absorbed it?

*Reading Strategies.* We've divided the reading strategies, some fifteen in all, into three sections: "Before You Read," "While You Read," and "After You Have Read." Stress that these form a very comprehensive approach to reading and that you do not expect them to apply each of the strategies every time they read something. But stress that they do need to try several, at least one or two in each section, just to see how well each might work for them. Following the strategies, we include a complete response to Lee Abbott's "The True Story of Why I Do What I Do," just to illustrate the range of responses each strategy in turn can evoke. Stress that this is an extended example, not a template that they must follow to respond correctly to a reading.

*Writing Paraphrases and Summaries.* Students often overlook the effectiveness of paraphrasing and summarizing what they read. Remark the differences between these two activities, and talk about when it's appropriate to do each. Focus on both as ways of understanding a reading and of retaining its main point(s). If we put someone else's words into our own words (paraphrasing) or if we boil down a longer piece of writing into only a few words (summarizing), we tend to retain its message longer than if we'd simply read it without doing anything more than just decoding its words.

*Dialogue Notes.* This interactive reading strategy engages the reader with a text by requiring her to take notes while she reads and then later to reflect on her notes and the piece read. Asking questions of her notes and of the text can help her grasp the text's meaning and so come to understand it.

*Writing a Response.* Stress the difference between summary and response. A summary captures the essence of the reading, while a response makes some sort of value judgment. Ask your students to assess the three sample responses we've given to Denise Knight's "No Hunting Here, Please." How is it that we can have three different responses to the same piece of writing? Point out to your students, however, that not all judgments are created equal and that they may have to defend their reading of a text. Be sure to focus on the significance in a reading, its importance or purpose.

# RESPONSES TO EXERCISES

## Exercise 4.1

How did you read each of these texts? Think back for a moment to your reading, and write a brief description of your reading process. Where did you read them? How did you read them; that is, what did you do while you read? Did you make any notes? Write a brief response to each piece in which you comment on whether you liked it or agreed or disagreed with it and why.

> *As I read these pieces, I sat in front of my computer, leaning as far back as I could, feet up, pages in my lap. I played with my hair, gazed off into the space above my printer and sucked down a soda, so I didn't just sit and read, even though I stayed at my desk, but it was more of a relaxed posture than while I study. I didn't take any notes with pen and paper, but I thought I probably should! Instead I made mental checks at the places that touched me.*

*I really agreed with the Knight piece on hunting. I used to live on 60 acres in rural New York, and we had to deal with the same thing. We had horses, and we used to have to pasture them in the lower fields during the hunting season, when they were used to having the run of the place normally. With seven kids, too, we were all rambunctious, and without the woods to explore, we often got antsy. Thank goodness we had a lot of land that didn't have trees and instead had hills for sledding and rolling down. We used to have to put new signs up every year because they'd get torn down by hunters. I think that Knight brought up a lot of good points about hunters and the mentality that often goes along with hunting.*

*The Abbott piece was fun to read, even though it was really a pretty sobering concept. The writer's style really made this an enjoyable essay. It isn't about an incredible number of things, but it does illustrate a lot about the author through the images we get of his father and that one afternoon. I really enjoyed reading this piece. I can really picture his dad in a frenzy--with a lot more details than the author actually included.*

*I read the poem a bit differently. I've never really liked much poetry, and I read it too fast to ever really understand it, which is why, I think, I don't like it much. This poem I had to go back and read a couple of times, which helped me to understand it much better, and also helped me to like it more. I had to reread a couple of individual stanzas even further to get the full gist, particularly that first one, which sets up what the whole poem is about.*

## Exercise 4.2

Writing a paraphrase requires you to rewrite a passage, perhaps a sentence or a paragraph, in other words. A paraphrase is a complete rendition of the original passage and generally approaches the original's length. While paraphrases are most often used in connection with research, the following exercise is designed to help you focus on the power of creative uses of language.

What images are evoked by the following examples of figurative language? After you read each one, paraphrase it; that is, put it into your own words. What differences do you notice between the original and your paraphrase?

And on this afternoon, the sense of illness lay so heavy that you could have gathered it in your hands like snow and rounded it into balls to throw. (Henry Louis Gates, Jr., "Change of Life," *Colored People*)

*That afternoon we really felt the palpability of the illness.*

She moved quickly, darting through the field like a rabbit startled by a hunter.

*She ran swiftly through the field.*

The cat moved sideways as it approached the mouse, looking for all the world as if a stiff wind were blowing it into the helpless prey.

*The cat sidled stiffly toward the mouse as if it couldn't help itself.*

By "language using" here I am referring to the employment of any system of symbols in order to make sense of the world–the primary means by which all of us run order through chaos, thereby giving ourselves the identities we have. (William E. Coles, Jr., *Seeing Through Writing*)

*By "language using" I mean using a set of symbols to make sense of things.*

*My paraphrases are not nearly as effective as the originals. They work; they get the point across, but the initial passages lose a bit of flair when I change the author's wording. Since I interpret the phrases in my own way, and not necessarily in the author's intended way, my paraphrases lose some of the impact and power that was there.*

## Exercise 4.3

A. Select two or three stories from a weekly magazine such as *Newsweek, Time,* or *Sports Illustrated,* and write a summary of each. Bring the articles you summarize with you to class, and exchange one of the articles and your summary of it with one of your classmates. Read your classmate's article and summary and discuss with him his summary's accuracy.

*Chater, Veronica. "In the Eye of the Storm." Women's World, July, 20, 1999, 10.*

*In this article, a couple and their four kids were trapped in their house during a tornado. Only one person escaped being injured in the storm, the younger boy who rescues his father and his stepmother and sister. The other two kids were not at home at the time. When the storm dissipated, the boy discovered his sister trapped behind a dresser, and his dad and stepmom were going into shock after having been picked up and flung around by the storm. He was able to get a rescue crew to his house and helped to pick his family out of the rubble of the house.*

B. Read and summarize an essay selected by your instructor from one of the chapters in this textbook. Exchange your summary with those of two of your classmates. How are their summaries similar to yours? Different? How do you account for any differences you find? How accurate do you think their summaries are, even though they may be different from yours?

*Verducci, Tom. "Nasty Stuff." Sports Illustrated, March 29, 1999, 64-72.*

*Kevin Brown is an amazing pitcher for the Los Angeles Dodgers who is paid an unbelievable amount of money to continue to play the game of baseball. He has a horrible temper, loves his family, doesn't communicate well with teammates or coaches and is very driven to succeed at what he does. He never expected to play baseball professionally, and in fact thought his baseball career was over after high school until he was persuaded to play in a semi-pro game and then the Mets scouted him. He was encouraged to play ball for Georgia Tech and then his career took off. Not many people like him because of his obliviousness to other people's feelings, and he has offended many, but no one can deny his talent on the mound.*

## Exercise 4.4

Write a dialogue notebook entry for an article from a weekly magazine such as *Newsweek, Time,* or *Sports Illustrated* that has both text and graphic elements. While you may use any of the reading strategies listed above, you should especially preview the article (strategy #4), looking particularly at its graphic elements. After completing your dialogue entry, write a summary of the article. What do you think of the article; what's your response to it?

Not presented

## Exercise 4.5

Read the following essay by Shelby Steele, using various of the reading strategies listed in this chapter. Then write a summary of it and a response to it. As you work with this essay, particularly as you begin to frame both your summary and response, consider these questions:

1. Steele takes what could be construed as a controversial and unpopular stance on affirmative action. How effectively does he justify his position?

2. Steele says that affirmative action has led to "racial representation" through "racial preference." What,

according to Steele, are the effects of such preferences?

3. Steele offers this statement about affirmative action:

> But after 20 years of implementation I think that affirmative action has shown itself to be more bad than good and that blacks–whom I will focus on in this essay–now stand to lose more from it than they gain. (¶4).

How effectively has he supported this assertion? Is it Steele's thesis? If so, how effectively does it guide the essay?

4. What do you think the purpose of this essay is? On what do you base your assessment?

*Shelby Steele believes that black kids of today haven't really experienced racial discrimination, at least not to the degree that the previous generation did, but they have experienced racial insensitivity. He believes that affirmative action has become an opportunity for blacks to gain many things, including diversity, development, and an education, but the entire population of people, both black and white, have ignored the means to gain true racial diversity. Instead, he says people have focused on who owes who and how to make sure they get what they think is due them. This method has forced a new sort of demoralization on the black race, and although the white race still feels doubt, that is all it feels. He also feels that much power has been lost through the process of victimization, because that has become a lifestyle, a creed, and with it, people have ignored the true problems and ways to gain power.*

*I believe that Steele has been effective in what he is arguing because he gives many examples of how these issues have come about. Allowing a race to take advantage of such a thing as victimization, which lulls them into a false sense of power is a huge mistake. From victimization comes so many other false senses of security which perpetuate a vicious cycle of abuse. Racial preference and racial presentation allow too many people to feel they are owed something, and so instead of working for goals intently, they are then advancing on false realities. This idea also allows a sense of inferior vs. superior roles, which have no place in society today, particularly between a black man and a white man.*

*Steele's assertion that these racial mandates have changed society although we have tried to eradicate them is true, because so many people still rely on these to get anywhere in anything. Women take advantage of the new mandates to reach that glass ceiling that Steele mentioned, and yet they still are unable to break it. Minorities are allowed many privileges for financial aid to get educations, yet they still think it is owed to them, and many blow it.*

*When Steele states in paragraph 4 that affirmative action is "more bad than good," he is stating a thesis. The entire essay is driven by this idea that it is problematic and must be eradicated for true racial or even individual power to manifest. Each individual must take advantage of what is offered them, and look to the means instead of the method of grabbing power. Steele has delivered a very effective essay on the new attitude people must take in order to gather what is rightfully theirs. The chance to get an education and to advance in society is not owed to anyone, no matter what their color or gender is. It is, instead, up to each individual to work to earn those things and to achieve what they can.*

### *Exercise 4.6*

Locate an essay on the internet. Read it online, and complete a reading log entry for it, including summary and response. How was your experience here different from reading and responding to a text in hard copy? Which do you prefer? Why?

> Hayden, Thomas. "Dinosaurs in the Dust." Newsweek.com July 11, 1999.
> http://www.newsweek.com/nw-srv/issue/o2_99b/prinited/us/st/sc0202_1.htm
>
> This article was about a relatively new excavation ground in Argentine Patagonia. The archaeological crew has been excavating clutches of fossilized Titanosaur (huge plant eating dinosaur) eggs. They break the eggs in half and check for fossilized embryos. Although most of the eggs contain mud, the crew had discovered several with intact embryos and some with double shells (formed when the egg is held too long in the reproductive tract, often due to stress). This gives a lot of information about the mother Titanosaurs, including observation of stress factors such as possible overcrowding (the closeness of the egg clutches suggests this), nesting habits such as digging pits for eggs, and embryo development.
>
> I really liked this article because it was fun to read and it was about something that interests me. I first came to school to study archaeology and often fantasized about discoveries such as this. It is very interesting what we can learn from fossils, and even fossilized eggs. We wouldn't expect fossilized eggs to offer many clues because we don't realize they can be broken to reveal such a wealth of information.
>
> Reading an article online is much more difficult to do than reading on paper. For one thing, there are the physical aspects. For me, words start to run together a bit on the computer screen, especially if the blue background is up. Also, I can't take notes next to the text; if I want notes, I have to jot them on paper, which means I have to try to figure out where my references fit! I think I still prefer hard copy, but it is nice to have an alternative. I think that eventually we will read most things on-line. Not having so many books in print (i.e., on paper) will be much easier on the environment.

Bill

# *Teaching Chapter 5*
# *Personal Essays*

## OVERVIEW

Writing is a whole-life sport. That is, writers write for many different occasions and in many different venues. Writing lets us range widely over topics, issues, ideas, forms, and purposes, whether academic, professional, or personal.

For many students, the bulk of writing they will do in their college careers will be academic, and that's simply a given. But not all the writing that our students do will be for academic purposes. While it's true that students will write to analyze, report, and argue various public issues, to take notes, and to complete tests, they also need to be able to write speculatively about themselves and their individual issues. Writing a personal essay offers the student this latter opportunity.

The opening chapter of Part 2, Writing Occasions, Chapter 5 offers the first of our extended applications of the rhetorical triangle. In this chapter, we spotlight the writer, focusing on the need of the writer to explore and make sense of a topic that's close to the self. The writer's job is to give her reader some insight into her thinking about and ordering of her topic, so that the reader experiences, however vicariously, what the writer experienced.

In presenting this chapter, then, you'll need to stress:

*Significance.* The assignment calls for the writer's response to a personal experience that he counts as important. In writing about this experience, the writer should grapple with a key moment, one of those moments when he realized something about himself or others that has stuck with him.

*Workable Topic.* As we noted in "Unpacking an Assignment" (see "Teaching Chapter 1 Invention"), some topics work better than others for this essay. Those with obvious, predictable outcomes tend to produce obvious, predictable papers.

*Narration and Description.* A personal essay is often called a personal narrative. And because it calls for the writer to detail a personal experience, it will in all likelihood involve the writer in telling a story. Thus, this essay relies heavily on using descriptive language to help tell a story.

## TEACHING TIPS

*Invention Strategies.* The less formal invention strategies presented in Chapter 1 should work well in helping your students generate information to use in their personal essays. If your first essay is the personal essay, then assign Chapters 1 and 5 as the first readings for the course.

*Visualization.* The visualization exercise in Chapter 1 can be a valuable starting point for the personal essay, because it asks students to bring their favorite place to life in their minds and then to write a paragraph describing that place. Oftentimes, we've found that the student's favorite place is a favorite because important things happened there. Have your students consider why they chose to write about a particular place instead of others, why that place is significant or important to them.

Teaching Chapter 5 *Personal Essays* 63

***Freewriting***. Another valuable starting point is freewriting. To begin, have your students write "I remember . . ." at the top of a sheet of paper, and give them fifteen minutes to write down anything that comes to mind. Then have them select one or two of the memories they listed and write for another fifteen minutes on each one. Use Arlene Yusnukis's freewriting in Chapter 1 as a model, talking about the range of topics she uncovers in the first freewrite and then how she develops one detail from that freewrite by completing a second freewrite. Note that in Arlene's second freewrite, she relies naturally on chronology as an ordering principle, which is a primary feature of narration.

***Clustering***. Because it evokes associations and graphically represents relationships among various entries, clustering can lead the writer to see what might be significant enough a topic for a personal essay. One way this works is by quantity–the more entries in a cluster, the more importance it's likely to hold. Look at the clustering exercise on gardens that Bill completed in Chapter 1. How many clusters have four or more terms surrounding a key term? Those are the ones more likely to carry significance.

***Shaping Strategies***. The various shaping strategies presented in Chapter 2 can help your students provide at least an initial order for their writing. To give them some experience with representing an essay visually, have your students draw Datus Proper's essay. Here's one example of how that piece could be drawn:

<u>Datus Proper's narrative</u>     <u>Betty Cave's narrative</u>

Have them represent Arlene's essay as a timeline, noting how one event follows another in turn. Finally, have your students remark the structural similarities of Arlene's and Ali's essays. Both begin in the present and then use flashback and chronological ordering of events to return to the present.

***Distinguishing Features of Personal Essays.*** In each of the writing occasions chapters, we outline what we see as the distinguishing features of the essay at hand. Having your students discuss these features can help them through their writing process, and you may use these features as part of their prewriting as well as part of their revising, as they look back to see whether they've included them or not.

***Conflict.*** Have your students diagram the conflict of a television program. I do this by talking about a thirty-minute situation comedy, asking my students to describe how a particular episode begins, how the characters interact, whether there's a point of conflict, and what happens just before each commercial. Then I ask how the program ends, how any conflict gets worked out or resolved. The point to be made is that plot proceeds on conflict and resolution and that we often learn important things from having to resolve conflict.

***Dialogue.*** An important feature of narration is dialogue, and you should encourage your students to incorporate dialogue when appropriate as part of the detail they present in their writing. But caution them not to overuse "said." Have them develop a synonym chart or list for "said." How many words may substitute for this overused verb? At least these: commented, remarked, shouted, yelled, whispered, whimpered, cried, sobbed, stated, posited–but not "go" or "goes," as in this dialogue:

So I go, "Well, that's bad."

And then she goes, "Well, yeah, it is."

You may also do synonym charts for such verbs as "entered" and "run." The point is that students have the vocabulary necessary for descriptive passages, but they often don't know that they do.

***Detail.*** You might refer to my comment to Marisol about what her essay needed: detail, detail, detail. Detail is crucial to all writing, but especially to the personal essay. To help students see the need for detail, have them work with sentences that don't say very much. I label such sentences as bland and have my students develop them into longer, more detailed sentences. Try this:

1. Write a bland sentence on the board or on an overhead. My favorite: The person entered the room.

2. Have students talk about this sentence in terms of good writing. They'll tell you fairly quickly that it really doesn't say very much.

3. Have your students identify bland words in the sentence, and list words that can substitute for them. In the sample sentence, "person," "entered," and "room" are words that need to be detailed. Identify these words as nouns and verb, also the nouns as the sentence's subject (person) and direct object (room). Using student response, generate a list of words to substitute for each of these bland words.

4. Have your students find other places to add detail: adjectives to modify the nouns, adverbs to modify the verb. Generate lists of adjectives and adverbs.

5. Have your students write three separate sentences using the word lists on the board or overhead, but tell them they may use words other than those listed. Write with them.

6. When they've finished writing, have each read his best sentence aloud. As they read aloud, stop frequently to point out details that really work, or sentence structures that vary from the usual. Talk about the placement of adverbs in the sentence and how moving adverbs around changes emphasis and so the sentence's meaning.

7. When everyone has read, ask the class which sentence is correct. The answer is that all of them are, because each one reflects its writer's vision of the action carried by the original sentence. Make the point that the writer's job is to capture as accurately as possible her vision of the topic.

And now for a word about using adjectives and adverbs sparingly and about naming parts of speech. Less-experienced writers working through this experience may want to layer one adjective or adverb atop another and another and yet another. Encourage your students to pick adjectives and adverbs judiciously so that they write in more specific terms than "a crystalline river flows laughingly through magnificent hills whose sides are dotted with beauteous trees." Focus on using very specific nouns and verbs as well. As for naming parts of speech such as noun, verb, adjective, adverb, subject, direct object, and predicate, it's ok in a writing class to talk about grammar, provided that you do so in the context of writing and that grammar instruction doesn't substitute for writing instruction.

***Writing Assignment***. Tie the suggested prewriting and shaping activities to chapters 1, 2, and 3, as well as to earlier work in this chapter. Several of the examples in those two chapters model the kind of writing that leads to the personal essay and so should serve as good models for you to use in helping students through this particular assignment. For example, Arlene's freewriting and Marisol's freewriting in Chapter 1 and subsequent essay development in Chapters 2 and 3 should prove useful.

While the sample focus statement we've shown in Chapter 5 is formulaic, it should give your students an idea of one way to develop such a statement and so a tentative plan for their writing.

Finally, in talking about this essay as one that spotlights the writer, do not assume that the reader is unimportant. Here you'll need to talk about when the writer should consider the reader most, and that's during revising, so that the writer provides sufficient detail to bring his reader into the essay.

## SAMPLE STUDENT PROCESS

The sample student process in this chapter is Chris Miller's. Point out to your students that Chris began with one topic in mind and actually worked through a fair amount of prewriting before deciding to change his topic. Have your students complete the "Important List" exercise that Chris did, listing important people, places, and ideas, then expanding those entries by identifying them more specifically, and then freewriting about each in turn. The procedure is one of expansion by adding detail at each level. As they write, have your students compare their responses with Chris's.

Work each draft of Chris's writing by comparing it to each preceding draft. Note the addition or deletion of details, the restructuring of paragraphs, and so on. Have your students estimate the number of words in each draft and then compare them. Finally, ask them to compare each draft for correctness, and make the point that Chris paid close attention to correctness only at the end of his writing process.

## RESPONSES TO EXERCISES

*Exercise 5.1*

Identify the verbs that report who said what in the conversation between Linda and her father. How many times does "said" appear? Write your own dialogue between two characters, paying particular attention to verbs, especially those used to report who said what and how they said it.

*In the argument between Linda and her father, the verb "said" appears only once, but different terms for "to say" appear in several places. Linda is described as shouting and whining; she presses on, explodes, sputters, and begs, and her words echo throughout the room. Her father weighs his words, mutters, pronounces his punishment, and begins with an endearment. He is the one who actually "says" something.*

*Sample Conversation:*

*"Hey, let me have another cigarette." The whine came from the right and was heard over the blaring jukebox.*

*"Didn't you buy a pack yesterday?" Brian demanded as he reluctantly shifted the pack down the bar.*

*Jeff smirked and picked up the half empty package of Camels. "I left them at your girlfriend's house last night!" His sarcasm struck a chord.*

*Brian looked up quickly and grumbled, "Always a kidder. Why can't you just get off it? She can't stand you."*

*"I know, that's the way I like it!" Jeff always spoke a little louder than he needed to.*

*Brad walked in just then and smiled at his buddies. They each did the obligatory handshakes, trying to see who could make the loudest clap when they slapped hands, and then he sat down. "Hey Jeff, got a cigarette?"*

*Brian started to laugh. "You're asking Mr. Chain Smoke Someone Else's Cigarettes if he has a cigarette? Here, take one of mine." His voice cracked as he passed the pack to Brad.*

*Jeff's beer spewed across his lap as his snigger turned to splutter against the new nickname he had been christened with. Brad and Brian just laughed at the spectacle.*

*This was a hard exercise to do, and I wonder if it is because of the dialogue I chose to write. I think it would be easier to do an argument like the one in the book, but I couldn't get original after reading the first one!*

## Exercise 5.2

1. "Dark Hollow" is arranged chronologically, with Proper taking us with him as he walks from his car to the stream, encounters and converses with Betty Page, and then fishes the stream. He doesn't tell everything that occurs on that trip; instead, he selects events that are important to the significance he's trying to present to his readers. Are there events that don't seem to be important enough to warrant inclusion in the essay, or does each event that Proper reports contribute something to the essay? Which events could, or should, have been deleted? Pick two events or details from this essay that carry special significance for you and explain what they contribute to it.

*I think everything in Proper's essay is important to the piece, although at first I thought that the paragraph about casting the fly was a bit unimportant. As I reread, though, I realized that it is just as vital to what is going on as anything else said. If we don't get a glimpse of how perfect casting the fly can be, especially in this special place, then we don't quite understand how important fishing is to Proper, and then we lose some of the importance of the fishing spot itself. This now becomes one of the most significant paragraphs, because it sets up the rest of the piece, showing the ideals and values that underlie Proper's essay.*

*Another detail that really makes this an important essay to me is the image of the author standing on the bank of this river in the rain, fishing. It just really gives me an image of freedom and peace and reflection that is often so hard to find when one lives in the city or even in a small town. I think this contributes to the piece because Proper has what Betty Cave no longer has--not only the land, but also the emotions that belong to it.*

2. Make a list of the details you think will be important in your essay. Then, create an order for them; is this order absolutely chronological or are there reasons to tell things out of sequence in places. If so, why? Using this second list as a guide, write a draft of your essay.

> *Important details:*
> *moment of conception*
> *Aidan's birth*
> *The way I have changed since I realized I was pregnant*
> *How much I have decided to do, what is important to me now, was not as important before*
> *How my relationship with my husband has changed*
> *What having a child means to me*
> *I never wanted to have kids*
> *I never wanted to get married*
> *I never wanted to quit playing rugby*
> *I wanted to always have a good time*
>
> *Ordering:*
> *Never wanted to have kids*
> *Never wanted to get married*
> *Wanted to always play rugby*
> *Wanted to always have a good time*
> *Conception*
> *How my attitudes changed when I realized I was pregnant*
> *Good times--that changed to different styles of good times*
> *Aidan's birth*
> *How I've changed even further*
> *How my marriage has changed*
> *What was important is not as important*
> *What having a child means to me*
>
> *I think some of these things are a bit out of place, but they are more focused now, as I am. I think I can start writing, we'll see how far I get.*
>
> *I never wanted to have kids. I was always a free spirit, very independent, always on the go, having a good time. I didn't have time for kids, much less a husband, and once I discovered rugby, forget about it. I was hooked. Rugby made me forget about everything--school, bills, even work sometimes. I wanted to play all the time. I was addicted to the game, and it was worse than drugs. I used to get so beat up out there on the field, but it was so fun to be able to do the same thing to other women, especially if they were bigger and thought they couldn't be stopped. It was a good thing I didn't have a boyfriend, because with all the bruises and bumps I had, people would think I was abused.*
>
> *I met Nick in the summer when the rugby season was put on hold. The only chances we got were when we could scrape together a motley sevens or tens team and drive up to Socorro to play New Mexico Tech. I met Nick at the end of May and fell in love. I didn't want to get married at first; I was*

*having way too much fun. I was bartending and trying to get through school, although I was very lazy about that aspect of my life. By September we had moved in together and we decided to get married in November. It was fast, but we knew it was right, and so we went ahead and plunged in. I forgot that I had never wanted to get married, and that "RUGBY IS LIFE," but not totally. I still played, but a couple of months before we got married, I put that on hold and focused on the wedding.*

*The next semester I played full force and we went to the Western championships, placing third. For such a young team, we did an outstanding job, but it wasn't as important to me anymore. I began to think about my future. Now that I had a husband, I had to focus on graduation and getting a job. Nick and I began to have our ups and downs, and I quit drinking altogether because it seemed that he and I just fought whenever we partied together. I wanted to have a good time with him, but I didn't find it so incredibly fun to get drunk and belligerent with the man I had to go home with.*

*Summer came and I started to work as a waitress at a small restaurant. The bar had to go. Bartending put me in too much contact with other men, and Nick became jealous. I wanted to ease our relationship, so I conceded and found other work. In June I got pregnant.*

*The minute we conceived, I knew. I felt a rush of emotions–fear, excitement, panic, and all the other adjectives that go with hysteria. I told Nick right then and he rolled over and told me to go to sleep. Six weeks later the test was positive. The emotions came right back, but excitement soon took over. In a matter of a few months, my life was nothing like what it had been. My idea of a good time was now shopping for baby clothes and furniture, and sitting at home with my feet up. Nick kept partying. He still wanted to have a good time, even if I had to stay home.*

## Exercise 5.3

1. Look again at the essays by Datus Proper, Steven Barboza, Arlene Yusnukis, Daniel Kinken, and Ali Duffy. How does each writer feature or emphasize the important moments in his or her essay? Identify any parts of each essay that you think to be extraneous or unnecessary. Why do you think these to be so? How vivid is the detail each writer provides? Is this detail sufficient to help you see the event? Why or why not? To what extent and how effectively does each writer use dialogue?

*Each writer has very different styles, and in their own ways, emphasize the importance of what ever is important to the individual. To Datus Proper, understatement is the key to emphasizing what is important, through the use of fishing and the scenery, and by inserting what Betty Cave finds important about the place. He inserts her history of the area with his present-time adventure of fishing in the rain. I think everything he says is vital to the image the reader gets of the place, as well as what is happening and has happened in that special spot. The imagery in this essay is vivid. At times I wish I were standing next to the man with a rod in my hand. His use of dialogue is a bit different from the standard style, because he doesn't really create a conversation, but more a sense of history through Betty's stories.*

*Steven Barboza's piece does a good job of relating how important religion has become to him, and how his views of religion have changed to make him who he is today. His beliefs have helped him through some tough times, and have also helped him to figure some things out about life and the trials one must go through. All that Barboza has to say about his journey and gathered knowledge is important to the reader, particularly if the reader is unaware of all of the details and history of Islam. His essay helped me to understand how he became the man he is. I think it flows together well and is very cohesive.*

*In Daniel Kinken's essay, there is only one paragraph that I think is irrelevant, but then again,*

> *it may not be so. It is the one where he states that he hasn't reached all of his goals. I feel a bit jarred when I get to that spot because up to that point the essay is very strong and cohesive and uses good tactics to keep the reader interested. There is a bit of dialogue, sound, smell and feel; all develop imagery.*
>
> *Ali Duffy's essay is awesome. How she moves from the classic prima donna with ribbons in her hair from the eighteenth century to twentieth century teenager in the space of a word or two shows that she's a writer. I love how she shifts gears to relate her thoughts and feelings as she moves from her "first kiss" through to the amazing ballerina who has gone nuts on the stage. Her essay is unified; it flows smoothly and is enjoyable to read.*

2. Identify the key moments in the event you've chosen to write about. How may you feature or emphasize them? Why do they figure as key or important? In what order do you think you should present them to your reader? Which event or events do you think you'll give more space to? Why? What kind of detail will help bring these moments to life? Does any lend itself to dialogue? If so, what will you have each character say?

> *The key points in my essay really need refining and development to make them stand out and not be just a string of details. I need to incorporate dialogue to make the issues stronger, and so if I do this, then I am going to have to narrow my ideas and just choose a couple to really dig into. I think I have figured out the order, but that may change depending on how I decide to narrow and define what I am writing about. I definitely want to talk about the birth and how amazing it was, but as it stands now, it doesn't fit with what I've said. I think I may have to give more space to Rugby and how it ended, because I start out really strong with that, and then it just disappears. If I don't do that, then I am going to have to just take it out. I'm not sure how to bring this essay to life. Right now it just drags along. I really need to deconstruct in order to construct.*

Bill

# *Teaching Chapter 6 Informative Essays*

## OVERVIEW

At the heart of informative writing is a basic contradiction. On the one hand, when we think of giving and receiving information we act as if we are dealing in a simple transaction. That is, we act as if we believe that some idea or concept exists in our brain and that we can package that idea into words, then deliver that package to some other person who will unwrap it (take the words off it) and thereby retrieve the concept or idea that we have sent. Of course, we know that this isn't possible; we know that the words we use to encode a message in fact help to constitute that message; and since those words do not mean exactly the same thing to the person sending and the person receiving the message, there can be no simple transaction of meaning.

In Chapter 6, we want to help students see how difficult this business of sharing concepts is. We want them to come to see that it is really impossible to get what is in their minds into words. At the same time, we want them to develop their abilities to shape information for a particular audience so that they can come as close as possible to sharing their meanings (their information) with readers.

## TEACHING TIPS

*The Nature of Information.* You'll note that we begin Chapter 6 with several humorous examples of situations in which obvious statements are made. Who needs to be told not to take a hair dryer into the shower or not to grab a running chain saw? While your students may laugh at these examples, many of them will need much practice in developing a sense of audience that will help them not to say silly things in their writing. What audience will need to be told that "raising children is hard work" or that "a college education offers one many wonderful opportunities"? Many of your students will be used to assuming that the only reader for their writing is the teacher and that the teacher doesn't care what they say as long as they say it correctly. You'll be introducing them to a new world of writing when you suggest that they take responsibility for what they say–and that they are responsible for tailoring what they say to a particular audience.

*Topic.* We suggest that you do a good deal in the prewriting stages to encourage students to explore topics they know something about or in which they have some expertise. Here you can refer them to the Interest Inventory and to the invention exercises in Chapter 1, which can also make connections between personal writing and informative writing. While the focus in informative writing is on the subject, it is nevertheless crucial that the writer make his paper personal in that the subject of his writing should be something he knows and cares about. Otherwise, he will not likely offer any real information to his readers.

*Readers.* Early in the planning for informative writing, you should help students begin developing a sense of an audience beyond the teacher. We usually encourage students to arrive at their own audience; however, this is very difficult for many students. Be sure not to allow students to settle for vague audience statements such as "people who want to know more about race horses." I always ask students where their audience holds its meetings. Where do you go to find "people who want to know more about race horses"? I am insistent that students either name a specific occasion on which they could speak to an audience or that they have in mind a publication where information can be shared.

If students come up with an actual audience (e.g., parents who attend the Parent/Teacher meetings at the local elementary school) or a publication (e.g., the school newspaper), then you can ask them to do an audience analysis, such as the following:

1. How many people do you suppose will attend this meeting or read this publication?

2. What will be their average age? What will be their median age?

3. What will be their educational background? How great a range in education will there be?

4. What will they already know about this subject? Where and/or how did they learn this?

5. What makes you think they will be or should be interested in this subject?

6. Is it likely that any members of the audience will know as much about the subject as you? If so, how will you deal with this potential problem?

Some students may have difficulty coming up with an audience; if so, point out that one natural audience is the other members of the class. If a student selects the class as his audience, have him answer the questions listed above for that audience–focusing on questions 4-6. As students in the class provide feedback to writers, they can help them gauge whether the information meets their needs as readers.

***Generalizing, Abstracting, and Stereotyping***. One of the keys to informative writing is generalization. The writer of an informative piece must know enough about the subject to generalize about it. You may want to spend some time in class working with students in exploring what it means to generalize. Our own teaching in this area owes much to the work of James Moffett. In *Teaching and the Universe of Discourse* (Houghton Mifflin, 1968) Moffett explains that as writers move into the world of informative writing, they tend to move from narrative (what happened) to exposition (what happens). If they know enough about cooking, they know what kind of foods tend to taste better when accented by rosemary. They know this because they have experienced (over and over) the addition of rosemary to certain foods and so they are in the position to say what happens in this particular situation.

You may want to spend a bit of time (and perhaps devise an exercise or two) to help students think about the difference between generalizing, abstracting, and stereotyping. Our teaching in this area is indebted to S.I. Hayakawa. In *Language in Thought and Action* (Harcourt, Brace & World, 1964), Hayakawa explains how language helps us to climb the ladder of abstraction. That is, we may look at a specific animal and name it "Bessie." In doing so, we are using language in a very concrete way. However, when we refer to that animal as a "cow," we are thinking of it as belonging to a certain class of animals. We are now moving up the ladder of abstraction. If we refer to the animal as a "bovine," we have moved even further up that ladder.

As you work with students in thinking about abstraction, you may want to fashion some exercises to help students think about what we gain, and what we lose, when we move up and down the ladder of abstraction. Students also find it interesting (and fun) to think about the various reasons people have for using abstraction. The farmer who refuses to allow his children to give names to farm animals is doing so because he knows what the consequences of naming will be when it is time to send the animals to the meat packing house. Although it is ancient history now, your students may find it interesting to examine the language of Watergate. When the "plumbers" (an interesting term itself) referred to their work as a "covert operation," they were referring to illegal acts that could be more specifically referred to as "breaking and entering." Students will enjoy and learn much about language by looking at various uses of abstraction.

The distinction between abstracting and generalizing is a difficult one to make. In fact, at times we may be doing both at the same time. If we label an animal as cow, we are abstracting. However, if we say of an animal: she's just an old cow, she won't hurt you, we are also generalizing. We have met many old cows and have found that (in general) they are not dangerous. Our reaction to the animal would be quite different if we were told that it was a bull.

Generalizing is one of the most powerful tools at our disposal to bring order to our worlds. If we could not generalize, we would have to deal with each animal we met on an individual basis. In fact, we would have to start fresh in every situation in our lives. Clearly, we could not live very efficient lives in this manner. However, there is a danger that we will become too efficient in generalizing, which leads to stereotyping. When we decide that our children cannot play with other people's children solely because those people belong to a certain race, religion, or ethnic group, our need to order has gone too far.

We suggest that you deal with issues of stereotyping in an open and forthright manner. In our own teaching, we admit to students that stereotypical thinking is seductive and that resisting it requires careful thinking and research. For example, when presented with data showing that men are responsible for a hugely disproportionate number of violent crimes, it is tempting to conclude that men are naturally (that is, genetically) more violent than women. That may be the case; researchers are currently studying the genetics of gender to gain insight into this question. However, that is not the only possible explanation for these data. It may well be that men have been programmed by thousands of years of culture to be more violent and that the effects of this programming could be undone. Until we know for sure, we would prefer to resist stereotyping men as violent, just as we would resist attributing stereotypical characteristics to African Americans, Native Americans, Southerners, Northerners, blondes, athletes, and so forth.

As you work through issues of generalizing, abstracting, and stereotyping with your students, we suggest you ask them to think about what they gain by using each type of thinking and what ulterior motivations they may have for using them. For example, if we didn't find a way to capture the behavioral differences between bulls and cows, we might well endanger ourselves needlessly. And we have no ulterior motives in using this thinking process. That is, in assuming these differences between bulls and cows, we don't denigrate cows or bulls or think of ourselves as somehow superior.

One could argue that we also lose something important if we do not stereotype the violent behavior of men (as opposed to women). This is not the case, however; we are well aware of the facts that men commit a hugely disproportionate number of violent crimes in our country. All of us know these data and use them in deciding how to react to certain situations. However, if we simply say that men are more violent than women and leave it at that, we run the risk of accepting actions as normal behavior that actually should be resisted. We may tend to blame women for not protecting themselves from male-initiated violence when we should be focusing on how to eradicate that violence. Or women may be tempted to feel they are superior to men by nature. In short, there is nothing to gain but quite a bit to lose by accepting this stereotypical thinking. [ NOTE: For an interesting discussion of this issue, see Susan Jacoby's "Common Decency" in Chapter 9 and Camille Paglia's "Rape and Modern Sex War" in Chapter 10.]

What we are saying, then, is that stereotyping has more to do with the motives of those who would use it than with the actual statement itself. It is certainly not a stereotype to say:

Boys are larger than girls.

Boys are stronger than girls.

Boys have a larger lung capacity than girls.

While these statements may be challenged on the basis of the physical abilities of any one girl, in general, these are true statements. But to move from these to say that boys are more athletic than girls is to define athleticism in terms of male abilities. What does it mean to be athletic? Depending on how one defines this term, a small, less strong person, could be just as athletic as a large, strong person.

***Clarity.*** Depending upon the sophistication of your students, you may want to simply stress that their goal in informative writing is to be as clear as possible. Once you have done this, you may want to assign exercises in the appropriate sections of Chapters 15 and 16 ("Strategies for Writing that Spotlights the Subject") and from relevant sections in the handbook–sections on wordy and vague usage. In this kind of straight-forward approach, you will focus on economy and precision; you can offer students such general principles as the following:

> Don't use the passive voice unless you can explain a reason to do so.
> Avoid "be" verbs when you can find more exact verbs.
> Avoid excessive use of prepositions.
> Don't use unnecessary words.
> Strive for the right word–not a close approximation.
> Make the relation of ideas clear by means of skillful use of sentence combining.

If your class is more sophisticated in their writing abilities and knowledge, you may want to explore clarity from a rhetorical standpoint. This is what we are attempting to do with the description of the automobile accident and with Exercise 6.3. When our students seem ready for them, we often use examples from the "The Uses of Obscurity" in Richard Lanham's *Style: An Anti-textbook* (Yale University Press, 1974; though the book was published many years ago, it is still one of the best discussions of style that we know.)

***Modes and Aims.*** In the introduction to Part 2, we introduce students to the differences between modes and aims of discourse. We also believe that one of the most important features of our text is its focus on aims of discourse. Our aims-based approach should be helpful to you in two ways. First, it will allow you to differentiate college-level writing from the writing most of your students did in high school. Many high school courses are modes-based; that is, their writing assignments call for students to write descriptions, narratives, expositions, and/or arguments. In introducing your students to aims-based assignments, you will be enriching their understanding of purpose and audience.

Second, an aims-based approach will allow you to enrich your students' appreciation for the role that modes can play in their writing. Rather than downplaying modes, an aims-based approach will allow you to use modes much more completely and fully in your teaching. Modes can be seen, not as containers or molds into which students pour information, but rather as tools for discovering and shaping material. In this chapter, we offer exercises in which students may use process, comparison/contrast, and cause to discover information to write about. And then, we show how these modes may be used as key organizing devices as students outline the structure of their essays. In Chapter 7, we show how analysis, classification, and definition may be used to discover and order information. We have grouped modes in this way for pedagogical purposes, not because there is any one-to-one association between the aim in question and the mode that may be used in achieving that aim. As you work through these chapters and the others in the text, be sure to remind your students that any mode may be used to discover and order material in any writing situation. For example, there are places where process is used in Datus Proper's personal essay, "Dark Hollow" (in Chapter 5), and there are descriptive and narrative passages in Martin Luther King's persuasive essay, "Letter from Birmingham Jail" (in Chapter 10).

# RESPONSES TO EXERCISES

## *Exercise 6.1*

In how many different situations have you shared information with others during the last week? In how many situations have you received information from others during this week? Can you group these different occasions? How many different groupings do you come up with? What role, if any, did writing–and here we include any type of keyboarding–play in your giving or receiving information?

> *Over the last week I have communicated with many people in many different contexts. I can group them into several categories including communication about love and affection; transportation and plans for the day/week; communication about who is taking care of the baby, when, why, how; communication about service at work; communication in writing about my progress with certain activities; and communication about feelings. I am sure there are several other groups, but those seem to be the main ones that I can focus on. Writing played a big role in several of these communication styles because most of it was done on a computer, while some of it was done by handwriting. I received an invitation to a baby shower, and left notes for certain people in my family.*

## *Exercise 6.2*

Not presented

## *Exercise 6.3*

Our example above makes the point that writers can have multiple purposes. The writer of passage C, the police officer, wants to present as factual and as clear an account of this event as possible. The writer of passage B, the young driver of the car, wants to tell what happened but also wants to draw attention to the complexities of the situation. This account has strong leanings toward persuasion; thus, clarity is not as important as is capturing a full accounting of all the factors in this situation. Look back at the sample essays at the beginning of the chapter and analyze them from the standpoint of purpose. Obviously, the writers intend to give their readers information. Can you discern other goals these writers are attempting to achieve in their essays? Are some of them more purely informational than others? How high a priority do the writers give to clarity in their writing?

> *Deborah Tannen, "Gender Gap in Cyberspace"*
>
> *Tannen's essay is a good example of an essay that is both personal and informative. The personal nature of the essay is clear from the first sentence: "I was a computer pioneer, but I'm still something of a novice." Clearly this is going to be a story about Tannen. But at the same time, she uses this story to give us information about the differences between men and women in terms of their approach to computer technology. It is proper to call this an informative essay (rather than a personal essay) because Tannen's overall purpose is to make generalizations about men and women.*
>
> *Michael Kinsley, "Orwell Got it Wrong"*
>
> *Kinsley's essay is an example of an essay that is both informative and argumentative. At the same time that he is informing his readers about the good and bad points of the information age we live in, he is arguing that the good outweighs the bad. That is why he titled his essay as he did. Orwell had been with those who feared that as more and more types of information became available, the government would exercise more and more control over its citizens. As his title suggests, Kinsley takes the other side of this argument. However, this an informative essay, rather than an argumentative (or position) essay, because Kinsley does not assume an audience that takes the other side. His purpose is to provide information to readers who are receptive to that information.*

## *Exercise 6.4*

Compare the directions on a household product such as cooking instructions on a common packaged food, with the directions on some prescription medicine. For what type of person are these directions written? For what situations? Is either of these insulting to your intelligence? Are the instructions equally clear?

*I compared directions on five-minute rice with directions on prescription medicine. The directions on the five-minute rice were easy to read, easy to follow and important. I was not sure if the rice was to be put in right away with the rest of the ingredients, but I was able to figure that out as I continued to read the package.*

*The directions on the prescription medicine were easy to read also, although I sometimes wish they would put more information on the bottle, such as whether this must be taken with food, or if it should be chilled, or if it is ok to take with another medicine. Once I have read the information sheet that comes with it, I often forget all of the information, and have long since thrown it away. When I have medicine for ear infections (which must be cold), some for congestion (which must be taken with food), baby Tylenol, and medicine for allergic reactions, then it can be confusing. I find myself calling the pharmacist a lot. (Just a few more directive stickers would work!)*

## Exercise 6.5

Although many essays use process as a major ordering device, many others make use of process as one means of order. For example, look at the role that process plays in Kubler-Ross's essay at the beginning of this chapter. A major part of her essay is the comparison of the process by which we used to handle death and dying with the process by which it is handled now. Reflect for a few minutes on the role that process may play in your essay. What, if any processes, will you need to inform your readers about? Sketch these now as a means of generating material for your essay.

*Processes in my essay.*

*Although I am writing an informative paper on what the major problems are in the first five years of marriage, I am using much material from the "process" by which my husband and I fell in love and then worked out a stable relationship. Thus, I might see that process as one that moves from meeting, to becoming interested in one another, to falling in love, to getting married, to experiencing disagreement, to working through disagreements. I could also see the working through those disagreements as a process in itself. First we recognize that there is a disagreement, then we get stuck in stubbornness and then we tire of the friction and begin to seek an accommodation.*

## Exercise 6.6

In Chapter 15, we discuss the differences in the use of metaphor for informative and for personal writing. Read those pages and decide whether Shalev's metaphor (comparing humans in Third-World countries to endangered animals, for which we tend to have much sympathy) is more like the metaphors we generally associate with informative writing or more like those we generally associate with personal writing. Or, is it different from both? Once you determine how Shalev is using metaphor in this essay, look at your information essay to see if this type of metaphor would be useful in it.

*Shalev's metaphor is more like the metaphor we associate with personal writing. In this type of metaphor, one attempts to chart new territory, to see things in ways that they are not normally seen. This is in contrast to the metaphor we often use in informative writing, since that metaphor often involves rather ordinary (if not trite) comparisons. These are comparisons that often don't even seem to be metaphorical since we're so used to them. Shalev is clearly attempting to do something fresh and original so that he can capture our attention and make us see what we don't do for fellow humans in light of what we do for certain animals.*

## Exercise 6.7

Comparison is such a basic ingredient in informative writing that you are likely to find it helpful in any subject you have chosen for this assignment. Think of several comparisons relevant to your topic and use them to generate material for your essay. After you have done so, reflect on what purposes these comparisons might serve in your essay.

> *I can easily compare the way Nick deals with stress as opposed to the way I deal with stress, and other similar situations. We both handle these things in our own way, but it is difficult for us to understand why the other does what he does. For example, I cry when I am furiously angry, and he holds it in until he explodes. I cry so that I don't explode, and I hope I am not around whenever he explodes.*

> *I might compare us to two elk fighting, since their antlers often get tangled, leaving them stuck together for days, still fighting, not eating or drinking, until one will finally give in and fall to the ground. Often this is the one that has lost, particularly if it is older, and it will get weaker and weaker, not having the energy to eat or get water, even after the fight is over. Winter invariably sets in just a few weeks after the rut season, and the elk perishes. Sometimes I feel like that elk; my relationship gets harder and harder, and my energy just gets less and less. Sometimes I just want to give in and not argue anymore.*

> *Another comparison I might make is between the dusk and the dawn, how sometimes the evenings show brilliant colors, and the dawn is just a gradual lightening of the horizon, and the differences between the two can really illustrate the depth of affection I feel for the man I married.*

## Exercise 6.8

Consider the following passage from Jonathon Kozol's "The Human Cost of An Illiterate Society":

> Illiterates cannot read the menu in a restaurant. They cannot read the cost of items on the menu in the *window* of the restaurant before they enter. Illiterates cannot read the letters that their children bring home from their teachers. They cannot study school department circulars that tell them of the courses that their children must be taking if they hope to write a letter to the teacher. They are afraid to visit in the classroom. They do not want to humiliate their child or themselves.

In this sample passage, Jonathon Kozol outlines some of the ways in which illiteracy affects people. Can you think of additional effects illiteracy might have on a person? Brainstorm for a few minutes, noting every possible effect of illiteracy that you can think of. After you have written your list, look over the list below, from the rest of Kozol's essay, then answer these questions: How does your list compare with Kozol's? What significant effects did you see that Kozol did not mention? What effects did Kozol mention that you did not imagine? After you have answered these questions, consider the implications of your findings. What caused you to overlook effects that Kozol saw?

> *My list:*
>
> *Illiterates:*
> *--cannot read the letter grades a child brings home*
> *--cannot pay their bills for fear of writing the wrong numbers in the columns*
> *--lose self-esteem because their spouses and children read at a level ten times superior to theirs.*
> *--stay in low-level jobs because they are afraid they will fail at higher-level job–after all, they cannot read new job descriptions, and if a new job requires any type of reading or writing, they will not be able to do it.*
> *--cannot put toys together for their kids, or if they follow the pictures, it is much tougher.*
> *--cannot read articles that will aid them in their field of employment.*
> *--cannot read directions to a new friend's house.*

*--cannot read the theater marquis to determine a time of showing.*

> *My list reflects much concern for enjoyment and entertainment; Kozol's reflects a lot of concern for ways of making money and doing the necessary things one has to do to live. I think our lists are complementary; we both have things that the other didn't think about. The differences in our lists make it clear that we have different priorities.*

## Exercise 6.9

Generate more material for your essay by exploring the role of causality in your thinking. You may want to return to the "What follows what?" and "What follows from what?" questions in our questions for analysis (in Chapter 1). We do not want to confuse chronological relations with causal relations–and hence be guilty of the post hoc, propter hoc fallacy. However, whenever one event follows another, it is worth asking whether there is a causal relationship between the two events.

> *Cause plays a big role in the relationship I have with my husband. It always has to be someone's fault that this or that has happened, and never an accident, or something that couldn't be helped. When we think this way, then our fights become much larger and omnipresent. It is harder for us to go back to our original way of thinking where each of us is intelligent, worthwhile, sensitive human beings. Our thinking degenerates and forces us into roles we would have originally rather not have even taken on. It is all a vicious cycle, and things get harder and harder to fix the longer they take to work out.*

> *I then reflect on what causes us to be so interested in the blame game. My parenting was very cause-oriented. If something went wrong at home, there had to be a cause and usually someone was to blame. By looking into these causes (for the obsession with cause), I gain some insight into how to break the cycle.*

## Exercise 6.10

Not presented


Ron

# Teaching Chapter 7
# Evaluation Essays

## OVERVIEW

Evaluation is something we do every day. In fact, it would be hard for us not to make value judgments about nearly everything we confront, however large or small, significant or insignificant. Evaluation requires judgment; thus, it forms an important element of critical thinking. As we weigh one idea, however abstract or concrete, against another, we compare, we contrast, and we come to some kind of conclusion about which idea is better. Working with evaluative essays is one way of strengthening our skill with critical inquiry.

Our evaluations are influenced heavily by terministic screens, the verbal filters that we bring to bear on experience. As we note in "Logology and *The Longwood Guide to Writing*: What We Owe to Kenneth Burke," our language actually forms a lens through which we experience reality. Sometimes that lens is crystal clear, but at other times it's clouded, opaque at best. We just don't always see things clearly or in quite the same light as others.

Language is essentially evaluative. Few terms are neutral; their connotations outstrip their denotations. How positive or negative are these terms: *proselyte* and *propaganda*? The denotations for these words are essentially neutral. A proselyte is one who attempts to convert others to a particular position, and the term is usually applied to one who tries to convert others to one religion or another. But how many shrill voices have you heard trying to convert you to think one way or another? In this sense, a proselyte has negative connotations. Propaganda is information designed to sway you to think in one way or another, which is, of course, the job of advertising. But during World War II, propaganda took on very negative connotations, because propaganda came to represent the misinformation and disinformation put forth by the Axis powers. Applying these terms—proselyte and propaganda—puts the person or information to which they refer, respectively, in a very negative light; hence, the value judgment implicit is negative.

Here's an exercise to illustrate the point that language involves value judgments. Have your students rank these terms from most positive to most negative: *sleek, anorexic, skinny, scrawny, svelte, thin, lean, beanpole, emaciated*. Then make the point that each of these terms could apply to a stereotypical fashion model, depending on who would be doing the labeling. Next, have your students list as many synonyms as they can for each of these terms: *athlete, police officer, politician*. After you list their terms on the board or on an overhead, have them rank the terms from most positive to most negative. Again, make the point that each term in a given set could refer to one individual, with each label depending on the point of view of the labeler.

The essay we suggest that students write while working through this chapter is called a criterion-based evaluation. That is, the writer establishes a set of criteria against which to hold her topic to decide its worth, in such terms as good or bad, worthy or unworthy, effective or ineffective, necessary or unnecessary. Begin working early on to help your students learn how to develop criteria, for the more clearly worded the criteria, the stronger the evaluation is likely to be.

# TEACHING TIPS

***Criterion-based Evaluation.*** As noted above, each student will develop criteria for evaluating her topic. To begin, have your students do Exercise 7.1. When you've completed working this exercise, continue by asking your students to list the traits of one or more of these:

> a quality *university*
> a great *sports team*
> a good *pizza, sub sandwich, lasagna*, and so on

Ask them to compare representatives of each italicized term. They should be able to decide fairly quickly whether their university is a quality school and how it measures up to another university. Similarly, they should be able to identify a great team (e.g., the Chicago Bulls of the mid- to late-90s, the Denver Broncos of the late 90s), to debate the merits of other teams in comparison, and to reach some agreement as to which teams are or were great and why. But they'll probably have a harder time in reaching agreement about examples of the third set, because what makes a pizza or a sub sandwich or a pan of lasagna good is more a matter of taste (no pun intended) than being able to measure that pizza against a set of criteria. Criteria provide benchmarks that help the student gauge the relative worth of his topic, a point you need to stress repeatedly.

You should also tie this discussion to Exercise 7.2, which follows discussion of establishing evaluative criteria.

***Sample Reading.*** Mark Twain's essay is the longest sample essay in *The Longwood Guide to Writing*, and your students may well need you to preview it for them. To begin, have your students talk about Twain, what they've read by him, what they know and think about him. If you need to strengthen your own background in Twain to lead this discussion, you'll need to learn about his take on Romanticism (he didn't like it). You'll also need to know who James Fenimore Cooper was and what his place in American literature is. Some of your students will have seen *The Last of the Mohicans*, the movie made in the early 90s that was based on this book by Cooper, and so will be familiar with the settings and types of characters Twain discusses in his essay. Such discussion will help your students prepare to read Twain's essay. For each reading, have your students identify the value judgment each writer makes about his or her topic, the criteria each establishes, and then the examples each provides to support that judgment.

***Modes of Discourse.*** Your students use modes daily to help them navigate in their world.

> ***Analysis*** involves examining the components of a given whole to see how effectively each part contributes to the whole. One example we've given involves the components of a personal computer. Given the amazing development of technology, it's quite possible that some of your students won't know what a 5.25" disk drive is, so you may need to update the terms there. You may, for example, have students debate the relative merits of a zip drive as part of the configuration of a new personal computer.
>
> ***Classification*** may be approached through a "bins" metaphor: individual examples are sorted into bins with others similar enough to warrant the grouping. Have your students talk about how they do their laundry. Do they wash whites only with whites? Do they wash everything together in a single load? What's the basis of their decision about what gets washed with what? When we hold a particular item against a group of several similar items and decide to include that item in the group or not, we're making a judgment based on classification.
>
> ***Definition*** can help us examine a particular term by establishing boundaries. Here's an exercise to help clarify this point. The following set of terms includes examples of post-secondary learning institutions:

community college, junior college, college, university. For each term, have your students list its primary traits, focusing on those traits that establish its difference from the other terms. For example, one trait that sets a university apart from the other schools listed is that a university will have a graduate program, while a college (that is, an independent institution that offers degrees in its own right instead of being one division of a larger institution) generally does not offer graduate degrees. Then have them write a single-sentence definition of each term that identifies the term and then one or two traits that set it apart from the others. Defining a topic as good or bad, effective or ineffective, and so on points to developing "because" support. As we note in this chapter, such support is critical to writing an evaluative essay.

# RESPONSES TO EXERCISES

## Exercise 7.1

List as many traits or characteristics of a good teacher as you can. Then think about the teachers you have had. Which of these were good teachers? List two or three of them by name; then decide how many of the traits you listed above that these teachers had. For each trait give one or two specific examples of how each teacher exemplified that trait.

> *Fun*
> *Caring*
> *Hard working Mrs. Nixon*
> *Dependable Mrs. Roselli*
> *Understanding Mrs. Andrews*
> *Responsible*
> *Fair*
> *Smart*
> *Expects a lot from students*
> *Respects students*
>
> *All three of these teachers exemplified these traits, and I think that is why I really respected them as teachers. Each one of these had something to do with why I chose to become an education major, especially Mrs. Nixon. They all expected a lot from their students and they respected them as well. This made us respect them in turn, and we wanted to work to keep that respect. All three loved to have fun, and that is why each of them was involved with separate clubs as advisors. I can't separate each teacher into having one or two of these characteristics, I think I define teachers by the qualities that were apparent in these three, and thus these are the role models I use when thinking of what good teachers and teaching are. Each worked hard to make sure we gained a positive, strong well rounded education, and they worked hard to make sure each student got this, not just one or two favorites.*

## Exercise 7.2

A. List the traits or characteristics of two or three of the following:

a good restaurant
a good romance novel or technothriller
an effective writing class
an important political announcement

a beneficial self-improvement program (e.g., an exercise or weight-loss program)
high quality children's television programming

After making your lists, name two or three examples that would exemplify the traits in each category.

*A good restaurant:*

*Pleasant atmosphere*
*Good food*
*Appropriate service*

*Lorenzo's Italian Food*
*El Comedor Mexican Restaurant*
*Chili's Grill and Bar*

*A good romance novel or technothriller (I chose some mysteries):*

*Keeps me turning the pages as fast as I can*
*Fun to read*
*Realistic*
*Fast paced*
*Makes me think--try to solve before we all figure it out*

<u>*Pretend You Don't See Her*</u>, <u>*Weep No More, My Lady*</u>, <u>*While My Pretty One Sleeps*</u> *(all by Mary Higgins Clark)*

*High quality children's programming:*

*Age appropriate*
*Educational*
*Uses bright colors*
*Exciting movements and sounds*
*Clean humor*

*"Sesame Street"*
*"Zoom"*
*"Barney"*

B. Are some of the traits you listed more important or essential than others? For one of the terms, rank your criteria from most to least important. Compare your ranked list with that of one of your classmates for the same term. Where do you agree? disagree? Other than personal taste, how may you justify your list and its differences in comparison to that of your classmate?

> *I think some of these traits that I listed are more important than others. For example, when it comes to children's programming, educational value is of utmost importance to me. To my son, however, bright colors and exciting sounds and movements bring him more enjoyment. With restaurants, everything is important, because enjoying good food is a total aesthetic experience. If one thing is off, say, the service, it often has a negative impact on my enjoying the food.*

*Exercise 7.3*

A. Look at the sample essays at the first of this chapter, and identify the thesis of each. How did the writer structure his or her thesis; what key value terms (such as "good" or "bad") did the writer use? How effectively does the thesis serve to guide the paper? What criteria does each writer use to develop the thesis? What kind of information does the writer use to support each criterion? How effective are the criteria and their support? Why?

> *Twain's thesis is very understated: "Cooper's art has some defects" (¶2). The key value term is "defects," which shows that he thinks writing is bad. This thesis very effectively guides the essay, because Twain has to support it, and he does. He uses three criteria, finding Cooper's "gifts of invention," "construction of dialogue," and "singularly-dull word sense" to be faulty. He supports each criterion with very specific details from Cooper's novels, lots of detail and specific quotes. And his attitude shows through his use of such adjectives as "odious" and "pathetic."*

> *Ellen Goodman's thesis comes at the end of her essay. In ¶16, she says, "[Brumberg's] book is a fine text [. . . .]" Goodman has only one criterion: the effectiveness of the comparison/contrast Brumberg offers between the attitudes of 19th and 20th century teenage girls about their bodies. Goodman effectively presents details that show how superficial today's teenage girls might be when compared to girls a hundred years ago. She does this to indict the beauty industry for being on an "evolutionary rampage."*

> *Stacy Birch's paper on Project Amnesty has a straightforward introduction with the thesis at the end of the first paragraph. Her paper is driven by this thesis, as she believes that Project Amnesty is a good thing and could prove very important to children of single parents. Stacy has only one criterion: forcing child support payments. She develops it by showing the effect of payment and non-payment on kids and their single parents, talking about the impact on money immediately available, health insurance costs, and single parents on welfare. Her criteria are effective for her topic because she supports each assertion with a strong example and fact.*

> *Michelle Lebsock's paper has a standard introduction with thesis as the last sentence in the first paragraph. She uses three criteria to judge Welch's CD: the strong vocal quality of Welch's voice, the lyrics that "paint" pictures, and the pacing (variety and continuity). She supports the first by describing the qualities of Welch's voice. She supports the next two with quotes from the songs on the CD.*

B. Below are several thesis statements. How effective do you think each thesis would be in guiding an evaluation essay? Why? What criteria could be developed in support of each thesis?

1. The NMSU Department of English is an exceptionally good academic department.

2. Skateboards should not have been banned from the NMSU campus.

3. The campus libraries are not open enough hours to meet student needs.

4. Drug-education programs aimed at educating elementary students are clearly not working.

5. Mark Twain was a great American novelist.

6. Despite having been first published over a century ago, *Little Women* succeeds today as a girl's book.

7. In making cartoon versions of fairytales, Disney Studios have not been faithful to the original versions.

> *I think that all of the thesis statements except for the second, third and seventh would be good theses for any of a number of evaluative papers. Each of these (#1, #4, #5, and #6) leads us to think of criteria we could use to support the assertion, because each is a "good/bad" evaluation. I think that any one of them could be for a positive or negative assertion also, because it depends on how the author feels about the NMSU writing program, or drug education programs in elementary schools, etc. It would be possible to develop several areas of support for each statement, and so I think in this*

*manner each of them would work. In sentences #2, #3, and #7, we have a topic, but we don't have an assertion of value. Without such an assertion, we don't have an evaluative thesis.*

## Exercise 7.4

Pick two of the sample essays at the first of this chapter and decide whether they use analysis in talking about their respective subjects. If so, how effective is the analysis? For each essay, identify the components or parts of the subject the writer discusses. How does each writer develop or support his or her analysis of the subject?

*Twain definitely uses analysis to develop his subject. He draws on Cooper's Leather Stocking Tales and shows how each negative aspect of his writing does not work. Twain maintains a high level of humor which allows the reader the opportunity to maintain and develop interest in what is being evaluated and how. This makes us want to go out and get the Tales to read for ourselves. Twain develops several areas of analysis primarily by listing and defining for the reader the things that work. We see a thorough critique of Cooper's style of writing, his use of dialogue and the poor method of switching dialects and intelligence levels of characters within paragraphs. We also are shown how bad Cooper was at architecture and gauging distances, and Twain shows us how the measurements Cooper gives aren't realistic at all. Twain's analysis is very thorough.*

*Michelle Lebsock's paper on the Gillian Welch CD is a very good analysis of an artist and her work. Michelle uses specific terms from the music field, which leads the reader to believe she has an extensive knowledge and grasp of what makes a good CD. Her tone and depth of involvement give the reader a feeling of trust that she knows what she is talking about, and so she develops a good essay that convinces us to try out the CD because she feels it is so good.*

*Michelle discusses several different aspects of good music and shows clearly how those aspects are at work in the CD that she evaluates. She uses bright adjectives and strong language to encourage us to trust her. Her development comes from a strong knowledge of the topic and that becomes apparent early on.*

## Exercise 7.5

Review the sample essays in this chapter. Which make use of definition; which define important terms for the reader? Why do you think it was necessary for the writer to do so? How effective are the definitions you find?

*The essay on Project Amnesty makes use of definition when it shows the reader what the program is and how vital it is to the kids of single parent homes. It is necessary for the author to define these ideas for the readers since Project Amnesty is a relatively new program designed to aid children and families. The definitions are highly effective because they sincerely back up the statements and assertions the author is making in her evaluation of the program. If we did not know what the program was or did, we would be unable to gather information and come to the same conclusion as the author.*

## Exercise 7.6

Apply this structure to the sample essays by Stacy Birch and Michelle Lebsock at the first of this chapter. How well do these essays follow this structure? How effective is this plan for structuring an essay?

*The essay by Stacy Birch does follow the sample structure very well. We are introduced to the topic; we immediately get a definition of the issue, and then we are given the criteria Stacey uses to determine that the program is a good one. Each reason is well supported by examples, and the conclusion is a cohesive summary of what the essay is about.*

*The essay by Michelle Lebsock also makes good use of the sample structure in that it gives the readers a good introduction with thesis, and then moves into the criteria Michelle uses to develop her argument that the CD is a good one and why Gillian Welch is a good artist. She gives the reader a wealth of information to support her views and supports each individual characteristic with strong language and reasoning. She makes quite a bit of use of quotation and paraphrase to illustrate her ideas and the conclusion to her paper is a strong summary of her feelings and evaluation of the CD.*

*I think this plan is effective for structuring an essay because it is straightforward and precise. It is easy to follow and gives a basic blueprint to help the writer not get lost. It is easy for the readers to follow, and we are not swimming in excess.*

## Exercise 7.7

1. Look again at the essays presented earlier in this chapter. For each essay, restate the writer's judgment of the topic and the evaluative criteria on which the judgment is based. How clearly stated is each judgment? How effectively do the criteria support it?

*The judgment in each of these essays is clearly stated; it's very clear where each writer stands on his or her topic.*

*Twain feels that Cooper's writing is not good and certainly doesn't deserve the praise it got. He feels that the dialogue is shoddy, that the details don't merit attention because they are poorly planned, that the tricks of the author in his character portrayal and plot development are overused and boring and simple, that the plot has no order or believable development and that the language is not up to par. He clearly states his judgements and backs them with examples from the text. He provides detailed support and uses many passages to illustrate his points.*

*Ellen Goodman's essay effectively evaluates a book about teenage girls and the changes they have undergone over the past hundred years when it comes to body image, the beauty industry and the trade offs they have made. Goodman feels it is important for girls and women today to read this book and to discuss in hopes of getting girls to see that they don't have to define their worth in terms of beauty.*

*Stacy Birch's essay on Project Amnesty clearly follows a simple structure of criterion, support, evaluation. She effectively supports each of her statements with several examples and facts to show the reader how vital this program is to kids from broken homes.*

*Michelle Lebsock's positive evaluation of a CD is well-developed. Lebsock states each judgement clearly and supports assertions with examples from the CD and from her personal experience.*

2. How detailed is the support each writer uses to develop his or her essay? How effectively does the support develop *"because"* statements?

*I had to infer "because" statements, but they're in each of the essays, even if they're only in the background. These statements probably helped direct each writer's prewriting. (Now there's a thought: did Mark Twain ever have to do any prewriting?) Anyway, I think these "because" statements are behind the essays:*

*Twain: Cooper's writing is defective "because" he isn't very inventive, "because" he doesn't write dialogue very well, and "because" his word choice is bad.*

*Goodman: <u>The Body Project</u> is an important book "because" it gives frank discussion about the* *manipulation of today's teenage girls by the beauty industry.*

*Stacey: Project Amnesty will be effective "because" it'll force deadbeat parents to pay the child support they owe.*

*Michelle: Gillian Welch's <u>Revival</u> is an excellent CD "because" the vocals are strong, "because" the lyrics are descriptive and paint images, and "because" the pacing creates variety without harming continuity.*

Bill

# Teaching Chapter 8
# Essays About and From Literature

## OVERVIEW

One purpose of this chapter is to help students strengthen their skills in reading and responding to literature. In the chapter, we present a way of reading literature that echoes the reading strategies of Chapter 4 but that does not derive from any particular school of literary criticism. The terms we use in talking about interpretation involve the mechanics of literature—plot, theme, symbols, characters—that many students will be familiar with from their high school English courses. This first purpose focuses on writing *about* literature.

A second purpose is to help students consider the possibilities of literature beyond the classroom, so that they interpret a piece of literature but then write beyond it, applying it their own experience. This second purpose focuses on writing *from* literature. In large part, this approach works out of Kenneth Burke's discussion of "literature as equipment for living," which he presents in *The Philosophy of Literary Form* (3rd ed., Berkeley: U Cal Pr, 1973). As we discuss in "Logology and *The Longwood Guide to Writing*: What We Owe to Kenneth Burke," Burke says that literature would comfort and protect us.

There is just a bit more to be said about Burke's comments. One of the things Burke decried was the riding of any one particular critical orientation. Instead of espousing one school of criticism or another, Burke stepped back to take a broader view. In the title essay of *The Philosophy of Literary Form*, Burke outlines what he sees as the nature of literature: "Critical and imaginative works are answers to questions posed by the situation in which they arose. They are not merely answers, they are *strategic* answers, *stylized* answers" (1). Then in an essay titled "Literature as Equipment for Living" (293-304), Burke suggests that we approach literature from a sociological perspective, which would:

> [. . .] seek to codify the various strategies which artists have developed with relation to the naming of situations. In a sense, much of it would even be "timeless," for many of the "typical, recurrent situations" are not peculiar to our own civilization at all. The situations and strategies frames in Aesop's Fables, for instance, apply to human relations now just as fully as they applied in Ancient Greece. (301)

Continuing in this essay, Burke offers this justification for his sociological approach:

> The method has these things to be said in its favor: It gives definite insight into the organization of literary works, and it automatically breaks down the barriers erected about literature as a specialized pursuit. People can classify novels by reference to three kinds, eight kinds, seventeen kinds. It doesn't matter. Students patiently copy down the professor's classification and pass examinations on it, because the range of academic classifications is endless. Sociological classification [. . .] would derive its relevance from the fact that it should apply both to works of art and to social situations outside of art. (303)

And finally, he states that a reader following his approach would:

[. . .] consider works of art [. . .] as strategies for selecting enemies and allies, for socializing losses, for warding off evil eye, for purification, propitiation, and desanctification, consolation and vengeance, admonition and exhortation, implicit commands or instructions of one sort of another. Art forms like "tragedy" or "comedy" would be treated as *equipments for living*, that size up situations in various ways and in keeping with correspondingly various attitudes. The typical ingredients of such forms would be sought. Their relation to typical situations would be stressed. Their comparative values would be considered, with the intention of formulating a "strategy of strategies," the "over-all" strategy obtained by inspection of the lot. (304. Italics Burke's.)

Burke, then, would have us see a piece of literature as more than an artifact to be dissected; he would have us see it as something to be considered and then applied to the situations we confront daily. In our terms, Burke would have us write *from* literature, not just *about* it.

# TEACHING TIPS

*Literature as Equipment for Living.* Early in the chapter, we invite students to consider literature from Burke's perspective. Invite your students to talk about their favorite pieces of literature. Why are these their favorites? How often have they read them? Why? Talk about your own responses to these questions as well.

*Reading Strategies.* Use short poems to teach the reading strategies we outline in our discussion of Robert Frost's "For Once, Then, Something." Try to find poetry your students aren't likely to be familiar with, ones they haven't read or don't know very well. (E.g., try working with Trumbull Stickney's "Six O'Clock.") Or use either of Sherman Alexie's poems (in Chapter 8) or return to Lorna Dee Cervantes's poem (in Chapter 4).

*Elements of Literature.* Your students will in all likelihood be familiar with the terms we use in talking about the structure or mechanics of a piece of literature. Reinforce their knowledge by talking about these elements (e.g., plot, conflict, and characters) in terms of a situation comedy, something they're likely to be familiar with. Draw the structure of a sitcom, showing how the action proceeds from initial conflict to its climax or resolution.

*Beyond Summary.* One of the biggest problems students have in writing about literature lies in plot summary. They will oftentimes offer elaborate, detailed summaries of the action of a piece of literature but never talk about what it means. Be sure to call your students' attention to the need to interpret, not just summarize. Have your students consider the extent to which the student essays we've included in this chapter offer the writer's interpretation of the stories with which they deal. Ask your students at what points they agree with the student authors and at what points they don't.

*Writing From Literature.* We offer one sample student essay written *from* Robert Frost's "The Road Not Taken." Ask your students to compare this essay to those by the other student writers in this chapter. You'll note that the essay by Jessica Edwards, "The Price of Freedom," has a lengthy introduction that involves personal narrative. What makes Jessica's essay one *about* literature as opposed to one *from* literature?

*Writing Assignments.* We offer specific advice on both writing *about* and *from* literature. You may specify either approach, or you may allow your students to choose. If the latter, consider rearranging your peer groups, so that students working on similar approaches will read and comment on each other's papers.

# RESPONSES TO EXERCISES

## Exercise 8.1

In "The Philosophy of Literary Form," Kenneth Burke uses the word "poetry" to stand for all types of literature. He defines poetry as "any work of a critical or imaginative cast" (PLF, p. 1), so poetry in this broad sense encompasses not only poems but also short stories, novels, plays, and even non-fiction prose. And in "Literature as Equipment for Living," he says that poetry is "produced for purposes of comfort," that it is "equipment for living," and that it "would protect us" (PLF, p. 61). In a short response, explain what Burke might have meant in saying that literature might "comfort" us. How might it become "equipment for living"? How might it "protect us"?

What pieces of literature have you read that you might think of as "equipment for living"? How did they "comfort" or "console" you?

> *I think that literature being "equipment for living" and "protection and comfort" is a good way to describe something that so many people look to in times of need. We read to learn about certain things, to determine what other people think about things, have learned, etc. Literature, even for enjoyment, can often be important to some people for protection and comfort in that some people need to read to be happy. Some literature allows a person to enter another world and leave the current one behind. I definitely believe that I read often to escape what is bothering me at the moment. I can become any number of different heroes or heroines, and the only intruders are those who belong within the novel. Literature can protect by educating us, allowing us to leave our present state, or by informing us. We can turn to it in tough times; we can return to a favorite passage that we value. Literature is valuable in these respects.*

> *Several novels have become a comfort to me: <u>Their Eyes Were Watching God</u>, by Zora Neale Hurston, and any of the novels by Mary Higgins Clark. I enjoy becoming the heroine in each, and they make me strong. These comfort and console me because they are about women who have often defied the odds and done great things. Sometimes I use the Bible as "equipment for living" because it keeps me on the straight and narrow. I can look to it for comfort and consolation because so many passages are beautiful and strength giving.*

## Exercise 8.2

Apply this reading procedure to Alexie's and Cervantes' poetry and to at least one of the three short stories presented at the first of this chapter. How did your applications enhance your reading and understanding of the poetry? The story?

> *By applying the suggested methods of interpretation to reading the poetry of Alexie and Cervantes, as well as the story "El Tonto del Barrio," I was able to gather a much more developed idea of what each is about, as well as why it was written. Alexie wanted to make a strong statement about the ill treatment of Native Americans. Cervantes also wanted to make a statement about society, but hers is more positive that Alexie's. And Armas wanted to say something about how the dynamic of a society can be upset by even the best of intentions. By applying the reading methods suggested, I was able to read each text more thoroughly and deeply.*

## Exercise 8.3

Describe or summarize the plot of any of the short stories or poetry you've read in this text. Then describe any conflict you may find in the piece of literature you're working with. How does the conflict drive or forward the plot?

*"El Tonto del Barrio" is a story about a man who is quite willing to do his own thing, and is successful and well liked, until he is faced with "progress." Romero spends his time sweeping and whistling, and is well liked for many years until a young man, who thinks that a man should be paid for the work he does in money, interferes. Seferino thinks that work should be rewarded in cash, but he does not realize that Romero has a good life, has everything he needs or wants, and is happy. Once Seferino starts to pay Romero, things change, and Romero begins to become unhappy. He demands a raise and goes on strike when he doesn't get it. He begins to drink heavily and becomes a real nuisance in the community. People even talk about having him committed to a mental institution. At the story's end, when Seferino leaves for school, Romero begins to reenter his old life, whistling and sweeping and talking to people when they talk to him. The community returns to the old style of life.*

*The conflict in the story comes with Seferino's view of life and work. Seferino does not seem to understand the neighborhood's benevolent treatment of Romero. When he "employs" Romero and pays him a regular salary, Seferino begins to conflict with the community's old values, and he causes Romero to enter into conflict with his neighbors as well. This conflict drives the plot. With the changes in attitudes (e.g., Romero toward the community and the community toward Romero), we see the conflict develop and fester. Only when Seferino (the catalyst for change) leaves for college do we see the community return to its old ways, and the problem with Romero is no longer a problem, because he no longer feels driven or compelled to work for money. He is incapable of holding a real job for real wages, but he gets what he needs from his friends in the community, who give willingly.*

## Exercise 8.4

For at least one of the short stories at the first of this chapter, make a list of characters. Which are major? Minor? Who is the protagonist? Antagonist? How do the protagonist and antagonist work against each other? To what effect?

*"El Tonto del Barrio"*

*Characters*

*Romero Estrado*
*Barelas*
*Seferino*
*Tino Gabaldon*
*Frank Avila*
*Manolo*
*Worker from Hotel*

*Main*

*Romero*
*Barelas*
*Seferino*

*Protagonist: Romero*

*Antagonist: Seferino*

*Romero has a system, as does the community, that Sefereino upsets by introducing a new concept. This made everything change, and as long as Seferino was in the picture, the entire community was affected because things were so different. The funny thing was, the community placed blame on the secondary source, because it was the more obvious one, and they didn't realize the actual root of the problem. When Romero asks for a raise and is denied, his attitude totally changes, and this is when everything begins to go downhill. Seferino's attempt to help backfires, setting up the clash between his society's old values and his new ones.*

## Exercise 8.5

In "Shopping," how does the wealth implicit in the mall as physical setting work with the bag lady, the reactions of other shoppers to her, and Noel's reactions to her? What does the mall represent or symbolize in American life? How does this aspect of "Shopping" reflect American culture?

> *The implicit wealth in "Shopping" is set clearly against the image of the woman in black. All around her, we imagine bright lights and bustling people, their arms laden with bags and packages. Smack in the middle, we see a woman in black clothing talking to herself. The reactions of the other shoppers remind us of reactions we have had when we have seen people in this situation before, and our own aversions, however unconscious, that we may have to the homeless. The mall represents the coldness and sterility of our material society. We consume a lot and do so conspicuously, but just how much real satisfaction do we get from it? The shoppers' faces I see in malls at Christmastime don't have very pleasant looks on them, many more scowls than smiles.*

## Exercise 8.6

A. What symbols (including colors, objects, and/or gestures) might represent these concepts?

| innocence | purity | anger | evil |
|---|---|---|---|
| life | growth | death | solidarity |

> *innocence: green; purity: white; anger: red; evil: snake*
> *life: a pregnant silhouette; growth: sapling; death: skull & crossbones*
> *solidarity: clasped hands*

B. What might these terms symbolize?

| eagle | skyscraper | hawk | open arms |
|---|---|---|---|
| dove | snake | river | apple |
| ocean | baseball | rain | water |
| house | mountain | hearth | |

> *eagle: freedom; skyscraper: progress, civilization; hawk: warlike*
> *open arms: love; dove: peace; snake: evil*
> *river: free spirit; apple: health; ocean: wildness, turbulence*
> *baseball: health, American spirit; rain: cleansing; water: life*
> *house: warmth; mountain: goals; hearth: home*

## Exercise 8.7

Write several questions that the titles of Sherman Alexie's poems raise, questions that you would want your reading of the poems to help you answer.

> "That Place Where Ghosts of Salmon Jump"
>
> *Why are these ghost-fish?*
> *Why is it important that they're ghosts?*
> *What kind of place would salmon ghosts go?*

> *Would anyone be able to see them, or is this a special vision?*
> *Do these ghost-fish jump with other fish or alone?*
> *Are they jumping for joy, or jumping to get upstream as they do in life to spawn?*

"The Powwow at the End of the World"

> *What does Alexie mean by the end of the world?*
> *Who will be there?*
> *What will happen at this Powwow?*
> *Why is it important for Alexie to write about?*

Bill

# Teaching Chapter 9
# Position Essays

## OVERVIEW

If your experience is anything like ours, you have found argumentative writing very difficult for many of your students. When you think about it, there is good reason for this difficulty. We are asking a lot of students in this chapter. As we have articulated it for ourselves, our goal is to help students develop the ability to see their beliefs and opinions as just that–beliefs and opinions. When the student argues that gun control is a bad thing, he must come to understand that others will argue that gun control is a good thing. And we hope that he will develop the ability to see that many fair-minded people will have opinions and beliefs that differ from his.

In order to reach this goal, we will have to help students locate their topics somewhere between statements of fact that need not be argued and foundational assumptions that allow for no argument. This will require a good bit of work for most of our students.

## TEACHING TIPS

*Syllogistic Reasoning.* As you help students deal with differences between various types of support, you may find it useful to introduce them to the basics of syllogistic reasoning. Below is a syllogism with its three parts identified:

| | |
|---|---|
| Major Premise: | All required courses in my curriculum should help prepare me for the job I will take after graduation. |
| Minor Premise: | This course will not help me prepare for my job after graduation. |
| Conclusion: | This course should not be required. |

As this example illustrates, a syllogism consists of a major premise, a minor premise, and a conclusion. A *valid* syllogism is one in which the conclusion follows logically from the two premises. The syllogism above is valid; given a situation in which one agrees that all required courses should help prepare one for his job and also accepts the fact that this course will not help one prepare for his job, it is irrefutable that this course should not be required. Of course, many people will balk at the assertion made in the major premise, but that is beside the point in determining that this is a valid syllogism.

Compare the valid syllogism above with the following invalid syllogism:

| | |
|---|---|
| Major Premise: | All required courses in my curriculum should help prepare me for the job I will take after graduation. |
| Minor Premise: | This course will not help prepare me for my job after graduation. |
| Conclusion: | I should not take this course. |

Note that one does not have to accept the conclusion even if the truth of the two premises is assumed. It may well be that students should enroll in elective courses even when they will not help prepare them for their careers. If this syllogism is to be valid, the major premise might be rewritten as follows: I should only take courses that will help prepare me for the job I will have after graduation. While one may well not agree with the major or minor premise, he would have to agree with the conclusion if he grants the truth of the two premises.

As you work with students in constructing arguments, you may want to show them how to connect a thesis sentence and the claims that support that thesis with syllogistic reasoning. For example, consider a thesis such as the following:

> UNC Charlotte should institute a curfew for all students living in university housing.

How might we build support for this thesis? We could support the thesis with a causal claim:

> Instituting a curfew on our campus would save students' lives.

How would we go about offering support for this claim? We might look to see if other campuses have (or have ever had) curfews and find whether there is data to support our claim. Or we might examine the number of accidents, muggings, and rapes that happen at various hours of the night and determine whether those data help support the claim. So far, we have looked at this thesis from the standpoint of the argument procedure outlined in Chapter 9. But how do we connect this procedure with syllogistic reasoning?

We can begin by stating the thesis as a conclusion. The causal claim can then function as a major premise for this argument. So far, then, we have the following parts of a syllogism.

| | |
|---|---|
| Major Premise: | unstated |
| Minor Premise: | Institution of a curfew on our campus would save students' lives. |
| Conclusion: | UNC Charlotte should institute a curfew for all students living in university housing. |

These two parts of a syllogism form an *enthymeme*, a syllogism with one of its premises missing. We often deal in enthymemes because we don't think it necessary to state (and support) one of the premises. Let's return to our enthymeme above. What major premise would make it into a valid syllogism? There is only one major premise that would force us (given that we accept both the major and minor premises) to accept the conclusion:

| | |
|---|---|
| Major Premise: | Anything that would save student lives should be done. |

We now have a valid syllogism:

| | |
|---|---|
| Major Premise: | Anything that would save student lives should be done. |
| Minor Premise: | Institution of a curfew on our campus would save students' lives. |
| Conclusion: | UNC Charlotte should institute a curfew for all students living in university housing. |

In stating the premise this way, we may well gain insight into how those who argue against this conclusion will frame their arguments. They may agree that the curfew would save lives, but they may point out that any number of other actions could save lives. For example, forbidding all students to take trips home to see their parents during the school term, disbanding the football team, and so forth. Thus, they may well argue that while not having a curfew does expose students to some risks, the loss of freedom that comes with a curfew is worse than the risk.

As you work with these concepts, you may find it useful to spend some time in asking your students to turn thesis sentences into syllogisms. Then you can discuss the insights these syllogisms provide into the ways in which arguments might be mounted against the theses. Let's look at one additional example. Given the following thesis, what syllogism might be constructed to support it?

| | |
|---|---|
| Major Premise: | We should support all proposals that produce economic benefits. |
| Minor Premise: | A new arena will produce economic benefits for the citizens of our city. |
| Conclusion: | We should build a new arena for our basketball team. |

As stated, this is a valid syllogism. Of course, that does not mean that opponents will accept the claims being made in the premises. Depending upon the opponent, there may be objections to one or both of the premises. Some people will argue that this arena will not produce these benefits. Others will argue that even should those benefits be forthcoming, some things are more important than money. They might point to the fact that a new team downtown will draw more people to the region, which in turn will cause such problems as increased traffic congestion and air pollution.

Below are some theses that you may ask your students to transform into syllogisms:

1. Our state should increase the salaries of public school teachers.

2. Our state should enact a "three-strikes and you're out" sentencing guideline.

3. Restaurants should have the right to dictate how their customers dress.

4. Our state should enact (or repeal) a no-fault insurance law.

5. Our state should repeal (or enact) a state income tax.

6. The federal government should enact a flat tax (or repeal current income tax laws).

7. Bicycles should not be allowed on sidewalks of our university.

8. Preference in admissions should be given to the children of alumni with a strong record of giving to the university.

9. The state should require applicants for a marriage license to pass a test showing basic knowledge about the dynamics of the marital relationship.

10. The state should license parents and require parenting classes as a part of that process.

***Developing Ethos.*** The concept of ethos is extremely important for the writer of argumentative essays, for ethos represents how the writer presents herself to her readers. Will her writing present her as informed and fair or as merely opinionated and shrill?

*Listening to the Opposition.* Many argument chapters ask writers to assume a goal of changing a reader's mind about a given topic. In a sense, our position chapter asks the writer to undertake a goal that is likely to produce more change in himself than in anyone reading his essay. The writer must attempt to see his opposition's point of view so clearly that he can articulate the opposing viewpoint in language acceptable to the opposition. Consider, for example, a writer who is arguing for the right to life. He must avoid the kind of slanted language that would characterize those who disagree with him as murderers or even as immoral. If he is to capture the opposing position in language that the reader can accept, he must say that this person believes that a woman's right to choose whether to complete a pregnancy is to be valued more highly than continuing a pregnancy at all costs.

This kind of sensitivity to language is not easy to come by. You may want to do some work designed to help your students pay attention to the ways in which their beliefs and biases can be reflected in their language, in ways that they are not conscious of. For example, consider the two sentences below:

During Columbus's time, many people believed the earth was flat.

During Columbus's time, many people realized the earth was flat.

What's wrong with the second sentence? It's problematic because *realize* is what linguists call a "factive" verb. It assumes that the statement in a "that" clause it introduces is true. There is a problem here because we know that the earth is not flat. There is no such problem with first sentence since "believe" is not a factive verb. We see a similar phenomenon in the following sentences.

She tells me that she has not lived with her husband for two years.

She claims that she has not lived with her husband for two years.

In the first sentence the welfare worker is simply reporting on a conversation she had with an applicant for aid. In the second, the worker is reporting on that conversation and registering some personal doubt as to the veracity of what the woman says–with the word *claim*.

As we suggested above, you may want to give students exercises in which they practice stating the opposition's case in language that is acceptable to the opposition. Your students will find it a difficult task to imagine how the opposition would want its case presented. They have been so accustomed to the argument of slash and burn that they have given little time to hearing what others will say. The example on pages 337-339 of the imaginary dialogue between me and a person who takes the opposing point of view on the issue of gun control is designed to suggest a way students can use role playing to develop their skills in "hearing" the other side. We would suggest that you make such a dialogue a part of your students' prewriting for the position paper; however, before you do so, your students may benefit from some role playing in class. On a given day, assign students the task of thinking about pro and con arguments for a particular argumentative thesis–you might want to use one of the theses in the exercise above. Then when students come to the next class, ask two volunteers to role play in a discussion about this issue, one arguing in favor, the other against. After this role playing, the class can discuss the relative effectiveness of each of the role players.

Your students may not know how to begin this dialogue. If so, encourage them to start talking and to keep talking, even if they think they don't know what to say. If you have the means to do so and think it won't intimidate the participants, record the conversation, so that the class can listen to the dialogue again and then discuss it.

***Triadic and Dyadic Arguing***. As you work to help students develop their ethos in this writing assignment, you may want to introduce them to the distinction between triadic and dyadic arguments. A triadic argument is one in which a speaker mounts an argument against an opponent whom he has no real hope of persuading. In such a situation, the writer really hopes to persuade people listening to the argument he is mounting against his opponent. Much of the argument that your students have been exposed to belongs in this category. A primary example would be a presidential debate. One candidate argues against another in order to win the approval, not of that candidate, but of the voters who witness the argument. An open letter to a Congressman published in a local newspaper on an issue that the Congressman has already declared his position on would fall into this category. If the Congressman has announced his intention to vote for a bill, no letter from a constituent is going to change his mind, and the constituent who writes such a letter is well aware of that fact. In such a case, the writer hopes to convince other constituents who may read the open letter in the newspaper.

When we engage in such triadic arguments, we can take much more liberty with our language than we could in a dyadic argument. We don't have to worry about alienating the person we are writing to, since we have no hope of convincing him. Of course, if our language makes us seem unfair or unreasonable, we may lose favor with the real audience we are writing for.

In Chapter 9, we ask students to write a dyadic argument, that is, to write to people who disagree with them. While they may not hope to change their readers' minds, they should aim to help give those readers a new understanding of the position they oppose, and they should strive to gain the readers' respect. Thus, it is crucial that students take care to use language that will foster the kind of ethical appeal needed to achieve these goals.

As an exercise, suggest that your students scan newspapers, especially the editorial pages, and magazines to find examples of dyadic and triadic arguments. We would guess that they will probably find a preponderance of triadic arguments. You can then discuss why there are so few dyadic arguments and how as writers they will benefit from engaging in the one called for in Chapter 9.

*Just The Facts*. Some of you will recognize the illusion in the header here to the television series "Dragnet." Sergeant Joe Friday was famous for his request that agitated citizens, usually hysterical women, give him "just the facts, ma'am." We would all like to believe that everything would be clear if we could just get the facts. Unfortunately, none of us ever really lets the facts get in the way when it comes to the important issues we disagree on.

I'm reminded of a personal example. Some years ago, I was in conversation with a good friend who is decidedly conservative in his political views. We were discussing the fall of the Soviet Union, and I was being very careful in my choice of words, since I did not want to insult him and add to his distress in being proved so wrong about our national policies. I knew that my friend had been a hawk, arguing that we should put more and more money into our military to guard against the U.S.S.R. Now that the entire structure of the Soviet government had fallen and we were getting glimpses into just how weak that country was, and had been for some time, I was sure that hawks like my friend would see the folly of their arguments. I wanted to be magnanimous, not to gloat over how right I had been and how wrong he had been. To my amazement, it was my friend who wanted to broach the issue; to my further amazement, he told me how right he and others had been to encourage our government to keep its defenses up against the U.S.S.R. By doing so, he argued, we had forced the U.S.S.R. to continue to put more and more of its money into defense, thereby leaving no resources to support the infrastructure of the country. We agreed on the facts. The U.S.S.R had been weakened and ultimately toppled because it could not sustain the arms race with the U.S. However, we disagreed entirely on whether the U.S. should have been engaging in this race with a country that was in such desperate straits. I had thought it a waste of our resources, since that government was going to collapse anyway. He thought it a very good use of our resources since it hastened the overthrow of the U.S.S.R.

As you work to help students differentiate between facts and beliefs, you may want to use this or another example, and ask students to come up with their own examples in which people on different sides of an argument agree on certain facts but interpret them differently.

*Arguments from Definition and Cause.* Our discussion of the way in which arguments may be supported by *definition* and *cause* is indebted to the work of Richard Weaver, especially to his famous article entitled "Language Is Sermonic" (*Language Is Sermonic: Richard M. Weaver on the Nature of Rhetoric*, ed Richard L. Johannesen, et al., Louisiana State University Press, 1970). In this work, Weaver lists four methods of argument:

Argument from Definition

Argument from Analogy

Argument from Cause

Argument from Circumstance.

Weaver sees this as a hierarchy, with the loftiest kind of argument being that which rests on definition. That is, it is more powerful to say that you should not take drugs because drugs are evil than to say that you should not take drugs because doing so will harm your health.

We have dropped two of Weaver's categories–analogy and circumstance. Weaver also gave these two types of argument less attention than the others because analogy is very close kin to definition and because circumstance is such a weak grounds for arguing. That is, if the only support we can offer for a particular action is the circumstance we find ourselves in, we have little power in our argument. Clearly, the two linchpins in Weaver's system are definition and cause.

Weaver is an interesting rhetorician. In "Language Is Sermonic," Weaver argues that the society of his day was suffering from a loss of any real belief in values. With the loss of agreed-upon values, those who would construct arguments were forced to build them on cause or circumstance. You may want to explore this issue with your class. Just what kinds of assumed values are available to them in constructing their arguments? Students could list values they and their readers are likely to accept by definition. Which of the following appear on their list: honesty, truthfulness, fairness, compassion, respect for human life? What others do they come up with? Once you have such a list, you might ask students to choose three values and rank them in terms of the weight they carry in their value system. That is, if truthfulness conflicts with compassion, which value generally wins in their world view? Students might bring brief essays on this topic to class and discuss them. You should find clear differences–for example, one student may value truthfulness more than compassion; another the reverse. This discussion should help you make the point that arguments from definition are going to need much support. That is, it is not enough to say that drugs should be illegal because drugs are evil. Someone else may well argue that legalizing drugs will save lives (cause fewer people to lose their lives in purchasing and using illegal drugs). They may go on to appeal to saving human life as a value that transcends, in their system, good and evil. That is, drugs are evil, but saving human life is a greater good.

*Appeals to Authority*. In Chapter 9, we talk about appeals to authority. We make the point that even though most of us rely on authority in certain areas of our lives, the appeal to authority has its limitations in logical argumentation. This is a sensitive subject for many of our students. And much of the sensitivity has to do with culture, as Nancy Pfingstag points out in her discussion of non-native student writing. (See her essay "Newcomers in First-year Composition: Teaching Writing to ESL Students" in this manual.) However, the cultural differences we are talking about here are not limited to differences between students who speak different languages. Many U.S. American students come from cultures that place great value in holy books (the Christian Bible being the chief authority for many of our students) and in religious teachers. It is important, we think, not to tell students that they cannot refer to holy books and teachers; to do so seems to disorient them and, thus, to be unproductive. More to the point, to tell students which authorities they may (or may not) use seems to make us guilty of the same type of narrowness we want to caution them against.

We have found it helpful at the very beginning of the argument unit to say that no one authority will be sufficient to support a claim. That is, if a student is going to argue that young people should practice abstinence from sexual relations before marriage, it is not sufficient to cite a Biblical passage in support of this thesis. The student may very well cite the Biblical passage, but then he should move on to other supports. There are many other authorities to appeal to on this issue. And there are many causal arguments that can be offered in support of this thesis.

You may find an exercise I have used many times helpful in dealing with this issue of authority.

It's called the Liar's Circle; it consists of drawing a circle on the board and placing certain sentences within that circle:

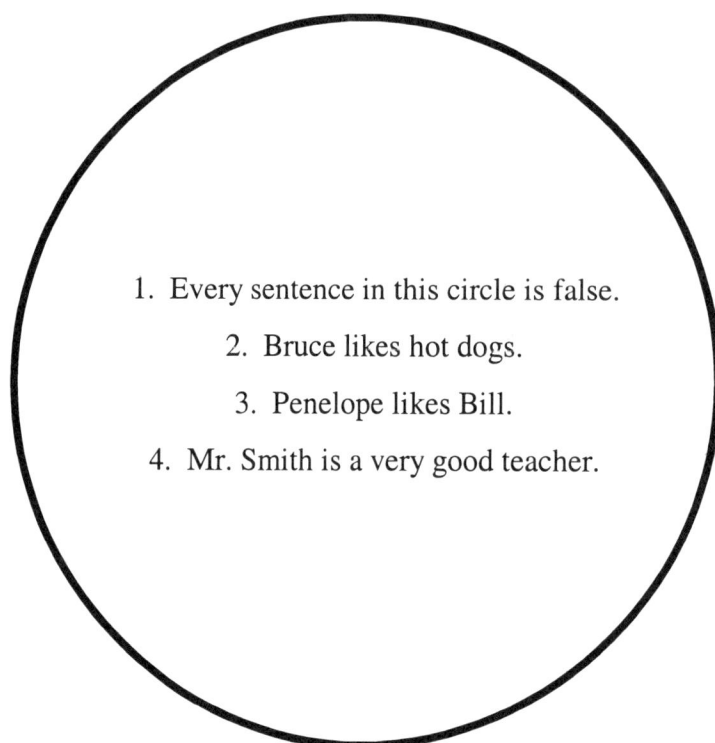

I then ask the students in the class whether sentence #1 is true. If it's true, then it's automatically false. Once students have struggled a bit with this question, I point out the essential problem–that is, sentence #1 attempts to make an assertion about itself. This in itself is not so usual. What is unusual is that the sentence asserts that its basic assertion is false. It sometimes helps for us to examine another sentence in the circle in regard to this issue. Take, for example, sentence #2, Bruce likes hot dogs. There is a sense in which this sentence could be seen to make the following assertions, one of them explicit and the other implicit:

 2. Bruce like hot dogs          EXPLICIT

 (This assertion is true.)       IMPLICIT

That is, we expect that any writer who says something to us will say what he thinks to be the truth. Otherwise, why would he speak to us? It would look exceedingly odd to have the following sentence.

Bruce likes hot dogs, and what I have just said is false.

We would wonder why the speaker bothered to make this false statement–that Bruce likes hot dogs. And we might go on to wonder about his statement that the first statement is false, since he is proving himself an unreliable source.

We're now in a position to return to the first sentence, which we could analyze as follows:

Every sentence in this circle is false, and this sentence is true.

We add the second assertion, "and this sentence is true," because we have to believe the writer thinks what he is saying is true. Otherwise, why would he take the trouble to say it. But then we have a problem because what he says explicitly contradicts this second implicit assertion. Our logic system breaks down.

How to solve the problem. We would advise the speaker to take this sentence out of the circle and modify it slightly.

1a. Every sentence in that circle is false. (And this sentence is true.)

Now, we have something we can process. This speaker is telling us that we should not pay attention to the sentences in that circle.

And that is precisely the point we are trying to make to our students who would want to rely on one authority for support. They are doing something of the same thing the liar's circle illustrates. They would tell us that one should not engage in premarital sex, offering as support for this thesis: "The Bible says that one should not engage in premarital sex." When asked why we should accept the authority of the Bible, they would say: "The Bible says that it's true." So we're back to the liar's circle.

The Bible says that one should not engage in premarital sex, and

what the Bible says is true

because the Bible says so.

This may seem like a lot of trouble to make a rather simple point. We have found that with many of our students, this isn't simple. And it is very sensitive. The laughter and head-scratching that goes on when I introduce the liar's circle to them is often very helpful in getting students to think about the closed thinking they have been engaging in.

*Opinions*. *Opinion* is a loaded term. Many of your students will arrive believing that all opinions are created equal. The assertion, "It's my opinion," is supposed to close off all debate. Of course, we know that not all opinions are created equal, and a large part of our work in argumentation consists in helping students come to understand what we mean in saying this.

As you work with students on this issue you may find an exercise I have used helpful. The game consists of setting up a scenario, listing three people, and then asking whose opinion would be more highly valued in that situation. Let's take a simple example first.

**The Situation:**

You find yourself staring at the wires of bomb that has been placed in a public building. The clock is ticking, showing 30 seconds remaining. You assume that if something isn't done, it will explode at that time. You have to do something. You believe you should disconnect one or more or the wires attached to the explosive. But which one(s)? You haven't a clue. Whose opinion will you value more?

**The Authorities:**

1. A noted authority on terrorism who teaches at a major university. He has documented the actions of numerous terrorist groups throughout the world in the last 50 years.

2. A skilled electrician with training in wiring buildings.

3. A former bomb maker. He has served time in prison but is now reformed and gives lectures on the subject of terrorism. He has constructed more different types of bombs than any other

person in the FBI files.

This one is pretty easy, eh? But how about the following one, entitled "Who you Gonna Call?"

**The Situation**:

You're on the brand new game show, "Wanna Win a Million Bucks?" You have to answer a certain number of questions correctly if you're to win the ultimate prize. The rules of the game say that if a particular question stumps you, you may call a friend to help you, but you may ask only one question. You find yourself facing the following question: How many presidents were elected in the 1970's. Now, this wouldn't be such a hard question, except for the fact that you were not born until 1980 and you have not been a student of presidential politics. You know that Ford was President sometime during the 1970's, but you don't think he was ever elected. You know that Nixon was President before Ford, but you're unsure of his dates. You know that Reagan became President about the time you were born, but was he elected in 1979. Face it, you don't know the answer to this question. So who will you call?

**The Authorities**

1. Your dad. He was an adult during the 1970's, and he pays attention to matters of politics.

2. Your friend, Bill. He loves history, and intends to study history in college. He probably paid close attention in his history class in high school on these issues.

3. Your uncle Bob. He owns an insurance agency. He knows more trivia than anyone else you know and usually wins handily in trivia games.

This one is hard isn't it? We expect it would lead to some interesting class discussion about what constitutes authority. You may want to ask your students to prepare two or three of these for a class period and play a game of "Who You Gonna Call?" in class.

# RESPONSE TO EXERCISES

*Exercise 9.1*

Not presented

*Exercise 9.2*

Look back to three of the essays at the beginning of this chapter (or essays that your instructor chooses). Identify any instances in which the writer presents as fact, information with which someone opposing his or her argument might disagree. Also identify instances in which these authors could have used more facts to support their arguments. How would their arguments be strengthened by the use of more facts?

*In "Don't Let Judges Set Crooks Free," Phil Gramm states that mandatory minimum sentencing will discourage a person from engaging in criminal activity because he knows he will get a stiff sentence. The opposing side of the argument could state that this is an entirely untrue statement, and that a criminal will engage in criminal behavior regardless of the punishment. They might argue that once a criminal becomes a criminal, that lifestyle is ingrained and cannot be changed. This may lead to alternative viewpoints.*

*In "Common Decency," Susan Jacoby states that young women initially resist sex as a part of the courtship rituals, and young men take pride in being able to get women to have sex with them. The author states these as facts and offers no support for the assertions. Those opposing her argument may disagree.*

*In "The War on Drugs is Self Defeating," Jack Weinstein makes the following assertion: "Now they [drug offenders] must serve an average of two additional years, and sometimes a 10-year minimum, leading to at least 800 more penal years, at millions of dollars of added expense for incarceration in our district alone." Clearly the judge is doing some estimating here, and his opponents may take him to task for it.*

*Each of these arguments could be countered by an opposing viewpoint. I do believe that in general the essays make good use of factual information. While the essay on date rape is an excellent essay and does its job of swaying readers' opinions, I do believe it could be stronger if it used more numbers and concrete facts.*

## Exercise 9.3

We compared an essay presented at the beginning of this chapter, "The Conservative Case for Abortion," with an essay presented at the beginning of Chapter Ten, "Dismemberment and Choice." Two other essays in these two chapters deal with the same issue: date rape. Compare the attitude that Jacoby ("Common Decency") exhibits toward those who would disagree with her with the attitude that Camille Paglia, "Rape and Modern Sex War" (in Chapter 10) takes toward those who would disagree with her. Do these writers seem to indicate that a sensible person could or could not disagree with them? Why or why not?

*Camille Paglia, in "Rape and Modern Sex War," puts forth the theory that men are driven by aggression. Susan Jacoby takes a very different view, arguing that men can control their impulses just as women can. I think both women believe that sensible readers would agree with them, but they differ in how they treat readers who might disagree. Paglia resorts to name calling in several places, presenting those who would disagree with her to be whiners. Jacoby is more even-handed toward her readers.*

## Exercise 9.4

Examine three of the sample essays from the beginning of this chapter (or essays chosen by your teacher). What is the thesis of each essay? What claim(s) does each thesis rest on? Explain.

*In "The Conservative Case for Abortion," Muller argues that abortion should remain legal. He builds his argument on the claim that abortion promotes family values. This makes his argument somewhat unique, since most times those arguing for family values are against abortion. Muller, however, argues that many times unwanted children disrupt families that already exist. In many other cases, there is no family waiting to accept a child and so the child has to live totally without family values.*

*Phil Gramm's thesis, in "Don't Let Judges Set Crooks Free," comes in his conclusion. At this point, he says he is in support of mandatory minimum sentencing and will be pushing for judges to impose harsher sentences on drug offenders. Throughout the essay, he supports this thesis with claims about how criminal activity is increasing and with facts that show the light sentences that result from our current system.*

*In "Common Decency," Susan Jacoby argues that date rape should be considered as rape, not some special case brought on by special circumstances. She supports this claim by arguing that most men and women act civilly toward each other in the most frustrating situations and that it is only the deviants in our society who don't know that "no" means "no."*

## Exercise 9.5

Examine the supports for the two essays dealing with drug laws–"The War on Drugs is Self-Defeating" and "Don't Let Judges Set Crooks Free." What kinds of authorities do these two essays appeal to? Which essay makes more use of appeals to authority? Why do you think it does? Is this an effective strategy?

> *Neither of the essays makes extensive use of authorities. Of the two, Weinstein ("Don't Let Judges") makes more use of authority. At the beginning of his essay he refers to Chief Justice William H. Rehnquist's statement that "The law by itself is not going to solve the problems of drugs and violence." He then moves to cite Attorney General Janet Reno who, according to Weinstein, - emphasized the importance of reconsidering the existing drug policy. Gramm does not appeal to authority at all. He cites one expert on statistics, Morgan Reynolds, but he simply uses Reynolds as a source for facts and figures on how bad things are. Gramm may shy away from authorities because he wants readers to feel that authorities, like Weinstein, are responsible for the trouble we're in. He's taking a position that the common man can look at the situation we're in and figure things out for himself. Weinstein, on the other hand, takes the position that things are often more complicated than they seem on the surface. Thus, an appeal to authority is in order.*

## Exercise 9.6

Choose a paragraph from two of the sample essays near the beginning of this chapter. List every opinion you find in these two paragraphs. Then label them according to the three types of opinion we discussed. What kinds of support for opinions of type 3–those needing support–are offered? What insights into these essays do you get by means of this analysis?

> *The fourth and fifth paragraphs of "The Age Requirement for Teen Drivers," are full of opinions. Two of these opinions need no support.*
>
> *Driving an automobile is an inherently dangerous activity.*
>
> *As a licensed driver, you must take the responsibility for the actions and decisions that you make while driving.*
>
> *The other seven opinions were claims that need support:*
>
> *Otherwise, you could be one of far too many teens responsible for a highway death.*
>
> *[Here, the writer needs support for the claim that many teens are responsible for highway deaths; she provides this evidence in her essay.]*
>
> *Teenagers are deadly drivers because of their inexperience and their tendency to take risks. [We need some support for the claim that teenagers tend to take risks; however, this is given as a quote from an authority, so that constitutes some support.]*
>
> *Teen drivers see driving as fun and do not take it seriously enough. [The writer says this is her experience, but she needs more support for this claim. She offers some support by detailing the numbers of accidents teens are involved in.]*
>
> *At sixteen, they don't have the necessary maturity to do so [i.e. take driving seriously]*
>
> *[This claim needs support. That is what the entire essay is designed to do.]*
>
> *Maturity is a key to safe driving. [In a sense this is what the essay is all about, so the whole essay will be supporting this claim.]*

*Mature drivers are cautious and abide by the rules of the road. [Needs support. She gives some support by comparing accident rates for "mature" vs. inexperienced drivers.]*

*Many young teens, however, get caught up in playing practical jokes and racing each other while they are driving. [How many? What's the evidence? She doesn't really offer any.]*

*In "The War on Drugs is Self Defeating," the eighth and ninth paragraphs include four opinion statements. One of these can be classed as obvious:*

> *... and, too frequently, ghetto youths seek to emulate sellers and thugs who brazenly walk city streets.*

*[It is obvious that many ghetto youths are attracted to this lifestyle.]*

*The remaining three claims are in need of support.*

> *Many parents have no place to send their children for help;*

*[Weinstein doesn't offer any support for this claim, but an opponent could certainly say that this isn't obviously true.]*

> *Educational and other nonpenal controls are ineffective [Some might argue that we haven't devoted enough effort to these measures. Weinstein's statistics on the problem as it now exists offer some support.]*

> *Largely because of drug prosecutions, our justice system is in crisis.*

*[Some evidence is needed that our system is in crisis, and Weinstein does give it. Then, evidence is needed that it is drug prosecutions that have caused the crisis. He provides some evidence by giving statistics on how much time these cases take in court.]*

*One thing I learned in doing this exercise is that opinions are sometimes obvious, but they can be hard to spot when the reader agrees with what the writer is saying. This leads us to nodding in agreement before we realize we are being offered opinions.*

*I was impressed overall with the fact that the writers usually offered support for those opinions that needed it.*

## *Exercise 9.7*

Write two or three "should" theses for each of the following claims.

1. Lowering taxes in our city will cause an increase in the number of businesses locating in our city.
2. Gambling is wrong.
3. Killing is immoral.
4. A good system of higher education will help cause an improved economy in our state.
5. Car telephones cause more accidents than alcohol.

   *1a. We should lower taxes in our city.*

   *1b. We should not lower taxes in our city.*

   *2a. Gambling should remain illegal.*

   *2b. Gamblers should be prosecuted.*

*3a. The state should have the right to take the life of anyone who commits murder.*

*3b. The state should not engage in killing.*

*4a. We should support higher education in our state.*

*4b. Our educational system should be strengthened.*

*5a. Car phones should be illegal.*

*5b. It should be illegal to use a car phone when operating a car.*

## *Exercise 9.8*

Below we offer several claims that might be offered in support of "should" theses. In each case, explain whether the claim is based on value or causality. Are there cases in which both cause and value are implicit in one claim?

1. <u>Thesis:</u>   Citizens of this state should not vote for Senator X.

    <u>Claim:</u>   He is the pawn of special interests such as the tobacco lobby.

*[This is primarily cause, since the writer wants to imply that his ties to the tobacco interest will keep the senator from representing the interests of all citizens of the state.]*

2. <u>Thesis:</u>   We should abolish capital punishment.

    <u>Claim:</u>   We do not have the right to play God.

*[This is a claim of value. The writer is implying that only God can take life and that when anyone else does so, it is wrong.]*

3. <u>Thesis:</u>   Euthanasia should not be illegal

    <u>Claim:</u>   It is inhumane for individuals to be made to exist when there is no quality to their lives.

*[This is both value and cause. First, the writer says that to allow suffering is inhumane, a value statement. The writer also implies that the decision to prevent euthanasia will cause suffering.]*

4. <u>Thesis:</u>   You should support the school bond issue.

    <u>Claim:</u>   Education is crucial if our society is going to make the progress necessary for the survival of the human race.

*[This is primarily a causal assertion. The writer implies that education will cause progress in our society, i.e., help us to survive. There is a hint at value, in that our survival is inherently good.]*

5. <u>Thesis:</u>   The referendum on a state lottery should be defeated.

    <u>Claim:</u>   The state should not encourage gambling.

*[This is a claim of value. The implication is that gambling is wrong in and of itself.]*

## Exercise 9.9

Not presented

## Exercise 9.10

Not presented

*Exercise 9.11*

After examining the structure of the two essays outlined above, use the classical structure as a means of analyzing one of the other essays in our sample essays or an essay selected by your instructor. Then discuss how the writer's purpose dictates the way the writer structures the argument.

> *"The Age Requirement for Teen Drivers"*
>
> *Thesis: We should support the new procedures for licensing drivers in North Carolina.*
>
> > *exordium (the writer gets the readers attention, paragraph 1)*
> > *narratio (the writer sets the background for the argument, paragraph 2, sentences 1-11)*
> > *partitio (the writer gives her position, paragraph 2, sentences 12-13)*
> > *confirmatio (the writer makes the case for her position, paragraphs 2-6)*
> > *confutatio (the writer offers refutation of major arguments against her, paragraphs 7-8)*
> > *peroratio (the writer concludes her argument, paragraph 9)*
>
> *This is a very traditional structure. The writer feels a need for all of the elements in the formal structure and she uses them well.*

*Exercise 9.12*

The following is the first paragraph of "For Pollsters, 'More' Doesn't Always Mean 'Better'" by John Shelton Reed:

> Just before the election of 1936, *The Literary Digest*, a widely read and influential magazine, announced the results of its presidential preference poll. The New Deal was going to be repudiated; FDR would be swept out of office. Alf Landon would be the next president, taking nearly 60 percent of the two-party popular vote. The announcement was made with a great deal of hoopla. The *Digest* quoted a reference to itself as an "oracle, which, since 1920, has foretold with almost uncanny accuracy the choice of the nation's voters[ . . .] ." And, after all, hadn't they mailed out over 10 million "secret ballots" to voters all over the nation, after ransacking tax rolls, telephone directories, automobile registration and magazine subscription lists for names? And hadn't they heard from more than 20 percent of the nation's voters in return?

Of course, President Roosevelt won by a large margin. Explain in a paragraph any problems you see in the reasoning of those who conducted the poll, using the terms of the discussion we have just completed.

> *There are several obvious problems with this data. We could call the entire process a "hasty generalization." However, there are more specific problems. First, there is the problem of whether the names came from--tax rolls, telephone directories and automobile registrations. These documents would tend to tap into the more affluent society of the day. Then there is the problem that a select group sent their opinions back in. Perhaps, these people selected themselves because they were more dissatisfied than most.*

*Exercise 9.13*

Find and explain the errors in causal reasoning in the statements below.

**Example**: Detroit automakers say they are building better cars and it must be, for since 1973 the number of highway deaths has decreased significantly.

**Explanation**: This is a rather obvious case of oversimplification. Automakers may be building better cars, but many other factors may be contributing to this decrease in highway deaths. A very important factor that must be taken into account is the reduction of maximum highway speed to 55 mph that occurred in 1973 and continued in most states until 1987. Other factors such as safe driving campaigns and reduced travel due to the increase in fuel cost may also have been causes.

1. The wives of successful men wear expensive clothing, so the best way for a woman to help her husband to be successful is to buy expensive clothing.

> *Wives probably wear these clothes as a RESULT of their husbands' success. There is not evidence that the clothes a wife wears can CAUSE her husband to be successful.*

2. Mr. Smith will surely support the ERA. After all, he has been active in civil rights work for twenty years.

> *This may well be a HASTY GENERALIZATION. There is reason to think that a person who has supported civil rights might be open to women's rights, but nothing to guarantee that he will be.*

3. Either you are for an increase in teachers' pay or you prefer your own pocketbook to the welfare of the youth of our society.

> *This is an example of either/or reasoning. A person could be very generous with his/her own funds and still feel that the economy in general cannot fund an increase in teachers' pay.*

4. It was obvious from the time that Jimmy Carter became president that Russia would become more aggressive in countries like Poland. An American president just cannot afford to give any indication of weakness to Russia.

> *There are several ways to counter this. First, there is a begging of the question as to whether Carter had shown any weakness to Russia. Where is the evidence for this assertion? Then, there is no attempt to make a connection between this supposed weakness and actions that Russia might be likely to take.*

5. We should never cut taxes again. We cut them in 1981 and unemployment rose immediately.

> *This is faulty causal reasoning. There is no attempt to show that the cutting of taxes in 1981 caused the rise in unemployment. Any number of other factors could have contributed to this rise.*

6. You were bound to be mugged sooner or later. A person just cannot subject herself to crowds the size of those at baseball games continually without being mugged.

> *Faulty causal reasoning--in particular, oversimplification. The speaker assumes a connection between large crowds and muggings, but offers no evidence of this connection.*

7. If I were you, I would take German from a native German. After all, you do want the best instruction for your money.

> *Begging the question. The person assumes that a native speaker of German will be a superior teacher of German. What is the evidence for this claim?*

8. If I were you, I would take German from a non-native speaker. After all, you do want to pass the course, don't you?

> *Begging the question. The person assumes that a non-native teacher will make it easier for a person to pass a German course. What is the evidence?*

## *Exercise 9.14*

When we label an assertion as an example of faulty reasoning, we do not mean to imply that it is impossible to treat the topic of that assertion in a reasonable and convincing fashion. For example, there is quite a bit of difference between the basic reasoning at work in statements 1 and 2 in the preceding exercise. Whereas statement 1 is unreasonable to the point of being humorous, there is some degree of reason involved in statement 2, even though we cannot accept the assertion as it stands. If you were going to argue that Smith will back the ERA, how would you develop your argument? Write a paragraph in which you plan a strategy for such an argument.

> *I might try to find data as to how many people at the forefront of the ERA movement were active in civil rights. I might explain my reasoning that the same kind of commitment to fairness that causes a person to be in favor of civil rights would likely make that person open to the tenets of ERA. I might speak to the qualities of fairness that I know Mr. Smith possesses.*

## Exercise 9.15

Label the fallacies of definition in the following examples and explain which term or terms cause the difficulty.

**Example:** That film should be given the Academy Award because it was the best picture of the year.

**Explanation:** This is a simple case of begging the question. There is really only one assertion stated twice. The film is the best because it is the best. The writer offers no insight into what "best film" means, or why he considers this the best film.

1. We all agree that each company should be free to set its own price. Therefore, how can we deny the companies the freedom to set prices as a group?

   *There is an equivocation here on free. Saying a company should be "free" to set its own price is not the same as saying that many companies should have the "freedom" to set prices as a group. In one case "free" is the backbone of competition; in the other, "freedom" is freedom from competition.*

2. I wouldn't choose only children to be camp counselors because they are not good in group situations.

   *This is begging the question. We are really saying that only children are not good in group situations because they are only children.*

3. Dad, how can you say I'm not dependable enough to have the car? Yesterday, you said you could depend on me to ask for the car every weekend.

   *This is a humorous equivocation. Clearly "dependable" and "depend" mean very different things here.*

4. I can't believe you voted for a Democrat.

   *This is a type of begging the question. One shouldn't vote for a Democrat because one shouldn't vote for a Democrat.*

5. The West wasn't won with a registered gun.

   *There is a problem of relevance here. What does that time period have to do with the present. There's also a problem with defining "won." What does "won" mean in this context, and what does its meaning have to do with registering guns?*

Ron

# Teaching Chapter 10
# Persuasion Essays

## OVERVIEW

Our distinction between argument and persuasion will likely be new to your students. Given the fact that the distinction between argumentative writing (Chapter 9, Position Essays) and persuasive writing (Chapter 10) is not the norm in writing textbooks, why do we make it? I can probably best answer this question by telling a story about my teaching of argument and persuasion. Some years ago, I attempted to illustrate successful argumentation by having students read two argumentative essays: Clarence Darrow's "Why I Am an Agnostic" and C. S. Lewis's "The Efficacy of Prayer." Darrow's is an impassioned essay (somewhat in the vein of Heaphy's "Dismemberment and Choice") in which he satirizes and spoofs those who hold a fundamentalist Christian belief system, showing the "ridiculous" beliefs that this system requires of its adherents. In very emotional language, he resorts to name calling and to questionable logic in his relentless offensive against what he sees as simple-mindedness. Lewis, on the other hand, offers a carefully reasoned, dispassionate argument that it is impossible to prove whether prayer works. His method is to give anecdotes from his own life that suggest to him that prayer has had effects on the situations in his life, but then to explain how a person who would disagree with him could undercut his argument. In the end, he admits that it is impossible to prove one way or another whether prayer has any effect.

In teaching argument, I used to ask students which of these was the more effective argument. To my amazement, my students–who were largely Christian, many of them fundamentalist–overwhelmingly chose Darrow's as the better essay. When asked why, they would say that Lewis was "wishy-washy" and that, at least you knew where Darrow stood. They liked the fact that he was passionate about his beliefs, even if they disagreed totally with those beliefs.

What was going on here? As we've observed our students in writing classes, it has become increasingly clear that a good bit of the instruction out there on argument is removed from the real-world arguing that our students know about. Lewis's argument was published and read by a very narrow circle of academics, but it is not the kind of writing or talk that students experience in their everyday lives. The writing and talk they're exposed to in advertisements, political speeches, talk shows, and so forth tends to be tendentious and shrill. Our students could imagine Darrow giving a speech in front of a group of leftist sympathizers and encouraging them to vote against a bill designed to introduce the teaching of creationism in our schools. Students would expect such an audience to cheer uproariously and to be energized to work for their cause. On the other hand, they had no model for Lewis's essay. Where would he deliver such a lecture? Who would be interested in hearing it? Why spend so much time on a thesis that seemed, in a sense, obvious?

We do not mean to suggest that the kind of arguing that Lewis was doing is not to be valued. In fact, we have devoted an entire chapter in our text to this reasoned argumentation–Chapter 9. However, we want to separate this kind of "positioning" from the arguing we do when we want to move readers to take some action. All too often, teachers have assigned an argument to students and then instructed them to write to a group of people who disagree with them. What happens? Students write such arguments, but in doing so they become shrill, even verge on name calling–if they don't actually do it–ignoring the counter arguments that could be offered against their point of view. And we, as teachers, pounce on these problems showing students that they have lost contact with their audience. We remonstrate with them: "You can't call someone who disagrees with you a *murderer* and expect that person to hear anything else you say." True enough. But our students weren't talking to these people. We told them to do so, but they knew better. They knew instinctively that in writing and talking that happens outside the classroom, you address a persuasive essay to people who already agree with you, or who are at least are receptive to your point of view. They do this naturally. If they are required to write the piece *to* the opposition, then they use this occasion to demolish the opposition so that a real audience of onlookers can be persuaded, much in the way that you would write an open letter to a lame-brained senator so that the local paper can publish your letter. You pretend to want to persuade the senator, but what you really want to do is to pummel him, or her, in front of those who can vote against him, or her, in the next election. In a sense, then, this is a chapter in which we give students the permission to take off the gloves. Within limits, that is. We insist that our students maintain an ethical stance, in that they should not argue for something that they cannot mount a logical argument for. We also insist that students avoid name calling and misrepresentation of all kinds. Working within these constraints, they are free to pull out all the stops of language use and move their readers to take the actions they want them to take.

# TEACHING TIPS

*Emotion.* Early in Chapter 10, we talk about the role that emotion plays in motivating actions. As you introduce students to this part of the chapter, focus their attention on emotion by asking such questions as:

- What is an emotion? (A dictionary definition will not likely be very helpful here.)

- Are there a finite number of emotions? If so, what are they? (We don't have an answer for this question. Your students will likely begin with such emotions as *love, hate, anger, fear, pity,* and *happiness.* You may want to prod by asking about other possible emotions such as *envy* or *lust.* Is *lust* an emotion? Does it have physiological causes and, if so, does that prevent it from being an emotion?)

- Are some emotions more effective than others in causing people to act? (For example, will *fear* motivate people to do things in ways that *happiness* will not?)

*Non-debatable Topics.* One of the key differences between position papers and persuasion papers is the inclusion, in persuasive writing, of non-debatable topics. Your students will probably need you to spend some time talking with them about persuasive essays on non-debatable topics. Most will have been led to believe that all persuasion involves debaters squaring off at each other, so you will need to draw their attention to how much persuasion in their daily lives involves non-debatable subjects. We spend a good bit of time in the text talking about the marketing of cigarettes. No one, or at least no one with any credibility, is going to argue that one should smoke cigarettes. Yet there is much need for persuasion aimed at getting people not to smoke. Two of the essays in our text, "Zero Tolerance for Abuse," and "No More" are aimed at persuading people that something needs to be done about spousal abuse. Who would argue in favor of such abuse?

As you work with your students on this issue, ask them to list some things that they know they should do, but don't. Then ask them to write a paragraph or two about each of these, reflecting upon what it might take to persuade them to take the action that they already agree they should take. Some examples of such topics would be:

Giving blood regularly;

Having one's bone marrow typed for a possible marrow donation;

Sending help to the Red Cross (or some similar agency) to aid victims of natural disasters such as hurricanes, tornados, earthquakes, and floods;

Spending more time with family.

***Ethical Arguing.*** In this chapter, we make the distinction between *effective* arguments and *ethical* arguments. Even though an argument can be effective without being ethical, we want our students to work toward constructing arguments that are both effective and ethical. In the text, we define ethical arguments as those that can be argued logically as well as emotionally. But there is actually more to effective arguing, as we indicate in Exercise 10.6 where we suggest that students think of the terms "ethical" and "unethical" as being on either end of a continuum. We can say that one essay is more (or less) ethical than another; however, to make a pronouncement as to whether a particular argument is ethical is difficult.

For example, let's take the issue of name calling. One of the key elements of ethical argumentation is fair treatment of one's opposition. Once a writer begins to call the opposition names, she begins to lose her ethical appeal. However, at the same time, the name calling may make her more effective in arousing the emotions of her chosen audience. Two examples of this tendency are presented in this chapter: Heaphy's "Dismemberment and Choice," and Paglia's "Rape and Modern Sex War." Even though the writers of these essays do resort to name calling at times, they are very effective in swaying the readers their writings are intended for. Are these arguments unethical? We don't think so. However, the writers would certainly have more ethical appeal if they left out the name calling.

Lest we seem to be contradicting ourselves, we need to explain a bit further. How exactly can we say that a writer could enhance his effectiveness and lose something in his ethical appeal. Keep in mind that the key benefit of ethical appeal is to cause those who disagree with you to consider (listen to) your point of view. If you assume an audience that already agrees with you (or at least leans toward your point of view), you do not have to worry so much about their listening to you. Your concern is to make sure that they will be affected by what you say. Thus, a loss in ethical appeal may, in fact, correlate with some gains in effectiveness--so long as you do not discredit yourself by seeming to be dishonest (to yourself or others) or self-serving.

As the teacher of this course, you'll have to decide exactly how to deal with this issue. Do you want to insist that your students maintain the same ethical standards in persuasion that they would aspire to in writing a position essay? While this can certainly be done, as Martin Luther King, Jr.'s essay illustrates, doing so requires much skill in language. As you work with your students toward developing this skill, you may find helpful an exercise that I have used on numerous occasions. Early in the persuasion assignment, I assign students a draft in which I encourage them to pull out all the stops, that is to violate every rule of ethical argument. They are free, for example to misrepresent their opposition's point of view and to do all manner of slandering and name calling. Once they believe that they are free to say exactly what they mean, my students really get into this assignment. Then, in class we discuss some of their drafts, talking about issues of ethical arguing and the difficult choices the writer must make between energizing an audience with powerful, but slanted language and maintaining an ethical stance by means of carefully-chosen and respectful language.

***Descriptive Language.*** One of the most important tools in persuasive writing is descriptive language. While students are writing the essay, you may want to spend some time working with the material in Chapters 15: Working with Words and 16: Shaping Sentences, particularly Strategies for Writing That Spotlights the Reader. Impress upon your students that in writing persuasively, it's not just what they say, but how they say it that counts. If a particularly astute student raises the issue of the difficulty of separating style and content, I am happy to explore this issue; otherwise, I tend to act as if this separation is possible when talking about the role of style in persuasion. We spend a good bit of time talking about the emotional weight of words. One activity I have found useful is to ask students to write a list of words that cause them to feel certain ways. For example, *home* may cause one to feel nostalgic. *Adventure* may cause one to feel excited. In the context of this type of discussion, I sometimes choose a particularly well-written passage and remove some of the key terms.

I then ask students to fill in those blanks, and we talk about what is missing when we choose words other than the ones used by the author.

Of course, effective sentences are also very important in persuasive writing. As you work with your students on adding power to their sentence structures, you may find an exercise helpful that I have used on numerous occasions. Reduce a powerful piece of writing to very basic sentences. For example, consider this sentence:

> Feeling slightly dejected and wondering if there was any real future in this company for him, John slowly walked to the parking lot, not noticing the three menacing youths approaching him.

You could rewrite it something like:

> John felt slightly dejected. John wondered about his future in this company. John walked slowly to the parking lot. John did not notice the three menacing youths. The three menacing youths were approaching him.

(This is not an attempt at linguistic "kernels," or even at the kind of sentence combining precision we work with in Chapter 16. What I'm doing here is just breaking a complicated sentence down into simpler sentences.)

Then give these simple sentences to your students and ask them to combine them into one sentence. You could have them do more than one rewrite, asking them to try one in which they reduced the number of sentences as much as possible and another in which they attempted to achieve a particular mood or effect by means of the sentence structures they selected. They you can discuss the sentences the students compose in light of the original. Students should begin to see how important sentence structure is to the overall effect they want their writing to have.

# RESPONSES TO EXERCISES

*Exercise 10.1*

Most readers would certainly agree with Jaime Sherrill (in "Zero Tolerance for Abuse") and Alysia Tucker (in "No More") that more should be done to protect women from violence, but they may not agree with all of the smaller arguments these writers use to build their cases. Find one or two issues in each essay with which reasonable people may disagree. Do the writers offer support in favor of their points of view on these matters? Explain. Do they acknowledge potential disagreements?

> *In "Zero Tolerance for Abuse," Jaime states that society as a whole must refuse to tolerate violence, else no meaningful changes can occur. I think that many people would disagree with this general statement, because many changes can occur whether the entire society comes to a consensus or not. Every day, people work hard to change the present situation, but in such a diverse culture, not every single person is going to wake up one day and say, "Ok, it's time to alleviate the domestic violence problem in this country. Today, I will not hit my spouse or child." She does try to support this generality, and she notes that many new shelters and homes have been developed to help these people who have been abused, but she insists that society as a whole must take action. I don't see it happening as a whole movement in every aspect of society.*

> *In another case, Jaime says of an abusive father: "Anyone can see that this man is an unfit father and does not deserve to be with a child he abused while it was still in the womb." Some people might argue that you can't make this statement categorically. Depending on the situation, visitation rights for a father could be called for.*

> In "No More," Alysia states that most abuse happens in communities or families where others know there is abuse occurring. I don't believe that this is always true. Often, people have no idea that there is abuse in a home unless that woman comes out and says that it is happening. Many abusers are very smart and are careful to leave bruises and marks only in places that can be covered by clothing. As for verbal abuse, many abusers are so controlling that they make the abused wonder whether a comment was an actual barb. Many abusers easily find ways to manipulate and hide the facts, and the abused often goes along with it, whether knowingly or unknowingly. Often, this does have to do with low self esteem or lack of education, but I don't think that is always the case either, and I would have to argue with some of the points the writer makes.
>
> I am not sure either of these authors is aware that someone might disagree with these underlying arguments because they are so involved in making their case as strong as it can be. I don't think it would occur to them to support these underlying assertions, and in fact they don't really need to, because their essays are very good as written.

## Exercise 10.2

We mentioned Michael Heaphy's essay is an example of a persuasive essay in which the writer seems to assume that his is the only point of view on a controversial issue. Compare Heaphy's tactics in this essay with those of two or three of the other writers whose essays are featured at the beginning of this chapter. Rank these essays in terms of the degree to which they show awareness of an opposing point of view.

> Heaphy's essay on abortion is much like the essay "Justice For Those Who Have Shown Us No Mercy" in that both arguments are very driven by personal beliefs and are not allowing the opposing sides to have any voice. Both essays are strictly focused on what the author believes. They do not at any point allow for dissent. Another essay that is very one-sided is Paglia's "Rape and Modern Sex War." Paglia does acknowledge that there is another side out there, but she belittles those on the other side by calling them names. The writer in this group who seems most aware of an opposing point of view is Martin Luther King, Jr. In "Letter From Birmingham Jail," he makes it clear that he knows those clergymen to whom he is writing disagree with him. He shows respect for their point of view and attempts to answer their possible objections one by one. My ranking, then, from, most one-sided to most open-minded, would be: Heaphy, Jaclyn, Paglia, and King.

## Exercise 10.3

Not presented

## Exercise 10.4

1. One of the mainstays of cigarette advertising for years has been "the Marlboro Man." Find two or three examples of advertisements (from magazines in your library) using this theme. Who is the Marlboro Man? What emotions are being appealed to by the use of this theme?

> The Marlboro Man is the epitome of the rugged, cool, strong man who can handle any adversity, no matter the source. He is a cowboy! He can do anything–ride a horse for a month straight, round up those dogies, smoke three packs a day and survive with flying colors. These are the emotions appealed to in these advertisements. If you smoke these cigarettes, you too can be like the lone strong cowboy out on the range, going back to the good old days of frontier land and wide open spaces. Horses, sunsets, mountains and good friends are other aspects of the advertisements

2. Another long-standing and controversial advertising campaign involved the mascot for Camel cigarettes, Joe Camel. Find two or three advertisements using this theme. What emotions do these advertisements appeal to? What readers would most likely be attracted to this advertisement?

*These advertisements depend primarily on the "cool" aspect of life. If you smoke these cigarettes, you can be cool, get all the girls, ride the Harley, wear a leather jacket and have a good time. These cigarettes also appeal to kids because the "mascot" is a camel drawn in bright colors, with a cool leather jacket and a smirk on his face. I think "cool" is the key; he is called "Joe Camel," which reminds us of Snoopy and "Joe COOL." I know that most of the people in my sphere who smoke these cigarettes, are obsessed with the notion of getting the girls (or the guys as the case may be), and they are always well dressed in the latest trend, and like to be thought of as cool.*

3. Find two or three other advertisements for cigarettes. Analyze the components of these advertisements: the pictures, the words, and the overall composition of the advertisement--that is, the way in which the words and pictures are combined. What emotions does the advertisement arouse in readers? What types of people are likely to be most affected by this type of appeal?

*Virginia Slims is another cigarette advertisement that plays on a certain group of people. The whole theme of these ads is "It's a woman thing." One picture has a couple of women laughing and smoking and drinking coffee, and a second has a picture of a woman with a journal, with her husband in the background, a little unfocused. Both ads have simple copy (the language of an ad); the one with the women says, "If our best friend seems to know everything about us, it's because she does," and the one with the woman and man (in the background) says, "Never come between a woman and her journal. Unless you want to be tomorrow's topic." Both of these are written in a flowing script, obviously a woman's, and tend to entice a woman reader to feel accepted, confided in, understood. These ads are obviously in tune with many women's needs and try to make them believe that if they smoke these cigarettes, those needs will be fulfilled.*

## *Exercise 10.5*

Examine three or four persuasive arguments you encounter in advertisements--in magazines, on radio or television, or in some other medium, such as the Internet. What does the advertisement seek to persuade you to do? What methods of persuasion are employed? How effective are they in persuading you to take the desired action? Given our discussion here, how ethical are these attempts at persuasion--that is, how effectively could the advertisers argue their cases logically?

*There used to be a commercial on TV that had a professional wrestler who would come flying through a wall with a handful of Slim Jim beef jerky. His whole purpose was to scream into the ear of whoever was in the room to "Snap Into a Slim Jim!" Obviously, the effect was made, because I remember the commercial vividly, although it did nothing to convince me to buy the product. I think the whole point was to get buyers to remember the product because of the humor. No reasons for buying this product. In fact, I don't think we are even asked to buy the product. However, there is nothing particularly unethical about this advertisement. A person could offer logical reasons as to why this is a good product to buy I would think.*

*Now there is a Little Caesar's commercial with two professional wrestlers who are about to beat each other up in the ring with chairs, until they notice the pizzas on a table in the middle of the ring. Instead, they sit on those chairs, which a second before were weapons, and eat pizza, trying to trade wrestling cards with each other. This commercial is designed to appeal to the younger audience that has become fascinated with the professional wrestling drama on television. Again, no reasons for buying this product are offered. One could argue that this is a good product (as far as pizza goes).*

*Billboards on the highway for hotels are very strategic. In large cities, you often find advertisements for distant hotels. These billboards try to entice you to keep driving that extra three or four hours and then stop for the night. They do this to encourage business, of course, but they are also trying to compete by calling attention to big city prices and hassles. If I want to stop in*

*Albuquerque for the night, I might have to pay $69 or $70 or more to stay, but if I keep driving to Santa Rosa, I can stay for $40. Here, there is a form of logical argumentation. It is logical to want to pay less for the same product.*

## Exercise 10.6

It should be clear from our discussion that there is no clear-cut line between ethical and unethical persuasion. It is probably best to think of a continuum, from most ethical to least ethical, on which individual pieces of writing may be placed. Examine three of the essays from this chapter (excepting Heaphy's, which we have discussed), or three essays selected by your instructor, and rank them from most ethical to least ethical. Use as your criteria for this ranking the fairness with which they represent the arguments of those who oppose them and the tendency to call their opposition names or to insult those who oppose them.

*Clearly the essay that treats its opposition most fairly is Martin Luther King Jr.'s "Letter From Birmingham Jail." King does not misrepresent those who oppose him, nor does he engage in name calling. The next, in terms of fairness, would be Jaclyn's "No Mercy for Those Who Have Shown Us No Mercy." Jaclyn does not misrepresent, and she does not name call. Her passion for the subject makes it seem as if she would be harder on those who disagree with her than King would be. The least fair is Paglia ("Rape and Modern Sex War"). Paglia calls her opposition names and, at times, seems to misrepresent her opposition, suggesting that they see every instance of spontaneous sex as "date rape."*

*I did not include Jaime's "Zero Tolerance" since there wouldn't be any opposition to her basic argument.*

## Exercise 10.7

Examine two or three of the sample essays at the beginning of this chapter to determine how they use description to persuade their readers. Select two or three especially effective passages and explain how they engage the readers' emotions

*Jaime begins her essay with the following description:*

*Most injuries were to the head and neck and, in addition to bruises, strangle marks, black eyes, and spilt lips, resulted in eye damage, fractured jaws, broken noses and permanent hearing loss. Assaults to the trunk of the body were almost as common and produced a broken collarbone, bruised and broken ribs, a fractured tail bone, internal hemorrhaging, and a lacerated liver.*

*This descriptive list of injuries captures the readers' attention and, at the same time, appalls readers who may not have given thought to the fact that this kind of abuse happens in our communities.*

*Another essay that uses description very effectively to get to readers' emotions is "Dismemberment and Choice." I thought I understood what abortion was all about, but I had never really thought of it in the terms Heaphy described to us. I wanted to cry, I wanted to jump up and do something, I wanted to hug my son. It affected my emotions very deeply, primarily because I have a son who I could never imagine living without. Days later, I don't have to reread the essay because I can remember the images I got of babies coming out still moving, heads crushed in and the rest. It is so vivid that it makes my stomach churn.*

## Exercise 10.8

Several of the essays at the beginning of this chapter make use of narratives. Choose two or three of those narratives and discuss the role they play in their respective essays. What is the writer attempting to persuade her or his readers of? What emotions do these narratives appeal to? How effective do you imagine they will be in helping the writers achieve their purposes?

> *The narratives that Jaclyn ("No Mercy For Those Who Have Shown Us No Mercy") chose to use in her essay on capital punishment are particularly effective, because they illustrate several situations that make the readers cringe at how easily murderers get off. We watch as Jaclyn's cousin is murdered and then shoved aside so that the criminal could drive her car. We are also involved in the story of the couple who adopted a kid who then killed them. We become incensed that people can act so callously, and we want to believe, as Jaclyn believes, that these people who have killed deserve to be killed. The use of narrative becomes an effective tool for Jaclyn.*

> *Similarly, King ("Letter From Birmingham Jail") uses narrative very effectively to engage his readers. When he tells the story of how his daughter watched the commercial for a theme park and then how he had to tell her "colored" children couldn't go there, any parent would have to feel sympathy for King, and thus be moved to taking the actions he calls for.*

## Exercise 10.9

We have discussed description, narrative, and prose style separately. In practice, the three often work together to make persuasive writing. Our discussion of the passage from Dr. King's essay, "Letter from Birmingham Jail," focused on his prose style. However, the passage also makes use of descriptive detail and narrative. Find examples of each and discuss how they add power to his argument.

> *Martin Luther King Jr.'s argument is that the move toward integration is too slow and limited to only a small part of society. He also argues that when it is difficult to relate to your kids why some things are not offered to them, or why people are mean to them because of the color of their skin, then things must change. King makes his points by means of his description of how mothers and fathers are lynched at will, sisters and brothers drowned on a whim. His use of narrative further affects us as we read how his children are reacting to segregation. When King talks about how hard it is to explain to his kids why things are the way they are, I think about how hard that would be to explain to my kids, or how hard that would have been for my parents to explain to me.*

> *In one particularly descriptive passage, King recounts how he read the signs that separate "whites" from "coloreds." The entire essay is very strong and should have an impact on a wide audience.*

## Exercise 10.10

You will note that two of our essays in this chapter–Jaime Sherrill's "Zero Tolerance for Abuse" and Alysia Tucker's "No More"–treat the same general topic. Although the topics are the same, the essays are very different. We would argue that both are very effective, however. Analyze these two essays in terms of the criteria for successful persuasion we have developed in this chapter. What makes each essay successful? Then choose a topic that is treated by one of the other writers in this chapter and sketch a plan for how an essay you might write on this topic would differ from the one that writer has written.

> *Both of the these writers (Jaime and Alysia) emphasize the pain and suffering that the victims of abuse suffer. We read in both essays several accounts of women who have been beaten and abused. This allows the writers to appeal to the emotions of their readers. They show how and why women are beaten, and then they show the endless cycles of this violence. They emphasize how women are often of low self esteem or have no other way of life, or how these women love the men in their lives and live with the abuse for one reason or another. Both writers rely on narrative and prose, as well as description to relate how women fit into this pattern.*

> *However, while Jaime relies almost exclusively on personal anecdotes and descriptions, Alysia*

*offers statistics and facts that document the way women are affected by abuse. Both try to remain highly ethical when delivering their argument; however, Jaime tends to slip on occasion. I think both essays are successful, and in many ways similar.*

*Plan for essay structure on Capital Punishment*

*If I were to write an essay in favor of capital punishment, I might focus (more than Jaclyn does) on statistics that show:*

*(1) How many murderers have gotten out of prison and then killed again.*

*(2) How crowded our prisons are.*

*(3) How likely each one of us is to be touched in some way by one of these killers.*

*I could also tell some stories that would be different from Jaclyn's. I might also spend more time on the refutation of the counter argument. I think it was difficult for Jaclyn to spend any time on this issue because she was personally and passionately involved in making sure her side of the argument received all of the focus. I believe it is difficult to write this essay in any other manner, but I would attempt to give the opposing side some time, and then as Paglia does in her essay, I would refute that other side logically, although I don't think I would be able to use much sarcasm on this issue.*

Ron

# Teaching Chapter 11 Problem/Solution Essays

## OVERVIEW

We solve problems everyday, most often as we weigh the benefits and/or liabilities of one thing over another. Sometimes these problems are small, having a short-term effect: should I play Nine Ball now and study later, or study now and play Nine Ball later? Should I buy another car, or repair the clunker I have one more time? At other times, the problems we face are anything but small, for they at least suggest a long-term, if not lifetime, effect: should I major in English or Computer Engineering? Should I stay in school, or should I drop out and begin my own business? As you begin this chapter, remind your students that they already have considerable experience with solving problems–if they're alive, then they're problem solvers.

Using writing to solve problems, whether small or large, whether their effect is short- or long-term, is one of the best uses we can make of writing. Given the number and potential seriousness of the problems we confront, we see Chapter 11 as being in many ways the most comprehensive of our writing occasions chapters. First, problem solving can be serious business, and writing through a problem offers the writer time to mull things over, to consider advantages and disadvantages to the various solutions that may present themselves for scrutiny. Second, thoroughly exploring a problem and offering a solution to it requires the writer to analyze, define, evaluate, research, and argue, activities your students were engaged in while writing essays in response to other of the occasions chapters. Remind your students of their experience with these skills, so that they come to see an essay requiring them to define and solve a problem as something of a culmination of their experience in your writing course.

## TEACHING TIPS

*Sources*. Problem solving is big business, with a sizable number of books and journals given to it. Two books that we've found helpful are these:

James Adams, *Conceptual Blockbusting: A Guide to Better Ideas*, 3rd ed. (Persesus Press, 1990).

Don Koeberg and Jim Bagnall, *The Universal Traveler: A Soft-Systems Guide to Creativity, Problem-Solving, & the Process of Reaching Goals* (Crisp Publications, 1991).

These two sources focus on innovative and creative ways of solving problems, including using imagery as well as language to think through a problem.

In addition, books that pose problems requiring the solver to use a range of activities (e.g., trial and error, logic, drawing) to find a solution may also be useful. We've found the following helpful:

Steve Odell. *Puzzles for Superbrains* (Prentice-Hall, 1979).

Jean-Claude Baillif, *Super-Puzzles* (Prentice-Hall, 1979).

***Students as Problem Solvers***. Ask your students to talk about how they've used writing to solve a problem, no matter how large or small, no matter how formal or informal the writing. What was the nature of the problem? What solution did they develop? How did writing help in reaching the solution?

***Research.*** If you haven't already assigned Chapter 12, Researching and Writing, do so at the outset of your work with Chapter 11. In fact, if you intend to use the problem/solution essay as the culminating assignment in your course, then you should assign parts of Chapters 11 and 12 much earlier in the semester than you might otherwise. In our discussion of Chapter 12 in this resource manual, we suggest a way of assigning a research paper that will require the student writer to begin early in the semester and to work on it continuously (see "Teaching Chapter 12" in this guide). Here's a brief adaptation of that process for a problem/solution essay:

**Week 3 or 4:** Assign a researched problem/solution essay, including a research notebook (see Chapter 12). Through in-class exercises and freewriting, have students identify a potential problem to be solved, with these written responses becoming the first entries in the research notebook.

**Week 5 or 6:** Have students write an essay proposal in which they identify the problem and tell why they're interested in it. Have them bring two copies of this proposal to class, one for you, the other to circulate in their writing group. Each group member reads the proposal and writes at least two questions she thinks the paper should answer. Before the next class period, respond to the proposals yourself: What looks promising? What potential pitfalls do you see? What resources or strategies can you suggest?

**Week 7:** Return the proposals and talk about research strategies, including how to use the internet.

**Week 8 or 9:** Have your students submit a more fully developed topic proposal, including a brief statement about some of the research methods they plan to use. Use this proposal to troubleshoot, to identify opportunities and potential problems with their intended strategies.

**Week 10 or 11:** Have your students submit a one- to two-page progress report about their research. How much exploration have they completed? What kind(s)? How many potential sources have they located? What problems are they having? (Note: At this point, you should be well into discussion of Chapter 11.)

**Week 12, 13, or 14:** Conduct peer reviews. Have your students bring one or two copies of their essay to class for review. Depending on the length of the essay you require, students may be able to complete only one thorough review in a given class meeting, something you'll have to gauge.

**End of semester:** Have your students submit their research notebooks to you, with the final copy of the formal essay appearing as the first document you'll turn to. Have them include every scrap of writing they did to complete the assignment: rough drafts, reviewer comments, prewriting, notes, and any photocopies they made of print sources or any printouts they made of internet materials.

***Workable Topics.*** Ground your discussion in problem solving: Given the context of Chapter 11, what is a problem? This question derives from the assertion that not all problems are created equal; that is, some are solvable within the constraints of an essay written for a first-year writing course, while others are not. See, for example, the list of problems in the "Subject" section of our discussion of the rhetorical triangle, where you'll see problems that vary in scope, from local to global. And in the list of problems in the "Choosing a Topic" section in the assignment guidelines, you'll see topics that vary in seriousness. Generally, student writers handle local problems better, because they're more familiar with their causes and effects. But this is not to suggest that you limit topics too narrowly. As the student essay at the end of this chapter shows, student writers can handle broader topics successfully.

How to identify a workable topic? Have your students look to the Interest Inventory for potential topics, and, of course, have them work through one or more of the invention exercises presented in Chapter 1. Exercise 11.5 is also aimed at helping students discover topics, with the Bug List (11.5.A) having been especially helpful for our students. (The Bug List was presented by James Adams in *Conceptual Blockbusting*, which we referenced above.) Have your students write a Bug List in class; then list several of their responses on the board. Talk about which of these seem solvable and unsolvable to you, and why.

***Problem Definition.*** Defining the problem to be solved is critical to the development of this essay. It's frequently true that we point to a problem's solution when we define the problem. As we work to sharpen a problem definition, we narrow the focus, and as we increasingly tighten that focus, we increase our chances of finding a workable solution. An example is in order.

As university faculty members, we've seen a number of bright students with high ACT or SAT scores and high grade point averages (GPAs) who don't do well in college in large part because they don't know how to study. They have trouble coping with the demands and expectations of their instructors, who expect students to complete reading and homework assignments on time and so to be ready for class each day. Many instructors with whom we've talked about this will say something like this: "These kids just don't study." While that may be true, such a problem definition doesn't capture what we think is the essence of the problem, that many students don't know how to study effectively. That statement–students do not know how to study effectively–is a more accurate, better defined problem statement than is "these kids just don't study."

Exploring this problem statement would lead us to think about why they don't know how to study, what caused their lack of knowledge. Were they not required to study for their high school classes? Were they so smart that they didn't have to study, or were the classes not challenging enough for them? Were their teachers' expectations too low? Were the students in regular instead of advanced classes, so that the teachers pitched their instruction to the majority of the students and required all students to complete the same assignments at the same level? Considering questions such as these would help us to explore the roots of this problem, and exploring these roots may well point to a solution or solutions.

The solutions we might offer to the problem of students having poor study skills would vary depending on whether we focus on the problem's causes or on its immediate effects. That is, if the problem we define is that the students' high school experiences with studying have been inadequate to prepare them for college, then any solutions we propose would probably involve curricular reform in the high schools (e.g., more honors courses, stronger college preparatory courses, or enriched instruction and requirements for these students). They could also involve finding ways to help teachers focus on students' study skills without substantially increasing the teachers' workloads. But if we focus on the immediate problem–students are now in college who do not know how to study--then our solution would focus on how best to help those students, perhaps through informal advice in first-year classes or through a formal course that would introduce them to the rigors of college.

***Writer's Ethos.*** Be sure to stress that the writer's *ethos* will be particularly important in this essay. The writer of a problem/solution paper wants his reader to take some sort of action to remedy the situation; generally, that calls for the reader to see the writer as knowledgeable and fair. The writer appeals to the reader through the quality and depth of the information he presents, through the reasoning he uses in developing his argument, and through keeping his emotions in check. This is not to say that he can't write about topics that are emotionally charged–look, for example, at Randy Fitzgerald's essay, "The War Against Witnesses," for an issue likely to cause anger in the reader. But look also at the lack of shrillness in Fitzgerald's essay. He treats a topic about which he's very much alarmed without letting his emotions spur him into making immoderate or emotional statements.

***Structure.*** Problem/solution essays readily lend themselves to blocking. Refer your students to the drawing of blocking in Chapter 2, and then lead them through the discussion of the structure of Julie Titone's "Balance of Power: Can Endangered Salmon and Hydroelectric Plants Share the Same Rivers?" (See "Planning Your Essay's Structure.") Suggest that your students use blocking as at least an initial structuring strategy, one that may also help them generate ideas for their writing.

# SAMPLE STUDENT PROCESS

Kristina Geray's essay on pet overpopulation illustrates that a writer may deal with a more global topic. In this case, Kristina writes about pet overpopulation, something we're probably all familiar with and would recognize as a problem–who would disagree that having too many stray dogs and cats wouldn't be problematic? But because of the universality of this issue, Kristina needed to find a way to bring something new to it. She elected to use her personal experience with strays and to localize the issue. The statistics she presents about the sheer number of unwanted pets in her home county in Southern New Mexico are indeed alarming. Bringing this issue from national to local proportions and then moving back to the national level is an effective strategy for helping potential readers, in this case, pet owners in her immediate vicinity, understand both the local and national scope of the problem. Note also Kristina's research strategies. She used the internet, but she also conducted two interviews with local people who could speak with authority on the issue.

# RESPONSES TO EXERCISES

*Exercise 11.1*

Speculate about the intended readers of Barbash's "Clean Up, or Pay Up," Titone's "Balance of Power," Fitzgerald's "The War Against Witnesses," and Andrew's "Change." How effectively did these writers seem to have considered their respective audiences? Identify any details that you think particularly effective for their readers. Why do think them to be effective?

> *Each of the writers of the essays in chapter 11 seems to have targeted broad audiences. Louis Barbash is targeting high school students intent on college/pro athletic careers, NCAA officials, university officials, college students in athletics, and any other person interested in college sports. With this large collection of people, it is hard to miss anybody. Barbash wants these people to read his article because although athletics are a huge part of the American mainstream, and particularly college athletics, change must occur within the scope of the current system. Some details that really work in his paper are examples of graduates like Tom Scates, of professional athletes who go to college in the off-season instead of during season, and of the current status of athletes in universities. Not only do they take classes that will boost their GPA so they can play, but once they graduate and take on jobs other than professional sports, or after professional sports, many of them are left with no viable career options.*
>
> *Titone's "Balance of Power" has a relatively broad audience also, although it is much more refined to a specific area of the country. Titone focuses on those fishermen in the Northwestern region who rely on the rivers for the salmon they catch. She also focuses on the people who get their power from any one of the power plants that use this water as a their source and on other local people in the area dependent on the rivers for their livelihoods. She wants people to recognize the economic and environmental loss that losing these fish will offer and to recognize that the devastating effects of the current system can be altered with minimal hassle. I think that Titone's discussion of how the power*

*and shipping systems were not altered too drastically when the drawdowns were lowered for the fish to swim upstream, is very effective to show her readers that the power and water companies can do a lot of good for the fish without losing too much money and business. Her explanation of the current cycle of fish spawning and egg hatching is another effective method to gain reader attention.*

*Fitzgerald targets a large audience of adults who could themselves become targets for murder simply by witnessing and reporting a crime. He wants America to take a look at how frightened and cowed American citizens have become. Each of the stories that he used to illustrate his points were attention getters, particularly because the people murdered were only trying to do their civic duty.*

*Andrew's essay on changing to the new dollar coin is intended for any person who uses American money, so he has a huge job of convincing the country of his point of view. His narrative, particularly the part with the sales clerk, was very effective, because it illustrated his points and helped to back up his claims and information.*

## Exercise 11.2

Look again at the essays presented at the first of this chapter. How engaged, knowledgeable, and fair does the writer of each seem to be? Point to specific places in each essay that demonstrate these three elements of the writer's ethos. What do those places show you about the writer?

*Barbash is very engaged in his topic, because he thinks it is unfair to the young kids of America who expect to grow up and play professional sports that the current system doesn't allow for that. Instead, only a certain percentage will ever play, and many of those will not have a valid education to back them up in any eventuality. His language shows his attempts to reveal his passion also, when he says things such as "the hypocrisy begins [ . . . ]" and "Not only are these athletes being cheated out of a promised education, but they and their universities are forced to erect elaborate, meretricious curricula [. . .]". He is knowledgeable and shows this through numerous examples, interviews and statistics. Barbash shows a lot about himself as he writes. He feels very strongly that it is an unfair system where is stands right now, and that things must change. Too many kids are growing up in a delusional atmosphere that will get many of them nowhere, when a solid education would be a better route. Despite his passion for the topic, he's fair. He doesn't resort to name calling, though he's clearly coming down on the NCAA and university officials for exploiting the student-athlete.*

*Titone is engaged with her topic throughout the paper; it's clear that she cares about the future of the salmon in the Northwest. Her language and her examples of devastation of fish and wildlife, as well as the problems society will face allow her reader to make valid decisions about what must be done to alleviate the problems that we face right now. Some places that really illustrate Titone's values are in the third paragraph when she says "Now the misery is flowing downstream [ . . .] the fish just aren't there anymore." And again when she says, "Without help, the Northwest's remaining wild salmon [ . . . ] will surely swim to extinction." Titone lets us know that she's knowledgeable by presenting statistics and information that show the research she's done. She shows fairness by constantly viewing the other side of the argument and trying to show that the two sides aren't so far apart. The essay itself tells a lot about the author, but her use of language gives a strong image of the concern Titone has for the situation in the Northwest. Without the salmon, things will change, and Titone does not believe things will get better, but worse.*

*Fitzgerald's engagement is deep, because he tells about people who are murdered for simply doing the right thing. We recognize how important this topic is to Fitzgerald, and we respect that immediately. He's knowledgeable, having taken the time to research a number of instances when witnesses have become murder victims. He's fair. He maintains a very serious tone that doesn't condone murder or any attempts at witness tampering, which is at it should be.*

> *Andrew is engaged with his topic. He's written a light essay on a topic many people don't know much about. But Andrew took the time to research it, and he knows his stuff, so he's knowledgeable. The narrative he uses shows his attempt to make the topic hit closer to home with his readers. Even though I don't like Jay (the narrative's protagonist), the examples work. Andrew is also fair. He lets us know that the dollar coin is on the way, that it makes sense, and that we might as well get ready for it. There's nothing shrill about his tone.*

## *Exercise 11.3*

For each of the essays presented at the first of this chapter, identify the problem statement. How effectively does the problem statement for a particular essay help shape that essay's structure? If you don't find a specific problem statement, write one. How might such a statement as the one you wrote have helped the writer during prewriting and drafting?

> *Barbash's problem statement is given in three consecutive sentences, which is ok because his essay is so extensive. At the end of the fourth paragraph and on into the fifth, Barbash says this: "Less than half the football and basketball scholarship athletes will graduate from college. And what education athletes do get is often so poor that it may be irrelevant whether they graduate or not. In addition to corrupting the university's basic academic mission, big-time sports have been a lightening rod for financial corruption." This extended statement helps shape the essay's structure, because Barbash then asks if there's a cure for these ills. The rest of the essay argues that there is.*

> *Titone: "The fish just aren't there anymore" (end of third paragraph). Titone then explores why the fish aren't as abundant as they once were, so she supports the problem statement. She also argues that there are cost-effective ways of saving the salmon population.*

> *Fitzgerald: "Alberta Burden's death is part of a growing trend of violence against witnesses that has often paralyzed American justice over the past decade" (in the fifth paragraph). Fitzgerald then shows other examples to reinforce this problem statement, so it's an effective statement.*

> *Andrew: At the end of his paper (in the fifteenth paragraph), Andrew says, "Ultimately, the problem to be solved is how to gain public acceptance of the new coin." This seems to come late in the paper, but it works, because he's spent time showing how inconvenient paper money is and how convenient a dollar coin will be. So he's spent time preparing his readers to accept the new coin.*

> *Problem statements seem to shape the structure in that they give the author an idea of where to go with his paper when he gets stuck. These statements act often like an outline or thesis, although not as strongly. I think these would help the author stay focused and remember the real issue at hand.*

## *Exercise 11.4*

In "Balance of Power," Julie Titone discusses the potential economic impact of saving the salmon, contrasting that with the feared negative impact on local and regional economies. Why did she spend several paragraphs talking about economic matters? How effectively does her speculation about economic benefits counter the fears of an economic downturn if her plan were to be adopted?

> *Titone spends so many paragraphs discussing the economic impact of saving the salmon on the regional economies because she realizes that that is what her audience is going to be primarily concerned with. People are driven by money, and when it is going to cost them more to have power in order to "save a few fish," then many will balk at the idea. Therefore, Titone sets up her argument so that her readers see their concerns expressed, but then answers those concerns, providing a*

*counterpoint that says "not to worry." I think her speculation counters the fears well, because she shows how certain changes would actually benefit the community in even greater numbers in the long run. She presents an effective argument by giving so much time to the opposing argument and then finishing off the argument with strong points and views.*

## Exercise 11.5

Respond to at least one of these:

A. Write a Bug List. Spending at least 15 minutes, make a list of anything that irritates you, no matter how big or small or serious or frivolous it may seem. Pick two of your entries and freewrite about each for ten minutes.

B. What problems do you confront or know about that you'd like to see solved? Make a list of all such problems that come to mind, spending at least 15 minutes developing this list. Pick two of your entries and freewrite about each for ten minutes.

C. Find places in your interest inventory where you've identified potential topics that are less than ideal. While any section could hold potential topics for this essay, take a look at the "Education," "Jobs," and "Attitudes and Issues" sections. Pick two and freewrite about each for ten minutes.

> *Bug List*
>
> *Customers who whistle at me to get my attention*
> *No tip*
> *Changing the cat litter*
> *Rude people*
> *Ingratitude*
> *Babysitter calling in at last minute on the day you really need her*
> *Aidan sitting on my lap driving his cars on the keyboard when I have work to do*
> *Procrastination*
> *Computer problems I can't figure out how to fix*
> *Ice cream trucks*
> *The music ice cream trucks play*
> *Other people's kids (especially when they teach mine to hit)*
> *Parents who don't parent*
> *Verbal abuse*
> *Blown light bulbs*
> *Going over budget at the grocery store*
> *Photographs with light streaks*
> *Cockroaches!*
> *CDs that skip*
> *Missing the first few minutes of an action movie and then being lost the rest of the two hours.*
>
> *Freewrite–computer problems*
>
> > *Every time I run into a computer problem, I have to try and screw around to figure it out, but I don't always have the time and energy to fix it. Most of the time I call my brother or my sister and try to work it out together, but that doesn't always work either, because my sister has an old computer and my brother doesn't have all of the stuff that I have either. My oldest brother would know, he seems to know everything, but he is a surgeon, and has a family, and therefore, I try not to bother him. If he isn't at work, I am convinced he is exhausted or spending time with his kids. I'd rather try to fix my problems otherwise. Still, it is difficult when I am trying to get a project*

*done and I run into problems. I need to just sit down and read the manuals, but who wants to do that? It's funny, since I have used the computer so much for school, a lot of people look to me to find the answers, and in fact, I was put in charge of my mother-in-law's computer when it wouldn't save to disk, but I had no clue as to what was wrong. I almost resented it because I was so busy at the time, and no one ever used the computer to try to figure it out on their own. I think that the key to learning how to work and play with a computer, and fix the problems is to spend time on the machine. There is no point having one if it is not going to be used. These things cost way too much money to let them sit dormant.*

*Freewrite–Aidan:*

*Every time the ice cream truck goes by my house, it plays this horrible music that wavers on the air like it was dying or something. All of the kids in the neighborhood start to shriek and whistle, which keeps the music playing even longer. Aidan, whenever he hears the music, stops what he is doing and runs for the door, but he doesn't even realize that the truck means ice cream. Unless of course, someone like a grandmother has made use of the damn service. I hope not, because I have asked time and again for them to avoid teaching him what it means. I don't need him running out in the street after the truck when he is so young, but not at any age, either. What really bugs me about the truck and the music, is that whenever I am trying to get him to take his nap in the afternoon, the truck invariably drives by, and he is wide awake, no matter how asleep he was the second before, and sitting bolt upright. That drives me crazy, because then it is another twenty minutes before he gets over being mad at me, and settles down to sleep. I think part of his fascination is that he loves trucks and cars, and he knows that the music means truck. He even says truck, which cracks me up, because he just loves them.*

*I think I could get a problem/solution paper out of the first freewrite by focusing on why learning to use a computer and fix whatever problems may come up is so time-consuming. Even the "help" sessions that are built into most programs nowadays are of little real use, so why can't the companies that provide these machines and the software they run make it easier to use them?*

Bill

# Teaching Chapter 12
# Researching and Writing

## OVERVIEW

The emphasis in this chapter is first on searching and discovering, then on focusing writing for a purpose and an audience. The passage from Ken Macrorie's *Searching Writing* (in the introduction to Part 3) makes an important statement about research–too many students engage a research paper because they have to, not because they see it as an opportunity for learning. They treat it as drudgery, put in as little time as they can, string together a bunch of quotes that seem hardly related, and call that a research paper. Our focus in this chapter, on using research to support one of the aims we discussed in Part 2, runs counter to this "look it up and tell about it" model. As your students work through an assignment requiring research, keep reminding them that their task is not simply to string together an arbitrary number of quotes from an arbitrary number of sources but to use others' thinking to help them strengthen their own.

Plagiarism is, of course, a knotty problem. At times, students who plagiarize truly do intend to cheat. They may take information directly from various print sources or from the internet and simply pass it off as their own. Or they may lift a file from a roommate's or friend's diskette, with or without the knowledge of that person. Or they may repair to a set of papers on file in somebody's dorm room. Or they may find a paper on any number of research paper mills on the internet.

But there are other instances of plagiarism when the student's intent to cheat isn't so clear. Many times, students engage in unintentional plagiarism because they simply don't understand what needs documentation. You have the opportunity to work with these students to help them learn that not only direct quotes but summarized and paraphrased information needs documenting. But instead of taking an enforcement approach to plagiarism, help your students understand why we document information:

- to give credit where it's due
- to provide another researcher with our sources to use as springboard to her own investigation of a topic
- to learn the conventions of an academic discipline
- to establish credibility as someone serious about looking deeply into a topic

Be sure to lay out your expectations about documentation of sources clearly for your students. The ideal place to do this is in a syllabus that you hand out early in the semester, but in the absence of a policy statement on your syllabus, include any discussion of and sanctions for plagiarism on your assignment sheet. Many schools have policy statements concerning plagiarism and other forms of academic dishonesty in a student handbook. Refer your students to any such statements that your school has.

## TEACHING TIPS

***Process Approach to Research.*** One of the ways to guard against plagiarism is to require that your students engage in a process approach to research. When you make your research assignment, require a research notebook. And make this assignment early in the semester; students are fully capable of working on a research paper while they're at work on another essay. Assuming that you're in the fall term, you could follow this a sample schedule:

**Third or fourth week of September:** Make the initial assignment of the research paper. Have students identify a potential topic, which may require that they do some freewriting or clustering or working with their Interest Inventory and Questions for Analysis. Give them about two weeks to find and explore a topic, however tentative that exploration might be. Then have them write a topic proposal in which they identify the topic and tell why they're interested in it. Tell them that they'll be required to submit every scrap of writing that they do in a folder along with their final draft, so stress that they must save all the writing that they do. Tell them that their paper will be incomplete and will not fulfill the assignment if they do not submit notes, prewriting, and rough drafts along with their final draft.

**First or second week of October:** On a specified day, have them bring two copies of their proposal to class, one for you, the other to circulate in their writing group. Each member of the group reads the proposal and writes at least two questions she thinks the paper should answer. While there's no formal audience analysis at this point, the writer must take into account a potential readership and what they might need the paper to present. Before the next class period, spend a little time in responding to the proposals yourself, talking about what looks promising, suggesting potential pitfalls to avoid, and so on. Hand these back to your students as soon as you can. Continue the research assignment by having students decide which of the aims they'll use to help direct their writing and so their research: to inform, to evaluate, to argue, or to solve a problem. You may also assign specific parts of Chapter 12 for short, in-class discussions, e.g., how to conduct an interview, how to use the internet, how to take notes, or how to decide the reliability of a source.

**Third or fourth week of October:** Have your students submit a more fully developed topic proposal. Have them include a brief statement about some of the research methods they plan to use. For example, if they intend to administer a questionnaire, have them tell you why they think it's important for them to do so, and have them submit a draft of it at this time. Use this proposal to troubleshoot, to identify opportunities and potential problems with their intended strategies.

**First or second week of November:** Have your students submit a one- to two-page progress report about their research. How much exploration have they done? How many potential sources have they located? What problems are they having? At this point, you should require those students who wish to change topics to do so now; otherwise, they'll have to live with what they've already proposed. Why this rigidity? First, students who try to develop an entire new research topic at this point in the semester will likely have trouble writing the kind of comprehensive, well-prepared paper that the assignment calls for. Second, and on an entirely different note, we've found that students who change topics at the last minute and submit nothing but a final copy of a paper tend to be up to something nefarious. Requiring students to keep a running file of all their writing, which should be available to you to check at any point, is one of the best ways of ensuring that they haven't gotten a paper from someone or somewhere else.

**End of November, first of December:** It's peer review time. Have your students bring one or two copies of their essay to class for review. Depending on the length of the essay you require, students may be able to complete only one thorough review in a given class meeting; this is something you'll have to gauge.

**End of semester:** Students submit their papers to you, each one in a folder covering rough drafts, reviewer comments, prewriting, notes, and any photocopies they made of print sources or any printouts they made of internet materials.

*Taking Notes.* Lead your students through note taking for print and internet sources. Make clear your expectations for documentation, whether on cards, in a research notebook, or on a diskette. Talk about the kinds of information that they may want to use and how to capture that information and save it for later use.

*Summarizing and Paraphrasing.* Stress that summarized or paraphrased material must be documented. To help your students learn to summarize and paraphrase, remind them of the work they did with summaries and paraphrases while working through Chapter 4. Then lead them through more exercises here. To work with summaries, have them tell what happened in the last movie they saw, and encourage them to provide as much detail as possible. Then have them write this report in no more than five sentences. They should see that summarizing requires them to put the essence of a source in their own words. To work with paraphrases, provide your students with quotations or with aphorisms and then have them translate these into their own words. For example, "a stitch in time saves nine" could become "take care of business early" or "fish and visitors stink after three days" could become "don't overstay your welcome." Students should see that to paraphrase they must recast a passage in their own words and use about the same number of words as the original.

*Dealing with Sources.* Focus on the need for the writer to evaluate his sources, to decide their reliability, accuracy, and currency. And a word here about currency. At times, students take currency to mean the most recent information, the last word. And certainly, currency may involve this. But currency isn't limited only to sources published in the last two or three years. Instead, currency may also speak to relevancy, to the relation of a source to the writer's topic and purpose. Stress to your students that not all sources are equally reliable, especially those on the internet. Exercises 12.3-12.8 ask students to locate and evaluate or assess the reliability of sources. You should work through these exercises carefully.

*Documenting Information.* Talk about the need to document sources beyond questions of plagiarism. Stress that much of what we know, whether in medicine, science, or literature, developed from a researcher's use of someone else's work on the same or a similar subject. When a researcher presents her work for scrutiny, and when her writing and sources provide a springboard or point of departure for another researcher, then she has contributed to the development of knowledge and to the discussion that research sparks in a given profession or discipline.

We've included sample bibliographical or works cited entries for a number of different sources, with these entries following first MLA and then APA guidelines. We do not in any way pretend that these samples are inclusive, nor should they obviate the student's use of a style manual in his chosen discipline. Instead, we intend them only as samples that can give your students an idea about what various documentation entries should look like.

## SAMPLE STUDENT ESSAYS

In this chapter, we present two student-written research projects. The first, by Clarita Brown, began as an investigation into the American Indian Movement (AIM). Clarita, a Native American student at New Mexico State University, wanted to know more about AIM, so she took AIM as her topic for a paper in a writing class that studied countercultures as a semester-long theme, with the class' reading and writing given to that theme. Clarita began her paper as a report designed to convey information about AIM, but note the tentative nature of the conclusion. Her exploration of AIM reinforced her pride in being Native American and suggests the possibility of activism on her part in the future. The paper is informative, its significance immediately personal.

The second essay, by Gardiner Rhoderick, offers a solution to a problem. Whether the solution can actually overcome a popularly-held view of graffiti as vandalism instead of art remains to be seen, but Gardiner takes on a topic of great interest to him. Gardiner's task, at least in part, is to overcome his reader's association of graffiti with gangs. Note that he uses definition as part of his essay, working to define what is graffiti and what isn't. Ultimately, he works to define graffiti as art.

# RESPONSES TO EXERCISES

## Exercise 12.1

What has been the best experience you've had with writing a research paper to date? The worst? Write a paragraph about each of these experiences. Next, develop a list of traits for a good research paper or research process; then compare your list with those of your classmates to help you clarify and expand your list. Finally, use this expanded list as a checklist to help guide your research writing.

> *The best experience I've had with research occurred when I was trying to write a paper for my communications class. Everything fell together--I got the right books, articles and information to support my ideas, and the quotes I chose worked well, and the writing process was simple. I got a good grade on the paper to top it off. The worst experiences have pretty much been all the rest. I have a good time searching for books and articles, but the actual reading is not my strong point for some reason. I seem to accumulate the texts, and then they accumulate dust. My last research paper left something to be desired, because I put all of the research off until the last minute, and then the writing really was hard to do. I couldn't fit any ideas together to match the sources, and so at that point finding quotations was a near impossibility. Revision was basically nonexistent, because I had procrastinated so long.*

> *Some traits of a good research paper and process:*

> *Define an idea, or at least a broad topic, something that will keep me interested for an extended period of time.*

> *See what types of information and sources are available on that topic.*

> *Talk with professors and others knowledgeable in the field for pointers.*

> *Clarify as a process of elimination–both of topics and sources (the more sources, the harder it is to do the research and the actual writing--have several, but not too many)*

> *Check out the books and READ THEM!!*

> *Write a discovery draft*

> *Write a rough draft with enough time to put it away for at least a week*

> *Revise*

> *Talk to professors again*

> *Revise*

> *Clarify again*

> *Revise*

*Exercise 12.2*

1. If you have even a tentative topic for a research project, then use it as you complete this exercise. If you don't have a topic, then pick one of the following subjects and freewrite on it for fifteen minutes, asking questions you think to be appropriate. Then read back over your freewriting and look for a focal point, something that might serve as the basis of a research project. If you find such a point, why do you think it might work into a research paper?

>   nuclear energy
>   alternatives to nuclear energy
>   good (bad) study habits
>   history of a favorite sport or hobby
>   buying something (for example, the best camera or microcomputer)
>   benefits of some kind of exercise (for example, running, swimming, biking)
>   job opportunities for college students
>   a social issue (for example, drunk driving)
>   a national, regional, or local environmental issue
>   a campus issue

> *Exercise is so good for a person. I have been so sluggish lately, and I always blame it on the kid, because he doesn't always let me sleep as long as I'd like, but I think it is because I haven't made the time for exercise like I used to. I used to do something every day, and these days, I don't do much of anything except chase after him, and I am so tired all the time. My diet is terrible also. I don't eat well at all. I make sure Aidan does, but I just snack , and then I grab a burger on my way to work or something. I need to take pointers from my kid and start doing something. It would be so much easier if I could run with him in the back pack carrier. If his little head wasn't so heavy, I think I would try it. The strollers I have aren't designed for running, so that is out of the question, and when we go to the park, I have my hands full keeping him out of the pond, much less doing anything else. Maybe I can take a ball and teach him to play soccer, but his attention span is still so questionable. He could play for awhile, or he could just take off in the other direction. Hard to say.*

> *Exercise could be used as a point, particularly the history of exercise, or the different types of exercise, but I really am not all that interested in that. I would rather talk about Aidan and exercise, but how can I research that?*

2. Later in this chapter, you will be assigned to write a research paper. If you are free to choose your own topic, begin thinking now about potential topics, or ask your instructor for suggested or assigned topics. Pick one, and freewrite on it for fifteen minutes, asking appropriate questions. Then read back over your freewriting, and look for a focal point, something that might serve as the basis of a research project. If you do not find one, freewrite for another fifteen minutes; then look again. Continue working with this process until you find at least a tentative topic. Why do you think it might work into a research paper?

> *There have been so many autobiographies and biographies written by men, and so few by women. Why? Where have all the voices of the women gone? We have some by women such as Margery Kempe and Harriet Martineau, but most of the autobiographies are so new and by women of the eighties and nineties of this century–Nancy Mairs, Audre Lorde, I can't think of any others form the last twenty years. Zora Neale Hurston, the woman who wrote <u>A Room of One's Own</u>, I'll be shot by my English professors if I don't remember her name, it'll come to me. Anyway, why aren't there more? Thomas Carlyle, John Stuart Mills, etc.etc.etc. We need more women! (Virginia Woolf–that's the one I couldn't think of!) It is such a comment on society that this is the way it is, and the fact that I can't even think of other women who have written autobiographies is pathetic! What about men?*

*Who can I think of who has written an autobiography? Well, Lee Iacocca, Michael Jordan, Michael Jackson–I think. Just about any one of the male superstars of athletics, Tupac Shakur, what about women? There are a few biographies, but I can't think of any autobiographies. Even the biography show on A&E is mostly about men. Lifetime is good about writing and showing women's biographies, but that is a channel for women. It isn't as if men generally flip to Lifetime to see who the biography is on, unless it is some beautiful goddess like what's her name oh, Shania Twain, or ??? Judd–Ashley Judd? Anyway, I always see biographies about men on ESPN (go figure) and A&E and the History channel and blah blah blah blah blah.*

*Ok, I like this better. I can research women and autobiography. I think it is important, particularly since so little research has been done on the issue itself. HMM. Probably hard though, since so little has been done. Wonder where to go from here with this one. Maybe I will focus on the beginnings of feminine autobiography. Margery Kempe. Harriet Martineau, Margaret Oliphant. I can relate them and discuss the significance of their work. Hey, what about suffrage--oh, what is her name? Not the nurse, the other, the one they ostracized after she spent years building the women's suffrage movement in this country. Elizabeth Cady Stanton!! There we go, I'm getting something now.*

## *Exercise 12.3*

Using the topic you wrote about in an exercise earlier in this chapter, or using the tentative topic you have chosen for your research paper, locate in your library the following sources relating to your topic, listing the title, author, and call number for each.

1. two books
2. two essays in popular journals (for example, *Time, Newsweek, Better Homes and Gardens, Popular Mechanics, National Geographic),* if applicable
3. two essays in scholarly or professional journals, if applicable
4. two items from a newspaper, including one from *The New York Times*
5. two items from a CD-ROM database
6. two government documents, if applicable.

How reliable is each potential source? On what do you base your decision?

*books:*

*McCracken, Ellen. Decoding Women's Magazines from Mademoiselle to MS. PN4879 M38*

*Forever Feminine: Women's Magazines and the Cult of Femininity. PN5124 W6 F47.*

*essays in popular journals:*

*Starr, Mark. "Keeping Her Own Score." Newsweek.*

*Hamilton, Kendall. "Oprah's Going Glossy." Newsweek.*

*essays in professional journals:*

*Stephenson, Theresa, Stover, William J., and Villamor, Mike. "Sell Me Some Prestige! The Portrayal of Women in Business-Related Ads." Journal of Popular Culture.*

*Burkhalter, Nancy. "Women's Magazines and the Suffrage Movement: Did they Help Or Hinder the Cause?" Journal of American Culture.*

*newspapers:*

*McCully, Martha. "Fat Debates, Sustacal Shakes: It's Life in the Diet Blender." <u>New York Times</u>.*

*Bianco, Robert. "The World According to TV: Everybody is White, Sex-crazed, Beautiful And Young–Just Like In Reality. Right?" <u>USA Today</u>.*

*Each of these sources should be reliable. The two books are in the NMSU library, and their screening procedures are professional. <u>Newsweek</u>, the <u>New York Times</u>, and <u>USA Today</u> are national publications and aren't known for riding any particular hobbyhorses, so they should be reliable sources. And the two journals are professional journals. Are they refereed? I don't know. If they are, then that's a good sign of reliability; if not, then I'd have to see them as less reliable.*

## *Exercise 12.4*

1. Find a topic of current interest in your local or campus community. What is at issue? Identify the thoughts of people on both sides. What is the position of each person? Find at least two published sources for each side, and summarize each. Identify at least one person for each side and prepare a list of questions you would ask in an interview. If possible, interview each, and summarize the results of your interviews. How reliable do you think the sources you have uncovered are? Why?

*One of the local bars has a popular "gay night" on Saturdays, and some people object to the fact that local newspapers advertise for this event. Some people think it is great that this community has a place for homosexuals to go locally to dance, have a few drinks and let loose. Others think that there is no room for this sort of activity, and they are very much against any support for this group. One opinion published in the feedback column of a local newspaper was very indignant. The person could not believe that the paper would support such an activity to the point of actually advertising that gay people could go to this bar and socialize. Responses to this opinion were varied; however, the primary response was that there was nothing wrong with advertising for the night, and there was nothing wrong with gay people wanting to socialize. What was wrong was the closed minded attitude of the first opinion.*

*Another local publication, a magazine, stated that gays and lesbians deserve the opportunity to congregate and mix in any atmosphere as well as heterosexuals. The only difference between the two had to do with who chose someone of the same sex as a partner, but the couple's basic needs and wants were the same.*

2. In a news magazine such *as Newsweek, Time,* and *U.S. News and World Reports,* find an interview of a national business, political, or religious leader. Summarize the interview's content and its key points. How would you characterize the questions asked? The answers? Are there any questions you would have asked that were not asked? If so, what are they? Why would you ask them?

Not presented

3. Interview one of your classmates. Prepare a list of questions, asking things you would like to know about him. After the interview, write a brief character sketch or biography of your classmate and have him check your writing for accuracy.

Not presented

## *Exercise 12.5*

Identify a current issue about which you are concerned. Devise a questionnaire of at least five questions to ascertain opinions of others on this issue. Administer the questionnaire to at least twenty people, drawing on as broad a range of respondents as possible. Summarize and analyze the results. How did your questions help to shape the results?

> I am very concerned with the issue of kids shooting kids in the schools these days, because they aren't just shooting other kids alone, but teachers and parents as well. I am a parent and a teacher, and don't want to see this happening anywhere and to anyone.
>
> Some questions I asked on my questionnaire were:
>
> How did the recent shooting at Columbine High School in Colorado affect you?
>
> The several incidents that have occurred over the last few years have been as the result of some sort of "difference" that the kids felt. Do you feel this is an understandable excuse?
>
> What kind of punishment do you think kids who perform these actions should receive?
>
> Do you think local kids take weapons to school?
>
> What can be done about this violence in the schools?
>
> Who should be taking responsibility for the actions these kids take?
>
> Every person I submitted the questionnaire to admitted concern and to some extent, disgust with the current situation of violence in the schools. The fact that kids are getting away with such violence is appalling and scary–whether one has kids in the public schools or not. Violence is blamed on so many things, and my results show the reasons are varied. Parents, music, the modern acceptance of violence as a way of dealing with stress, the lack of concern for displays of violence, lack of teacher involvement–the list goes on. Most people in this area don't quite believe that we are touched by this in our schools, but others recognize that unfortunately the potential is there. Every day at least one kid sticks a weapon in his bag because he feels he needs protection. The questions I asked helped to clarify the thoughts I had, because my beliefs were reaffirmed on many fronts by what others believe also.

## *Exercise 12.6*

Spend an hour at a busy spot on campus. Describe the scene before you. Who is there? For what purpose? Are there any dominant patterns that emerge, things that are striking about what you see? If so, identify them. What makes them dominant or striking? What conclusions do you draw from your observation?

> I am in the student union downstairs in the main food court. There are many people here, it looks like several kids from around the state, because I know there are many conferences going on at this time. Most of these kids look very young, but attractive, as most kids are these days. It looks like just about everyone here is here to eat, although I notice several people drinking coffee or sodas, and they are content to just sit and talk while others eat lunch. It's early too--maybe 10:30 or so, I guess everyone else is like me--up early and hungry before long. Most of the people in here are dressed in shorts and tee shirts, because it is hot outside. I think it is part of the getup for the conference, also--a cliquish sort of dress. You recognize who is here for which conference by the clothes they wear. I recognize some of the t-shirts because before I had my son I used to be a counselor for one group. None of them recognize me though because it has been two years, and every year the groups change. I think this group is so dominant in my vision because I recognize why they are here, and so my attention is absorbed by them. They are high school juniors, about to be seniors, here to get college credit for a two week program. Pretty fun too. The kids get to do all kinds of stuff and take some classes with some of the most brilliant professors here. Dan Pinti used to do this conference--he taught Dante, and he is pretty high rate stuff. The patterns I see are all the same. Separate groups. Usually

*3-4 girls, or 3-4 guys. It must be early in the program, because by next week, those groups will be mingled, and although the numbers will stay the same, they will be split about in half for the most part, and the other groups will probably be 1 (girl or guy), 3 or 4. It is funny how adolescent relationships develop. So easy and stress free–compared to when it is time to get serious.*

## Exercise 12.7

1. Using the net search engine of your choice, base an internet search on any of the following key terms:

> skateboards
> grammar
> your favorite celebrity (e.g., singer or actor)
> the President
> skiing (either snow or water)
> your home state
> your home town

Click on two of the first ten hits listed and read them. How reliable do these sites seem? On what do you base this assessment? Next, record the number of total hits your search generated and then bibliographical information about the two sites you visited, including the relevancy rating.

> *I used Alta Vista to search Adam Sandler, because he is a funny guy. Two of the first ten hits revealed biographical sites about him, and I think one of them was developed by an older person, because it was much more sophisticated, but the one written by the kid was pretty amazing too. (Kids have so much talent these days) I thought that the first one was more reliable because it seemed to be more professional, with much more detail and professional links. The second used quite a bit of juvenile language and tone, although he did a good job of putting together a professional biography. The search generated 13,967 sites, probably because I only typed in the name Adam Sandler. I did not notice any relevancy rating, and in fact when I asked the technician about it, she didn't know anything about it either. I rechecked the info I had against the text, and I think it is because I was using a different type of search engine. There wasn't much bibliographical information about the authors of the websites, except the younger guy was using what looked to be a parent's address, and his name was written under the header ("this website was created by Seth Newton.")*

2. Select either of the two sites you visited. Click on the "More Like This" line. Scan the first 10 sites that come up and decide how similar to or different from your selected site they are.

> *The closest I could find to a "more about this" icon was "About.com," and of these, eight out of the ten on the screen were about movies he is in. This related to the websites I visited, because they had mentioned these, but the links were about each individual movie, or about a group of movies. They included reviews and info about each film. The other two were about humor and "college drinking games."*

## Exercise 12.8

1. Using the topic you wrote about in an exercise earlier in this chapter, or using the tentative topic you have chosen for your research paper, use a search engine to locate the following sources relating to your topic, listing the title, author, and website address for each.

> a. two books
> b. two essays in popular journals (for example, *Time, Newsweek, Better Homes and Gardens, Popular Mechanics, National Geographic*), if applicable

c. two essays in scholarly or professional journals, if applicable
d. two items from a newspaper, including one from *The New York Times*
e. an item you locate through the Library of Congress
f. a government document, if applicable

How reliable is each potential source? On what do you base your decision?

*I found some books at sales sites like Amazon.com.*

*Atwood, Lynne. <u>Creating the New Soviet Woman: Women's Magazines as Engineers of Female Identity, 1922-53</u> (Studies in Russian And East European History and Society.) www.amazon.com*

*Zuckerman, Mary Ellen. <u>A History of Popular Women's Magazines in the United States</u> (1995). http://info.greenwood.com/books*

*Sarasohn, Lisa. "The Goddess Ungirdled: How I Learned to Love My Belly And Found The Sacred Feminine Within." www.voiceofwomen.com*

*www.sojourner.org was the only journal site I could come up with that I could use, although the information in it would not have been directly in touch with my topic of women in magazines, but more as a way of supporting how women have changed and what sorts of things are available to them professionally these days.*

2. Visit the Allyn and Bacon Compsite, and locate information on the following:

a. documenting information
b. evaluating information from the internet
c. problems with grammar and mechanics
d. links to two search engines

*www.abacon.com/compsite/research/citation.html*

*This comprehensive site is designed for both teachers and students alike and is very easy to use because everything is set up in categories which are briefly summarized and clearly titled.*

*a. documenting information included things such as MLA style and citation guides for online documentation, which is vital today when everyone uses the computer to do a lot of research.*

*b. Evaluating information on the internet is another extremely important section, because there is so much available on the web, that one has to be very discerning to know what is good information and what can be overlooked. This also gives a lot of information about the different types of online services.*

*c. Problems with grammar and mechanics offers all types of aids and activities for improvement in writing the English language.*

*d. Links to two search engines. I am not sure I found the right links, but I found two links to the A&B home page and the English Home page. These both offer information about Allyn and Bacon and they also have several textbooks reviewed and up for sale. In the "more like this" section, there were several other publishers' websites.*

Bill

# Teaching Chapter 13
# Essay Examinations

## OVERVIEW

If your school is like ours, first-year writing is required of all students. Why should that be the case? Various composition theorists have made careers of exploring this question, but to many of the faculty in other disciplines, the answer is not complicated. They want their students to take first-year writing courses so that they will become better writers. And, for these teachers, one of the primary indicators of how well students write is the essay examination.

Although there are many differences between the writing students do in composition classes and the writing they do in essay examination situations, there are some important similarities. In Chapter 13, we hope to help students see the connections between the types of writing they do in the other sections of this text and the writing they will do on essay examinations in various courses they take in the college.

## TEACHING TIPS

In introducing your students to the material in this chapter, it would be very helpful to consult with a colleague who teaches courses in which essay exams are required. As I drafted this chapter, I wrote to several of my colleagues asking them to give me examples of questions that they used in their exams; I also asked for samples of excellent answers to these questions and received many excellent examples. If you have such colleagues in other disciplines, I would suggest that you do the same. You might then use some of the questions you receive for in-class discussion about taking essay examinations.

Some of my colleagues at UNC-Charlotte have taken this one step further. The Director of Rhetoric and Writing (in English) has arranged for an entire class in our first-year writing sequence to be composed of students who are enrolled in a particular history course. This history professor is working with the teacher of the writing course to fashion writing assignments and essay examinations that help students develop the writing skills being taught in the writing course. Such collaboration gives students a sense that the various parts of their education are connected to one another.

*Summary.* The ability to summarize is a crucial skill for college students. Your students will assume they know how to summarize, and it will be tempting to gloss over summary on the way to bigger and better things. However, I would suggest that you have your students read a relatively lengthy essay and then write summaries of varying lengths. For example, ask them to write 500- and 250-word summaries of an essay that is about 5 pages long. After you have taken up these summaries, reproduce several of each length and discuss them in class. No doubt you will find significant differences in the information in these summaries; thus, you will be able to lead students into discussion of the ways in which they read these essays. You may also pair this activity with the discussion of summary in Chapter 4.

*Synthesis.* In working with synthesis, we have found it useful to focus students on the concept of voice. In summary, the writer tells us what one other person (or source) says. In synthesis, the writer brings together the thoughts (or voices) of more than one person, or source. Of course, since the writer is the one doing the introducing, her voice is also present. In reading a passage, then, the reader must be able to tell at all points what voices are speaking.

Another way to get at this is to ask "who says" of every assertion made in a passage. To illustrate, I'll analyze the first two sentences of a passage presented on page 507 in the text.

> "Noam Chomsky and Jean Piaget do agree about several aspects of how humans develop their language abilities;"

*Explanation:* The speaker (or writer, in this case) says that Chomsky and Piaget agree on several aspects of human development. [What we are doing here seems painfully obvious, but the concept we are developing is very important. The point is that whenever a person says (or writes) something, we assume that she (the speaker/writer) is the one taking responsibility for her words. Of course, there are exceptions to this rule, as would be the case if a speaker introduces another possible speaker–for example, "John says it is raining." In such a situation as this, the speaker is no longer responsible for the assertion that it is raining–John is.]

Here is the second part of the first sentence in this passage:

> "however, there is a crucial difference in their theories about language development."

*Explanation:* The speaker says that there is a crucial difference between Chomsky's and Piaget's theories.

And here is the second sentence from the passage:

> "Both Chomsky and Piaget recognize the importance of nature in the development of speech."

*Explanation:* Here matters become more complex. In using the word "recognize," the speaker is doing two things at once. He tells us that both Chomsky and Piaget would say that nature plays an important role in the development of speech. So, it is Chomsky and Piaget who are making the assertions, right? Well, not exactly. The speaker tells us that Chomsky and Piaget make these assertions, but at the same time the speaker implies that they are right in their opinions. If she did not want to put herself on the spot in this way, she would not have used the word "recognize." For example, she could have said: "Both Chomsky and Piaget claim that nature is important in the development of speech."

You may find it helpful to ask your students to ask "who says" of several sentences in this passage (or other passages of your choosing). In doing so, it will be helpful to focus on the various ways in which writers introduce assertions, that is, how they signal readers who is to take responsibility for which assertions. While you are doing so, you may want to refer to some of the sentence strategies offered in Chapter 15, particularly the Strategies for Writing that Spotlights the Subject.

***Evaluation.*** Much of what we said in Chapter 7 will apply to the evaluating your students will do in essay examinations. In particular, you may want to refresh students on what is meant by "criterion-based evaluation" and be sure they can deduce criteria from the same evaluation questions in the text.

***Interpretation***–you may find it helpful to begin your discussion of interpretation with the question of just what it means to interpret. This discussion should move your students toward two key points. The first is that no meaning is possible without interpretation. You could make this point by taking your students back to the old question of whether a tree makes noise if it falls when no one is listening. The point here is that meaning, as we know it, is a human phenomenon; anything that happens becomes meaningful only when it is processed through the intelligence of a human being. Another name for this processing is interpreting.

The second point alluded to above is the crucial role that context plays in interpretation. Meaning happens when we perceive wholeness or completion. In fact, we don't think we know what something means until we can place it into a holistic frame. Whether we're talking about discovering the "meaning" of a puzzle piece by finding where it goes in the puzzle, or finding the "meaning" of a comment made by a Presidential contender by placing it in the context of the outcome of that election, we arrive at meaning by seeing how parts fit into wholes. As you work with interpretation here, you may find it helpful to ask your students to examine the interpretive reading strategies we offer in Chapter 4 and the role that interpretation plays in the ways that we find meaning in literature as explained in Chapter 8.

*Planning Your Essay's Structure.* As you lead your students through this section, have students review our treatment of modes in Chapter 6 and Chapter 7. What we said about organizing essays in those chapters applies to organization of essay exams. Early on in planning an essay, your students should think about the shape (or form) of that essay. The simplest tool they can use for this task is an expository mode.

You will notice that we have not given students a list of key terms that will allow them to decide what the teacher is calling for in an essay examination. While we could have called students' attention to such words as: *describe, explain, discuss,* and *compare*, we have not done so because it is very difficult to give formulas for interpreting what a teacher means in a question. For example, examine the following test directions:

Discuss the ways in which Chomsky and Piaget approach language development.

Compare Chomsky and Piaget's theories of language development.

The second question is more straightforward in calling for a comparison, but an astute reader will see that the first question also asks for a comparison. The best thing you can do for your students is to give them practice in reading exam questions and analyzing what types of essays the questions seem to call for. By type, I mean what expository mode will provide the structure for the essay. And, once you have determined mode, you will want to ask students whether the question calls for a summary, a synthesis, an evaluation, an interpretation, a practical application, or some combination of these.

While there is no one-to-one correlation between key words and modes, there are some words that occur more frequently in certain modes. Below we list some of these words:

| **MODE** | **KEY WORDS** |
| --- | --- |
| *Process* | process, stages, how |
| *Comparison/Contrast* | compare/contrast, differ/different |
| | good/better/best, agree/disagree |
| *Cause/Effect* | cause/effect, impact, change |
| *Analysis* | analyze, part, whole |
| *Classification* | classify, type, category |
| *Definition* | define, what |

*Planning Sample Essays.* Below I will attempt to provide answers for the questions asked in Exercises 13.21-13.31. Please do not view these as the correct answers. Since we are looking at essay questions (rather than the essays written to those questions), there is no such thing as a correct answer. You and your students will likely come up with some possibilities that I have not included here.

13.21. Pick two of the following decades and discuss what course of action you would have taken to deal with the problems faced by the colonies of North Carolina during that time. Be sure to identify the problems and use facts. (1) 1675 to 1685 (2) 1720 to 1729 ( 3) 1760 to 1769.

> *This question asks students to write a practical application. They have studied the various problems faced by the colonies and the types of solutions that were attempted, and they have also looked at the effects of those attempted solutions, so that they might be in a good position to second-guess some of those solutions.*

> *The most logical means of structuring this essay would be comparison/contrast–though causality would also play a large role in the answer. The student might compare the problems (and potential solutions) of one time period with the problems (and potential solutions) of the second. Or the student might lump the two time periods together and compare the solutions that he would recommend for the problems with the solutions that were actually attempted. In addition to comparison, the student could make use of some definition in explaining what the key problems were and of cause/effect in discussing what results various solutions to these problems might be expected to produce.*

13.22. Contrast the theatrical conventions, the themes, and the audiences of Restoration Theatre of the late 17th century in England with those of the bourgeois tragedy of 18th century England.

> *This essay would likely be summary of materials in a text, in class lectures, or both. As the question makes clear, the essay will be structured by comparison/contrast–of the theatre in one period with that in another. A second structuring device is provided by the question, in that the theatre is broken down (analysis) into its parts: theatrical conventions, themes, and audiences. [For an actual essay written on this topic, see David Wilson's essay in Chapter 13.]*

13.23. Leadership has always been a problem for North Carolina. During the period from 1660 to 1775, what individuals provided the best leadership for the colony? Be sure to discuss their accomplishments and the obstacles they had to overcome.

> *This question could be viewed as calling for interpretation or evaluation. I would lean toward calling it evaluation because of the two criteria for leadership offered in the last sentence: accomplishments and obstacles. An essay in response to this question could be structured in any number of ways, but two very likely structures would be narration, in which the story of this period is told with each leader's role constituting a major part of that story, or comparison/contrast, with each of these leaders being compared and contrasted to the others. However, if there are several different leaders to be discussed, they could be classified into groups, such as total failures, moderate successes, and excellent leaders. Or the writer could use cause and effect, showing what things various leaders did (and what the effects of these actions were). Finally, the writer could structure an essay by defining leadership and using that definition as a means of critiquing the actions of various leaders.*

13.24. Explain the relationship between the terms "enthymeme," "responsive chord," "nonverbal communication" and "electronic media." In what way(s) are these important concepts for political communication?

> *This question probably calls for summary of information given in a textbook, class notes, or both. If the student is being asked to come up with an answer to the last question (i.e. what ways these are important concepts) on his/her own, the question involves interpretation.*

> *It is hard to know what the best structuring device for the question is without knowing what the relationship between these terms is. In fact, the word "relationship" is probably code for a teacher's desire to have students summarize connections made in class lectures and discussions. For*

*example, the teacher may have explained how ads or messages delivered via electronic media rely on enthymemes, responsive chords, and non-verbal communication to get messages across to audiences. In such a case the relationship is that these are all tools of electronic media; thus a primary structuring device would be cause/effect--the student would show how these terms can be used to explain how electronic media can achieve the effect that it achieves.*

13.25 What are ad bites? Why have they become popular? Why is Jamieson concerned about them?

*This question likely calls for summary of information given in the text, in class, or both. If the student is being asked to come up with answers not given to him (as to why ad bites are so popular and/or why Jamieson is so concerned about them), then the question would necessitate interpretation.*

*The essay would seem to suggest a structure provided by definition; that is, the writer is asked to define ad bites. However, there is a suggestion that causality plays a part, in that the student is asked why ad bites have become so popular (what has caused this?) and why Jamieson is concerned (what causes his concern?).*

13.26 You've decided to run for mayor of Las Cruces, New Mexico, and you've decided to make an appeal based on myth. Which American myth would you use for your appeal? Using the general characteristics of myths, explain your choice.

*This question calls for an application. The student who has studied political myths and the way they are used in political campaigns must now apply this knowledge to a specific hypothetical situation. The question requires the writer to interpret, in that she must assess Las Cruces' political climate and determine which myth would be best suited for such a climate.*

*The writer could use almost any structuring device. An obvious one would be cause and effect, in that she could introduce a myth and explain why this myth would cause the desired result, i.e., voters to vote for her. She could just as well use analysis, breaking the political climate in Las Cruces into its various parts in order to explain them.*

13.27 In many works we have studied, characters experience an initiation or illumination–a recognition about themselves, a situation, another person. Choose three pieces of literature we have studied and show how they depict this experience. What is the nature of the illumination? Does the recognition promise change for the better or is it presented as coming too late, or as ironic?

*This essay could be calling for summary of information given in a text, in class or both; however, it seems most likely that the student is being asked to figure this out for herself–and thus to interpret. The question provides something of a road map for this interpretation by offering clarifying questions.*

*An obvious means of structuring the essay would be comparison–each of the characters could be compared as to the nature of their illumination and the promised effects of that recognition. As this last phrase makes clear, the writer will be using elements of definition (nature of illumination) and cause/effect (effects of recognition).*

13.28 How has the media's notion of newsworthiness given rise to the pseudo-event? Be very specific in your explanation. Use an example to illustrate your answer.

*This question could be calling for interpretation or summary, depending on whether the specific information asked for has been provided.*

*The essay could be structured by means of definition, since two key definitions called for are* "newsworthiness" and "pseudo-event." However, its structure could also be provided by cause/effect, in that the media's evolving definition of "newsworthiness" has brought about (caused) the "pseudo-event." [For an actual essay written on this topic, see page 522.]

14.29 Using as your examples a play by Shaw, a story by Lawrence or Mansfield, and a story from Joyce's *Dubliners*, discuss how these writers represent various social classes. What conflicts and problems do these characters experience? Who has power? Who is powerless and why?

> *It is likely that this question calls for interpretation. The student may have been given various types of information on power and power relationships as they apply to these writers, but here the student is being asked to pull these various pieces together for himself. Of course, if he simply gives back examples that he has been given in class, he is summarizing, and that will likely be all right since the question does not prohibit such.*

> *There are various ways to structure this response. One obvious tool would be analysis, since the question suggests various "parts" of the puzzle being put together. The writer may begin by discussing each work as a whole and then breaking it down into its components in order to show the power relationships. Another mode of organizing would be comparison/contrast; the writer could compare the ways these power relationships are depicted by the three writers. [For an actual essay written on this topic, see pages 521 and 522.]*

14.30 North Carolina's early history has been dictated by a series of conflicts and their resolutions. Culpepper's Rebellion, the North Carolina Regulator Movement, and the American Revolution were major conflicts impacting North Carolina's development. Compare the causes of these events, show their similarities and differences, and indicate how the results aided or hindered North Carolina's unity.

> *This question likely calls for interpretation, in that the teacher wants students to come up with their own appraisal of how various factors have affected North Carolina's unity.*

> *Clearly the question calls for the student to use comparison/contrast and cause/effect as structuring devices. As stated, the question suggests an overriding comparison structure, but the student could subordinate comparison to cause/effect if he chose to.*

14.31. Hugh Lefler writes, "Geographical factors contributed to economic differences in agriculture, industry, and trade in the various regions. Economic differences created social distinctions. Racial and social factors were involved in religious rivalries. And all of these factors contributed to political controversies." From your knowledge of North Carolina history, comment on the validity of the above quotation. Be sure to describe the political controversies and relate the statement to them. Which factor had the greatest impact on political controversies? Why? Be sure to use facts.

> *This question calls for evaluation. The student is to decide which of the factors mentioned had the greatest impact on political controversies. At the same time, the question calls for the student to evaluate the quotation given.*

> *The two primary modes of organizing would seem to be comparison/contrast (of these various factors) or cause/effect (the various effects these factors had on political matters.)*

## Additional Essays

Below I give my answers for the questions asked about each of the sample essays.

### David Wilson (Page 520)

1. What type of essay is it? Summary, Synthesis, Evaluative, Interpretative, or Application? Does this essay

call for more than one of these processes?

> *This essay is primarily summary. David rehearses the various characteristics of these plays as they were presented in his text and in discussions by his instructor.*

2. What mode provides its primary structure? Does it use other modes? What are they?

> *David's primary structuring mode is comparison/contrast: the drama of the Restoration theatre is contrasted with the 18th century bourgeois tragedies. In addition to comparison/contrast, David also uses analysis, looking at the various components of the theatre in these two different periods. David also uses cause/effect in showing how the tastes and desires of the two different audiences caused these differences in the theatre of the two periods.*

3. Using criteria outlined in this chapter, how effective do you find each essay?

> *We will leave this for you and your students to determine.*

## Ann Long   (Page 521)

1. What type of essay is it? Summary, Synthesis, Evaluative, Interpretative, or Application? Does this essay call for more than one of these processes?

> *Ann's essay is interpretive. That is, she tells us what happened in works by these three authors and interprets what these various events mean.*

2. What mode provides its primary structure? Does it use other modes? What are they?

> *The primary structuring device for this essay is comparison/contrast. Ann compares the works of these three writers, in that all of them deal with social conflicts, and contrasts the ways they treat this theme. Within each of her subsections, Ann's primary structuring device is narrative--she tells us the relevant parts of the plots of these works.*

3. Using criteria outlined in this chapter, how effective do you find each essay?

> *We will leave this for you and your students to determine.*

## Cherish Smith   (Page 522)

1. What type of essay is it? Summary, Synthesis, Evaluative, Interpretative, or Application? Does this essay call for more than one of these processes?

> *This essay summarizes material provided by a text or a class lecture.*

2. What mode provides its primary structure? Does it use other modes? What are they?

> *The primary organization structure here is definition. Cherish defines "newsworthy" in terms of the criteria that those in charge of the media bring to this term and then uses this definition to explain how a pseudo-event has been created to meet these criteria.*

3. Using criteria outlined in this chapter, how effective do you find each essay?

> *We will leave this for you and your students to determine.*

## Kim Coan   (Page 522)

1. What type of essay is it? Summary, Synthesis, Evaluative, Interpretative, or Application? Does this essay call for more than one of these processes?

> *Kim makes it clear at the beginning of her essay that she is summarizing material in her textbook.*

2. What mode provides its primary structure? Does it use other modes? What are they?

> *Kim's primary structuring device is cause/effect. She shows why these ads were not effective in achieving their purposes (to cause people to reject the Clinton Health plan); she also shows why they were effective in causing attention to be brought to the health care issue.*

3. Using criteria outlined in this chapter, how effective do you find each essay?

> *We will leave this for you and your students to determine.*

Ron

# Teaching Chapter 14
# Portfolios

## OVERVIEW

There isn't much to be added to what we've said in the text about the theory of portfolios. We see them as consistent with a process approach to the teaching of writing. Once you've decided that you will use a portfolio in your teaching, there are several questions that should be answered at the outset:

1. Will the portfolio consist of all the students' writing in your course, or will it be a selection from that work? If it is a selection, on what basis will writings be selected?

2. Will students be allowed (or required) to submit writing from other courses? If so, what guidelines will you give them for what writing they may submit and how to contextualize that writing? Will you accept that writing with another teacher's marks on it, or do you want the student to retype a clean draft of the paper?

3. Will you require (as Bill and I do) a reflective piece with the portfolio? Obviously, Bill and I think this is an important ingredient in our portfolio project, but reflective writing is not easy. And if it is not done well, it can be a waste of time, yours and the student's.

## TEACHING TIP

**Self-Assessment: Preparing for the Reflective Essay.** If your students are going to do well on this assignment, they will need practice. One way for them to get this practice is to do short reflective pieces on several writing assignments as they turn them in. That is, you can ask students at the end of a position paper, for example, to submit a self-assessment of that piece of writing in which the writer discusses both the strengths and weaknesses of the paper at hand. In preparing students for a self-assessment, have them write in response to such questions as the following:

### TOPIC

1. Why did you choose this topic?

2. How do you feel about the topic at this point? Are you tired of it, more interested than ever, or what?

3. Are there any specific problems with this topic. Does it work for a Position Paper? Have you found a way to treat it that allows for reasonable people to disagree with you?

### PROCESS

4. How long did you spend writing this paper from beginning to end? Do you feel you allowed yourself enough time, or would you allow more time if you had it to do over?

5. How many drafts did you do of the paper? Is this more (or less, or about the same) as (than) you normally do?

6. Where have you made global revisions (as opposed to local revisions)? (See Chapter 3 for discussion of local and global revision.)

## PEER REVIEW

7. Who has read your paper? In what context–in class or out? What kind(s) of feedback have they given you? A response letter, verbal comments in group critiques? Other?

8. List two or three peer suggestions that helped you in writing this paper? Point to specific changes you made in your paper in response to these suggestions.

9. List two or three peer suggestions that you did not use. Explain why.

## PAPER AS A WHOLE

10. What do you like best about this paper?

11. If you had time for more work on this paper, what would you give attention to?

12. What did you learn about your subject and/or your writing process in writing this paper?

When the student submits her essay, have her cover it with the self-assessment, so that you see the assessment first. And you should comment in your written remarks to the writer about the effectiveness or accuracy of the self-assessment. But you should not use the assessment as a guide to evaluation. Keep in mind that one of the reasons for requiring the assessment is to help the student learn to read her own writing better. If she's read well and noted that the overall organization of the third paragraph needs tightening, then praise her for reading closely and remind her that in her next paper you'll be looking particularly at paragraph structure.

Ron

# Teaching Style
# Chapter 15   Working with Words
# Chapter 16   Shaping Sentences

## OVERVIEW

As we move to these two chapters having to do with style, we are reminded of the constant tension between theory and practice. When people talk about putting writing theory into practice, they often offer strange (and sometimes humorous)advice? I'm reminded of Monroe C. Beardsley's famous quip in "Style and Good Style," about one particular piece of stylistic advice. Beardsley is remarking on an example from *The Elements of Style* (Strunk and White, MacMillan, 1959) in which writers are encouraged to improve their style by replacing empty *be* verbs with action verbs–so that the first sentence below is revised to produce the second sentence:

*There were a great number of dead leaves lying on the ground*

revised to become

*Dead leaves covered the ground.*

Beardsley's remark: "Stylistic advice is a rather odd sort of thing if it consists in telling students to pile up the leaves in their descriptions" (*Contemporary Essays on Style*, ed. Glen Love and Michael Payne, Scott, Foresman and Company, 1969)

We all know that it is impossible to separate matters of style and content. But when it comes to writing textbooks, we are forced into divisions that seem to suggest otherwise. The medium leaves us adding on style chapters at the end of a book, as if style is something we can come back to as an afterthought. Yet, all teachers of writing know that stylistic matters are at the heart of good writing. We know that we have succeeded any time we see a student struggling to get the right word or to arrange her words so that they say exactly what she means.

We trust that you will use the stylistic chapters here *while* students are in the midst of composing, not as add on chapters. That is why we have created divisions within these chapters that correspond to the major divisions in our occasional chapters.

## TEACHING TIPS

### Words and the Rhetorical Triangle

The Rhetorical Triangle provides us with the device by which we connect the occasional chapters with our chapters on words and sentences. That is, we divide both Chapter 15 and Chapter 16 into sections having to do with writing that spotlights the subject, writing that spotlights the writer, and writing that spotlights the reader. We do not mean to imply that a one-to-one correlation exists between the types of words or sentences in a piece of writing and the aim of that writing. We do mean to point out the fact that there are certain concerns, such as originality of metaphors, that tend to be more prominent in one type of writing than another. Thus, you may want to focus your students' attention on metaphor when they are working on personal writing (Chapter 5); similarly, students may benefit from instruction in professional language and jargon in informative writing (Chapter 6); and they may profit from delving into connotative language when working on persuasive writing (Chapter 10).

## Strategies for Writing that Spotlights the Subject

***Learned and Popular Words.*** As you work with learned and popular words, you will want to be sure that students see the connection between the types of words they will use and the audience for whom they are writing. A good way to do that is to ask students to look at different types of journals. Ask students to select a passage from a very technical journal, such as *The Journal of the American Medical Association* or *Linguistic Inquiry* or some such. Then have them look at a passage from a popular journal, such as *Newsweek* or *Reader's Digest*. Have them analyze learned and popular words in a brief passage in two very different journals.

***Technical Writing and Jargon.*** As you make students aware of the issue of technical writing and jargon, you will want to keep them focused on audience. A good teaching strategy is to have students look at how the same topic is handled in different sources. Ask students to choose a topic, for example, the role of carbohydrates in a healthy diet, and look at how that topic is treated in:

- a diet book
- a popular journal, such as a health magazine
- a journal intended for health professionals

***Sentence Structure.*** Of course the same journal articles may be mined as sources for sentence structures. You can ask students to examine the various types of sentences strategies discussed in Strategies that Spotlight the Subject, and then look for these strategies in these journal passages.

## Strategies for Writing that Spotlights the Writer

***Metaphoric Language.*** In this section of the text, we discuss the differences between original and non-original metaphors. In working with these concepts, I have found the following exercise (introduced to me by my one of my colleagues at Clemson University, John Idol) very useful. First, ask your students to write a brief essay on a topic of their choosing in which they use as many clichés as they can possibly come up with. Then ask your students to remove the clichés and to find fresh language to take their place. Students should gain appreciation for the fact that it is virtually impossible to use language free of metaphor. Then they should develop appreciation for the difference between established metaphors (that don't even sound like metaphors any longer) and fresh metaphors.

## Strategies for Writing that Spotlights the Readers

***Denotation and Connotation.*** Depending on the verbal sophistication of your students, you may want to move them further into the issue of just what denotative and connotative meanings are. Ask your students to study the history of certain words (ones you have looked up and know) in the *Oxford English Dictionary* to see how various changes in the words' denotative meaning may reflect the progression by which connotative meanings have moved into denotative meanings.

# RESPONSES TO EXERCISES: CHAPTER 15

## Exercise 15.1

Take a minute and list the various words that you use to refer to a person or object that is important to you. Choose something that you can associate at least three different terms with. Examine the situations in which you use these various terms? How do they differ? Are there any differences in the meanings you associate with these terms?

> *I refer to my cat as <u>Ripken</u> when I'm talking to him in general or feeding him. I call him <u>That Cat</u> when he sheds on the baby's bed or gets under my feet. I call him <u>Kitties</u> when I'm loving him or talking to the baby about him.*
>
> *These terms differ in that one is his name, one is an expression of aggravation or exasperation, and the third is of love, affection. These differences come about depending on my mood or whom I'm talking to. Aidan usually hears the cat referred to as <u>Kitties</u>, because that is what he calls him (well, actually it is <u>tickles</u>, but he tries). <u>That Cat</u> is what he is called quite often, because he is a three-year-old Tom cat who thinks he runs the roost. And he was named <u>Ripken</u> because my favorite baseball player is Cal Ripken, Jr.*

## Exercise 15.2

Reread paragraph 7 of Amy Tan's "Mother Tongue." On the whole, Tan's language in this passage is very direct and clear. However, in a few places she uses rather formal words. For example, she says that her mother's expressive language "belies" how much her mother understands. Also, she tells us that her mother "converses" with her stockbroker daily. What less formal words or phrases might Tan have used in place of these two words? What would she gain or lose in making such a *change?*

> *Some less formal terms for "belies" and "converses" could be "misrepresents" and "talks." If these terms are used, however, then a different image of her mother is presented from the one we actually get. The original words reveal Tan's respect for her mother, for someone who "converses" on a topic has more authority and knows more about it than a person who just "talks" about a subject.*

## Exercise 15.3

Despite the very real purpose that learned words can serve, there is no shortage of humor aimed at those who tend to use overly pretentious language. You may have heard of the alleged cheer of a university where the students were reputed to be enamored of their intelligence:

Repel the blackguards,
Repel the blackguards,
Force them to relinquish the spheroid.

Another easy target are the malapropisms of a character like Archie Bunker (from the television situation comedy *All in the Family*). Archie often talked about being "exacerbated" with the younger generation, when he actually meant "exasperated."

Then is the story of a political candidate who won his election by spreading the word that his opponent had a daughter who was a thespian in New York City and a son who had been seen openly matriculating at a local university.

There is another story of a plumber who once wrote to a research bureau saying that he had used hydrochloric acid to clean out sewer pipes and inquiring if there was any possible harm in doing so. According to the story, he received the following reply: "The efficacy of hydrochloric acid is indisputable, but the corrosive residue is incompatible with metallic permanence." The plumber took this as a compliment and thanked the person who sent the letter. After two or three interchanges with higher and higher officials, a top scientist wrote the plumber saying:

> "Don't use hydrochloric acid. It eats hell out of the pipes."

The plumber finally understood.

Find a couple of examples of your own (from your readings or from your own or other people's experience) of humor that arises from pretentious language. In each case, what causes the humor? Who, or what, is being made fun of? What, if any, point about language does the story (or situation) make? (By the way, if you don't know the word *malapropism*, you will want to look it up. Have you or your friends used any malapropisms recently?)

> *One time I tried to say I had to go home and feed my "brood," but I said it like "broad" and my mother-in-law thought I had a hooker in the back room!*

> *The humor came from me trying to be cute, but totally mispronouncing the word, and then ending up looking like an idiot! The point this situation makes about language is that even though someone knows what they are talking about, it can often be misconstrued in a simple fashion, and very quickly.*

> *Another time my brother asked, "What is the significance of that paper on the floor?" He was actually wondering why the paper was on the floor, but I launched into a description of what the paper said and who wrote it, etc. The humor came about because his use of <u>significance</u>. He was consciously trying to be smart and made me misunderstand what he wanted to know. I was not expecting a sophisticated word for such a simple question. This situation can show us that when someone uses words unexpectedly, they can often cause misunderstanding. <u>Significance</u> can be used there, but it usually isn't used in such a casual situation.*

## Exercise 15.4

Choose three pairs of words from the list of examples of popular and learned words, and explain the difference in meanings you assign to the words in each pair.. Look up the words in an unabridged dictionary, preferably the *Oxford English Dictionary*, to see whether the historical meanings of the words correspond with the differences you see in the words' meanings. Then, use each of the words in a context that helps illustrate the differences you intuit. Are there any pairs in the list that seem completely interchangeable to you? Why or why not?

*leave*: to go to the store, not be in the house for a little while; to give something to someone

*depart*: to go on a trip of an extended sort, a cruise or vacation (i.e. departure time on a flight or ship)

> <u>*leave*</u>: *"to go out of or away from," "to abandon or forsake"*

> <u>*depart*</u>: *"to go away, set forth or leave"*

> <u>*leave*</u>: *I am leaving to get some apples, but I will be back in a few minutes.*

> <u>*depart*</u>: *We depart on Saturday at 10:05, and won't be back for two weeks.*

*choose*: to pick one over the other

*select*: to pick the best ones with much more care in the decision

> <u>*choose*</u>: *"to desire, select from a number of possible alternatives"*

> *select*: "to choose from among several; singled out in preference, of special value or quality"
>
> *choose*: I choose to take that bucket of peaches and this box of pears.
>
> *select*: I will select only the best peaches for my pie, because I want this to be a special desert.

*evil*: not good, wrong, horrible, scary

*sinister*: creepy, evil looking,

> *evil*: "morally bad or wrong, wicked, malevolent, sinful"
>
> *sinister*: "suggesting an evil force or motive, ominous"
>
> *evil*: The character in the movie was evil and killed many of the other characters for fun.
>
> *sinister*: The character looked sinister because of the way he walked and was dressed.
>
> *None of these pairs seems absolutely interchangeable.*

## Exercise 15.5

We would expect popular words to predominate in your writing. This is as it should be, because good writing cannot be equated with "big" words. In fact anytime you use a learned word when you could have chosen a popular word, you should have a definite reason for doing so. To gain some insight into your word choices, review an essay you have written in this course, preferably one that spotlights the subject. Look carefully at a paragraph or two in that essay, focusing on any learned words you find in that passage. How many do you find? Are these words well chosen? Why or why not?

> *In one essay I wrote recently, I used several learned words. These were valid and necessary to the topic, because I was discussing the attitudes of women who allowed themselves to be debased and submit, while they walked around whining about their lot in life. This was a research paper to a professor who had done a lot of study on this area of women in history, and I felt that using popular language was a little shallow. I did this unconsciously though, and when I spoke about my topic to my sister, who is a freshman and has never taken a literature course, I had to popularize the terms.*

## Exercise 15.6

Reread Amy Tan's essay, "Mother Tongue," in the introduction to this part. In this piece, Tan deals with the complicated issues of how language and thought are connected. In particular, she discusses ways in which Asian Americans may be affected by the lack of English, or of proper English, in their homes. She also talks about the ways in which those who speak a nonstandard language are treated in U.S. society. Does Tan use technical terms? If so, are you familiar with them, or do they seem like jargon to you? Note any that you feel unsure of.

> *In paragraphs 2 and 3 (and others later in the essay), Tan uses the word <u>Englishes</u>. At first I thought this was something she made up, but when she continued to use it, I suspected it was a technical term. After consulting an introduction to linguistics book, I find that it is a term that refers to the various dialects of English spoken in the world. This isn't exactly the way Tan is using it; she is stretching the term to allow it to refer to the various dialects of English that she grew up with.*
>
> *In paragraph 3, Tan uses the word <u>nominalized</u>. I didn't know this one. A grammar book tells me that <u>nominalization</u> is "the process of turning another part of speech, particularly a verb, into a noun." I can see why Tan needs to use this technical term.*
>
> *In paragraphs 8 and 9, Tan introduces a technical term <u>Limited English</u>. At first I thought this was a normal use of these two words. But since it was in quotes, I wondered about it. When I came to*

> *the term the second time (again in quotes), I knew it was a speical term. I found that it is a kind of euphemism for a person who doesn't speak English fully. This term is especially important to Tan because she uses it to contrast Tan's mother's "limited" English with her "unlimited" intelligence. She goes on to show that her mother's "limited" English actually "limited" Tan's ability to understand her mother's abilities.*

## Exercise 15.7

What areas do you have expertise in? If you need to do so, look back at your responses to the Interest Inventory, particularly items 4 and 5. Pick one of these areas and list some of the technical language that you have to know in order to understand conversations about this subject. Are there particular technical or professional journals or magazines that deal with topics in this subject? If so, what kinds of specific knowledge can we assume the readers of these publications have?

> *I have a lot of expertise in the area of education, since I have been working on my degree in that field. I have picked up a lot of terms including <u>transgression</u>, <u>inclusion</u>, <u>invention</u> and <u>rhetoric</u>. I have also learned that there are many facets to the life of an educator that are discussed in popular terms, but one must have knowledge of the politics and system in order to understand what is going on, and actually join in a logical (or illogical, as the case may be) conversation.*

> *There are particular journals that deal with this subject, and though these are not necessary to enter into conversation, often it helps to have a starting point. When I was a younger student, I was expected to read many of these professional journals, and since I had such limited experience in the field, I had a tough time understanding most of the texts and lost interest very quickly. Readers of these journals must have some background in order to use them to gain more knowledge.*

## Exercise 15.8

The following passage from a seminal article on style by Monroe C. Beardsley, entitled "Style and Good Style."

> The clearest way to say what style is, I think, is to say what a *difference* in style is. Take two sentences or parts of sentences, S1 and S2. We say that they differ in style when two things are true about them. First, they differ to some extent in *meaning*. And second, the difference is not on the plane of overt or explicit meaning, but on the plane of covert or implicit meaning. The distinction between explicit and implicit meaning is one that requires a certain amount of analysis to elucidate, but let me say in a general way what sorts of things I have in mind, and leave it to the examples to clarify the distinction. Implicit meaning includes what we would ascribe to the connotations rather than to the plain dictionary sense of a word, and it includes what we would consider to be merely suggested, or hinted, or intimated by a sentence rather than to what the sentence plainly states.

> It is relatively easy to see what we are talking about when we compare two similar English expressions with respect to their style. If they don't differ at all in meaning, there is no difference in style (but this, as Pascal says, is almost impossible, for if there are different words, or the same words in a different order, there is almost certain to be some difference in meaning, however small and subtle.). If the meanings differ in some explicit way, there is no difference in style. It follows from this analysis that the concept of style is inherently comparative, and therefore variable with the context of concern. To isolate a particular stylistic feature in any discourse is always to think of a particular element of implicit meaning in terms of which that discourse might differ from some other one. This is the first of my two theses, then: that style is detail of implicit meaning.

Write a brief answer to each of the following questions:

1. How does Beardsley's passage compare to our comments on style in the introduction to this unit? What connections can you make between Beardsley's passage and what we said there?

> *What Beardsley says could be compared with what Lunsford and Bridges say in the following way. Beardsley says that a difference in style is a difference in "implicit" meaning, as opposed to a difference in "explicit" meaning, which would be a difference in content. Lunsford and Bridges talk about the comfort that comes when a writer gets the style right. That is, good style is that kind of writing that makes the reader comfortable. In Beardsley's terms, that could be put this way. The reader is comfortable when the writer gets the "implicit" meaning right.*

2. Do you find many learned words in this passage? Choose one or two words and examine them carefully. Write a brief essay in which you explain how they help Beardsley achieve his purpose in this passage.

> *There are many learned words in this passage and I believe that they help to illustrate exactly what Beardsley is trying to say. His point in the passage is to show that the style of language can have two different meanings, and that we must compare language to determine what sort of style it holds. His language shows how much he loves words and also that he knows how to use them to his advantage.*

> *One word Beardsley uses in this passage is <u>elucidate</u>. This term means to make clear or plain. The way he uses it in his sentence makes it obvious to the reader what it means. This word is difficult for the modern reader, however, because it is a term rarely used in common conversation.*

> *Two other words that Beardsley uses to help illustrate his points are <u>explicit</u> and <u>implicit</u>. Beardsley is using them to separate a "content" meaning from a "style" meaning.*

3. Does Beardsley use technical or professional language? Are there terms you do not know? Examine one or two terms carefully explaining whether they seem to be useful technical terms or problematic jargon.

> *Beardsley uses both technical and professional language in his passage. Some of the words I am unsure of, but when I read through a second time, I can gather the general meaning for the most part. I did decide to check the dictionary to make sure I was on the right track.*

> *One term that I initially felt was just problematic jargon, but which I now believe is very good use of language, is the phrase "ascribe to the connotations." I felt that this phrase was an overuse of big words that the average reader would have a difficult time understanding. As I reread, though, I recognized what the author was trying to do. He wants to illustrate his points as well as let the reader read the words. We can see what he is saying in action as we read.*

4. What type of audience do you imagine this essay being written for? Be as specific as you can in terms of their education, their interest in, and knowledge about, this topic. How do you know these things?

> *The audience for this piece has to be a group of well educated professionals with a broad vocabulary, probably English teachers and professors. This must be the audience because the context is clearly about language, something most English professors have an interest in. Second, the level of language is designed to be understood by people with an expanded vocabulary, and by people who enjoy language and how it works.*

### *Exercise 15.9*

After you have read this passage, from a recently published book by Ernest Pascarella entitled *How College Affects Students,* answer the questions that follow.

> With the development of more sophisticated, user-oriented statistical packages such as SPSS (Nie,

1983) and SAS (SAS Institute, 1985), the power of multivariate analysis has become available to novitiate and experienced researchers alike. Arguably, the consequences of this have not been uniformly positive. The uniformed use of sophisticated analytical routines is often more likely to obfuscate and mislead than to clarify. Nevertheless, the impressive advances in computing power during the last twenty years have permitted scholars to analyze large and complex national data sets with relative (though perhaps not absolute) ease and efficiency. Such analyses have made major contributions to our understanding of such issues as the impact of college on status attainment and the influence of institutional characteristics on learning. Moreover, they represent a new emphasis or direction in the research literature, which is not nearly so apparent in the studies reviewed by Feldman and Newcomb.

1. What audience do you think this book is written for? Why? How heavily does the writer depend on learned words? On technical language? How appropriate is the language in this passage for that audience? (Here is another way of asking this question: Do you think the technical language and the learned words used in this paragraph are necessary?)

*This passage is written for highly educated, technically-minded people who are interested in the administrative aspects of education. Because the level of language is high above the average reader's vocabulary, it would be difficult for many people with few reading and writing skills to understand. The author relies heavily on learned and technical language. I suppose to a certain extent the words used are necessary, but at the same time, I only feel that way after reading through it several times. My first response to the question about necessity of all the technical terms was that it was too difficult and thick to get through. Some of the terms could have been replaced with simpler ones, but others are necessary.*

2. Assuming that you agree with us that this piece is not very appropriate for college students, identify words or phrases that need to be explained. Look up any words you do not know. Then rewrite the passage in a fashion that would make it appropriate for an audience of college students.

*Some terms that need defining for college students would probably be <u>multivariate</u>, <u>novitiate</u>, <u>obfuscate</u>, and the phrase "status attainment and the influence of institutional characteristics on learning." To rewrite this passage, I would do the following:*

*Inexperienced and novice researchers can now have the benefit of multivariate analysis since more sophisticated and user-friendly statistical packages have been developed. However, some people would argue that this is not entirely a good thing. Things often become unclear and misleading when sophisticated analytical routines are used incorrectly. Nevertheless, scholars have had the benefit of impressive advances in computing power during the last twenty years; these advances have allowed them to analyze large and complex national data sets with relative ease and efficiency. As a result, we have much more understanding of how college is related to status and of how institutions contribute to learning. In addition, these analyses reflect the new direction in research, which is not nearly so apparent in the studies reviewed by Feldman and Newcomb.*

*Exercise 15.10*

Not presented

*Exercise 15. 11*

Not presented

*Exercise 15.12*

Although we encourage you to look for original and fresh metaphors in your writing–particularly in writing that focuses on the writer–you will find that even in this type of writing, you will often use standard, or dead metaphors. Below are passages that contain several metaphors that Gates uses in his essay, "Change of Life." What is being compared to what in each example? Note that some passages may contain more than one metaphor. Which of these metaphors are original and which are dead metaphors? Do you have difficulty in deciding in some cases? Write a brief discussion of your findings.

I can say that a veil passed over her life, dimming her radiance, and then never quite lifted away. [2]

> *This seems fairly original. Although we often refer to this world as a "veil of tears," to see what happened to his mother as a veil dropping over her is fresh.*

I only knew that something had eclipsed the woman who gave birth to me [. . .] . [3]

> *Again this seems fresh. Planets are eclipsed literally. We sometimes see this extended to talk about something getting cut off, but to think of one's mother as being eclipsed seems fairly original.*

Mama's "change" was the great crisis in my life, the crossroads of my childhood. [3]

> *This is pretty much a dead metaphor. We often see turning points referred to as "crossroads" in life.*

[. . .] she would buy canned goods obsessively, as if to stock a bomb shelter [. . .] [5]

> *Again, this is a pretty common comparison, especially for children who grew up in the early part of the cold war.*

[. . .] spurring a pack rat's notion of providence–a contained panic about running short. [5]

> *This seems very fresh. In fact, it's so fresh that it made me stop to figure out just what a pack rat's notion of providence is.*

I could not break the spell, no matter how ardently I labored. [ 6]

> *This is a very well-used metaphor, in which any inability to act is compared to being under a spell.*

And on this afternoon, the sense of illness lay so heavy you could have gathered it in your hands like snow and rounded it into balls to throw. [10]

> *This is a very fresh and original metaphor. I wonder what made him think of snow? Is he thinking of cold and freezing and how they eventually lead to paralysis?*

She had weathered acute depression [. . .] [11]

> *This is a very well-used metaphor. To get through something is to "weather" it.*

But Mama felt her life had been shaken by just such an earthquake; she knew how easy it was to fall off the edge. [11]

> *This is an ordinary metaphor that is made fresh when it is continued. The earthquake is usual, but falling off the edge is novel.*

My mother was an untethered craft, battered by frigid waters, too far out for me to bring back to shore. [12]

> *This metaphor brings together much of the passage around the concept of drifting and paralysis, as caused by cold. It's an ordinary metaphor that is made fresh by the way it is developed.*

Mama, quietly wrestling with her own devils, was more tolerant [. . .] [14]

> *This is a well-used metaphor. Dealing with difficulties is wrestling with devils.*

My stomach was doing flip-flops. [16]

> *This is a very ordinary metaphor.*

In the end, as I say, joining the church gave me a space of my own [. . .] [27]

> *An ordinary metaphor. Doing something to help one develop is getting one's space.*

(The responses to this exercise were written by Ron.)

*Exercise 15.13*

Not presented

*Exercise 15.14*

Think for a minute about the associations you bring the two terms "lawyer" and "attorney." Both regularly refer to someone with a law degree who earns a living by working in the legal profession. The connotations of the two terms are quite different. A person with an office in a house just off main street may be called a lawyer. A person who has just been named as a partner in a prestigious law firm will more likely be referred to as an attorney. If we look more closely, however, we will find that these two words do not have exactly the same denotative meanings. An attorney is someone who is given the legal right to act in place of someone else. Of course, lawyers are often given such power, but someone could be an attorney without being a lawyer. That is, "attorney" is a broader term than "lawyer." The following pairs of words are similar to the pair we've just considered: professor/teacher; evening/night; preacher/pastor; singer/musician. In each case, explain the difference in denotative meaning. Then attempt to capture your sense of the connotative differences in the two words' meanings. Finally, speculate on how the two words' differing contexts have helped create this connotative difference in meaning.

> *Professor/Teacher*
>
> **Denotation.** *A <u>professor</u> is someone who holds a teaching and/or research position in an institution of higher learning, such as a college or university. A <u>teacher</u> is someone who teaches, usually in a public school. Most <u>professors</u> would also be properly called <u>teachers</u>, but a <u>teacher</u> would not be a <u>professor</u> unless he or she had a position in a college or university.*
>
> **Connotation.** <u>*Professor*</u> *carries with it prestige and honor. To call someone a <u>professor</u> is to recognize their position.*
>
> **Speculation.** *The two words have come to have these different connotations because of their associations. Since colleges have historically had more prestige than public schools, the term associated with college (<u>professor</u>) carries more prestige.*
>
> *Preacher/Pastor*
>
> **Denotation.** *A person can be a <u>preacher</u> if he or she gives hortatorical talks on religious matters in some type of formal situation, as in a church service. A person is a <u>pastor</u> if he or she is the spiritual leader of some group of people. A <u>pastor</u> will almost always be considered a <u>preacher</u>; however, a <u>preacher</u> may not be a <u>pastor</u>.*
>
> **Connotation.** <u>*Pastor*</u> *carries with it the connotation of concern and care. A <u>pastor</u> is someone who looks after those in his or her church or congregation. <u>Preacher</u> has no such favorable*

*connotations.*

**Speculation.** *The word <u>pastor</u> has probably taken on the favorable connotations of caring because this is what people in spiritual leadership roles do. The etymological associations of the word may also have contributed to this connotation: Latin, <u>pastor</u> [shepherd], from <u>pascere</u> [to feed.]*

### Evening/Night

**Denotation.** <u>Evening</u> *is the latter part of the day. Often considered to be that time of day when one's work is over. During <u>evening</u> one eats the evening meal and rests or recreates before going to bed. <u>Night</u> is that time when there is no sunlight. It is the opposite of day, the time when there is sunlight.*

**Connotation.** <u>Evening</u> *has connotations of rest and relaxation. One associates sleep with <u>night</u>.*

**Speculation.** *This seems fairly straightforward. Since <u>evening</u> is the time when most people are no longer working on their jobs, it is associated with rest and a slower pace.*

### Policeman/Officer

**Denotation**. *A <u>policeman</u> is a member of a police force. An <u>officer</u> is someone who holds a position of trust and authority, such as that held by a <u>policeman</u>, a leader in the military, or a leader an organization, such as a bank officer.*

**Connotation.** *The word <u>officer</u> has connotations of importance and respect that the word <u>policeman</u> does not have.*

**Speculation.** *Even though the role that <u>policemen</u> play is a crucial one, <u>policemen</u> have not traditionally had the respect that is accorded to many other professions. Thus, the word <u>policeman</u> does not carry with it much in the way of prestige. The word <u>officer</u>, on the other hand, is associated with more prestigious positions. Its derivation, from the phrase one who holds office, seems to carry prestige with it. Thus, when one calls a <u>policeman</u> an <u>officer</u> one is usually thought to be showing respect.*

(The responses to this exercise were written by Ron.)

### Exercise 15.15

1. For each of the sets of words below, state what you see as the shared denotative meaning. Then, determine which words you would label as positive, which neutral, and which negative? On what do you base your labeling? Write sentences that cause readers to see the words as you do. In addition to these positive/negative differences, what other differences do you see between these words? Are these additional differences denotative, connotative, or both?

    a. thin, scrawny, lean, gaunt, slender, lanky, scraggy

    b. rash, heady, impetuous, hasty

*1.a. Each of these words shares the meaning of "not fat or heavy."*

*Positive: thin, lean, slender*

*Negative: scrawny, gaunt, scraggy*

*These differences are based on the experiences I have had with these words.*

*In addition to the negative connotations, <u>scrawny</u> carries a suggestion of boniness, perhaps in part* because of its sound. <u>Scraggy</u> connotes a state of being unkempt or unclean. <u>Lanky</u> doesn't seem to be positive or negative; it does carry a meaning of tall (and thin).

***Sample sentences***

1. The ballet dancer was exceedingly beautiful and very <u>thin</u>.

2. The athlete was <u>lean</u> and muscular.

3. Her classmate had undergone a weight reduction plan and looked <u>slender</u> and svelte.

4. The <u>scrawny</u> little boy looked as if he hadn't eaten in days.

5. Her ex-boyfriend looked anxious and <u>gaunt</u>.

6. The <u>lanky</u> man had a three-day <u>scraggy</u> beard.

*1.b. Each of these words carries a suggestion of speed and lack of deliberation.*

*Positive: heady*

*Negative: rash, impetuous, hasty*

<u>Heady</u> can be positive since it means something like <u>intoxicated</u> or <u>exhilarated</u>.

<u>Rash</u>, <u>impetuous</u>, and <u>hasty</u> all carry with them connotations of youth and inexperience. While <u>heady</u> also has this connotation, it does not connote the same negative judgments implied by the others.

***Sample Sentences***

1. The <u>heady</u> young man made good decisions quickly, while some of the older members of the firm deliberated for interminable amounts of time and then, still, made wrong decisions.

2. The <u>rash</u> young man grabbed the old woman by the arm and "escorted" her across the street, without bothering to find out that she didn't want to cross the street.

3. Before he knew what he was going to do, the <u>impetuous</u> young man found he had kissed the young woman on the cheek.

4. If one is to do well in investing, he cannot afford to make <u>hasty</u> trades when a stock has a sudden downturn.

2. For each of the words below, develop a set of synonyms. Then, rank your words from most positive to most negative. If you were to use each word to describe someone or something, how would your attitude towards that person or thing change as your language changed?

   lazy   small   satirical   sweet   large   motive   feisty

### *lazy, sluggish, lethargic, worthless*

*In essence <u>lazy</u> is a pejorative term, but it is mild in its criticism. If one wants to be extremely critical, one might use <u>worthless</u>. <u>Sluggish</u> carries less criticism because it has a connotation of cause. Something is caused to be <u>sluggish</u>, either a medical condition, or a problem in mechanics, as with a <u>sluggish</u> motor. <u>Lethargic</u> is usually applied to people, and again there is a hint of medical cause. Something causes one to be <u>lethargic</u>.*

### *small, little, petite, miniature peewee*

*<u>Small</u> is a fairly objective description, as is <u>little</u>. <u>Miniature</u> carries with it the suggestion that*

*something is a smaller version of the real thing. But even here, there is no pejorative implication. If one wants to be pejorative, one can use the very informal word <u>peewee</u>. On the other hand, if something is small and good (or pretty), it is <u>petite</u>.*

### satirical, critical, sardonic, biting

*All of these words tend to be pejorative in various degrees. The word <u>satirical</u> suggests that fault has been found in something and, at the same time, that that something (or someone) is being made fun of. However, in <u>satirical</u>, there is also a suggestion that the criticism has a purpose of showing how the thing (or person) criticized could be better. In its most basic sense, <u>critical</u>, simply means passing judgment on something. In this sense, it would not be pejorative at all. However, there is a strong connotation of fault finding usually associated with <u>critical</u>. <u>Sardonic</u> suggests that some fault is being found. There may also be humor in the <u>sarcasm</u>, but if so it is a dark humor, since there is a sense in which the thing criticized may be beyond redemption. <u>Biting</u> suggests a criticism that is hurtful. It is not necessarily more or less pejorative than <u>sardonic</u>, but the focus in the word <u>biting</u> is on the hurt inflicted.*

### sweet, nice, lovely

*All of these are fairly positive terms. <u>Sweet</u> is often used to describe a person who has a pleasant disposition. <u>Nice</u> is also used to describe such a person. However, <u>nice</u> doesn't imply as much about the person, or the relationship, between the two people, the speaker and the person being described. If one knows someone to be <u>sweet</u>, one has had more close contact with them than if one knows someone to be <u>nice</u>. <u>Lovely</u> seems to be even more removed than <u>sweet</u> or <u>nice</u>. Or, perhaps, it's just more formal: "What a <u>lovely</u> person!" With <u>lovely</u> and <u>nice</u>, there is also a sense that the person is being described more holistically than with <u>sweet</u>, where there seems to be some particular thing about the person that makes him (or more likely her) <u>sweet</u>.*

### large, gargantuan, big, plus-sized

*<u>Large</u> is a fairly descriptive term, referring to the relative size of something. If it's large, it's not small. <u>Big</u> would seem to be the closest in meaning to <u>large</u>. The only real difference between the two would seem to be that <u>large</u> is a more formal word than <u>big</u>. <u>Gargantuan</u> differs from <u>large</u> and <u>big</u>, first by being bigger (or larger). If something is <u>gargantuan</u>, it is so large as to be unexpected and surprising. In its context, a <u>gargantuan</u> thing leaves one almost stunned. There is a slight negative connotation sometimes associated with <u>gargantuan</u>, because it is too irregular for the context. <u>Plus-sized</u> on the other hand refers to something (usually a person) who is large, but it does so in such a way as to avoid any negative association.*

### motive, reason, purpose, design

*<u>Reason</u> and <u>purpose</u> are the most neutral words here. But <u>purpose</u> differs from <u>reason</u> in that one does not even have to be conscious of his <u>reason</u> for doing something. If he has a <u>purpose</u>, then he knows why he's doing something. <u>Motive</u> and <u>design</u> both suggest some type of calculated action. Of these two, <u>motive</u> seems to be more neutral. If one has a <u>design</u>, he's working behind the scenes in a way he may not be with a <u>motive</u>.*

### feisty, spunky, full of vim, energetic

*<u>Energetic</u> and <u>full of vim</u> are both reasonably neutral. The second term is a bit more chatty, a bit less formal, than the first. Both <u>spunky</u> and <u>feisty</u> suggest energy with attitude, with <u>feisty</u> a little more confrontational and in-your-face than <u>spunky</u>.*

*Exercise 15.16*

Reread the following passages from essays presented in Chapter 10 (we added the underlining.)

The news organizations' reticence about mentioning the actual nature of abortion may arise in part from a chink in the gleaming semantic armor that otherwise encases the subject. *The abortion advocates forgot to re-name the body parts encountered in abortion.*

Presumably the "conscientious practitioners" of abortion (as the AMA now calls them–in slight departure from its own earlier description of them as "modern day Herods"), would be loath to admit to killing unborn children. They would rather say that they *terminate pregnancies*, an odd assistance for a process that invariably terminates itself.

As long as the discussion is couched in such genteel terms, there isn't much room for primitive, natural words like "arm" and "leg." They are gaucheries. On the other hand, if we could simply introduce a few Choice words into the vocabulary, then our mass media would no longer need to shy away from the topic of abortion techniques. The unborn child won't be called a child but just a "fetus" (Latin for "offspring"), and the arm is only a "potential arm" or, say, a *"brachium."*

Michael Heaphy, "Dismemberment and Choice"


The Italian philosophy of life espouses high-energy confrontation. A male student makes a vulgar remark about your breasts? Don't slink off to whimper and simper with the campus shrinking violets. Deal with it. On the spot. Say, "Shut up, you jerk! And crawl back to the barnyard where you belong!" In general, women who project this take-charge attitude toward life get harassed less often. I see too many dopey, immature, self-pitying women walking around like melting sticks of butter. It's the Yvette Mimieux syndrome: Make me happy. And listen to me weep when I'm not.

Camille Paglia, "Rape and Modern Sex War"

Write a brief explanation of how the connotations of the underlined words in each passage help the writers achieve their overall purposes in the essay. Also note any other words that you find particularly effective. Explain their effectiveness.

**From: Michael Heaphy, "Dismemberment and Choice"**

gleaming semantic armor

*By referring to the news media's gleaming semantic armor, Heaphy immediately puts abortion advocates on the defensive. If they have to have armor, then they must need protection from something. Of course, Heaphy would say they need protection from the truth. But their protection is only semantic. This word has connotations of fake or false. So theirs is a false protection that gleams much like false gold would gleam.*

would be loath to admit to killing unborn children.

*The word loath is put into the mouths, as it were, of these advocates. They would use such fancy, foppish words as this in talking about anything, because this is the type of fancy, foppish, unreal people we are talking about. With admit, Heaphy again puts the pro-choice advocates on the defensive. We admit things that are true, but embarrassing. So rather than saying that they wouldn't want to call abortion killing, Heaphy assumes the truth of his position, by using admit rather than call.*

*As long as the discussion is couched in such <u>genteel</u> terms, there isn't much room for primitive, natural words like "arm" and "leg." They are <u>gaucheries</u>.*

> *Again, Heaphy is using foppish and fancy words to characterize people who don't want to face the truth.*

*On the other hand, if we could simply introduce a few Choice words into the vocabulary, then our mass media would no longer need to <u>shy</u> away from the topic of abortion*

> *Here Heaphy continues his theme that these are really weak and timid people, people who can't face up to the truth.*

### From Camille Paglia, "Rape and Modern Sex War"

*The Italian philosophy of life espouses high-energy confrontation. A male student makes a vulgar remark about your breasts? Don't <u>slink</u> off to <u>whimper</u> and simper with the campus <u>shrinking violets</u>.*

> *Here Paglia is characterizing her opposition as weak. All three of these underlined words suggest people who can't face up to things in a realistic and effective way. It's one thing to leave, but to <u>slink</u> away is to leave in a cowardly way. It's one thing to cry, but to <u>whimper</u> is to cry and be ashamed of your crying at the same time. And <u>shrinking violets</u> is a cliché for people who don't stick around when the going gets tough.*

*I see too many <u>dopey</u>, immature, self-pitying women walking around like melting sticks of butter.*

> *In using <u>dopey</u>, Paglia shows her utter disgust and disregard for those who take the position she is challenging. <u>Dopey</u> is worse than <u>dumb</u>. To be <u>dopey</u> is to somehow be responsible for one's dumbness.*

(The responses to this exercise were written by Ron.)

### Exercise 15.17

Note presented

### Exercise 15.18

Imagine a situation in which you are writing to an audience that agrees with Muller on the issue of abortion. Rewrite Muller's passage above, using language that takes a satirical tone toward those who oppose that point of view. Would your rewritten passage be more persuasive for those already leaning toward Muller's argument? Why or why not?

> **Rewrite.** *The right-to-life movement regards human "life" as a good, a claim most of us are broadly inclined to accept. But the right-to-life movement cannot be satisfied with such a reasonable generality. It must push the issue to its limits; it must make equal all forms of life, with no thought to the mental, emotional or intellectual capacities of that life form. To the inflexible right-to-lifers, keeping alive anencephalic infants (children missing all or most of their brain) is a moral imperative. The right-to-life movement continually propounds its "gospel" that every degree of human life is equal to the most complete development of human life: that is why the moral status of a fetus two weeks into its development is the same as that of children and adults.*

> **Discussion.** *It's hard to say whether this rewriting would be more effective for a given audience, without knowing more about that audience or situation. What we can say is that it would certainly lose its ability to be heard by those on the other side of the issue. When they hear of themselves as "inflexible," and as "propounding a gospel of equality," they are going to turn away from the*

160  *The Longwood Guide to Writing* Instructor's Resource Manual

*argument.*

*Exercise 15.19*

Not presented

# RESPONSES TO EXERCISES: CHAPTER 16

*Exercise 16.1*

Not presented

*Exercise 16.2*

Not presented

*Exercise 16.3*

**Practice in Combining**. Below we offer several model sentences that were formed by using the strategies just presented. Under each of these models are two sentences that can be combined to form one sentence with that structure. Produce that sentence. Then create a sentence of your own with a structure like that of the model sentence.

**Example**     **The boy whom they called refused their request**.

    The tree was in a protected forest.

    They cut down the tree.

    The tree that they cut down was in a protected forest.

    The man who likes hot dogs is my father.

***1. That is the man who ran for Congress.***

    *That is the person.*

    *The person works hard.*

    *That is the person who works hard.*

    *She is the one I saw at the party.*

***2. The dog that bit the postman was held for observation.***

    *The trees were cut back.*

    *The trees were blocking the drivers' vision.*

    *The trees that were blocking the drivers' vision were cut back.*

    *The balls that fell from the tree were broken.*

***3. If the results prove positive, the team is likely to publish its findings.***

    *The game will likely be canceled.*

    *The weather does not improve.*

    *If the weather does not improve, the game will likely be canceled.*

*If the boys don't begin to study soon, they will fail the course.*

**4. Until the report is finished, we will not know what our profits are.**

> *The coach will not allow the player to return to the team until <u>sometime</u>.*
>
> *The player apologizes for his mistakes.*
>
> *Until the player apologizes for his mistakes, the coach will not allow him to return to the team.*
>
> *Until the last inning of the game, the crowd remained glued to their seats.*

**5. Although the crash destroyed both cars, no one was hurt in the accident.**

> *The house is in a good location.*
>
> *The house did not sell for its full value.*
>
> *Although the house is in a good location, it did not sell for its full value.*
>
> *Although he had many friends in Springfield, he finally decided to leave.*

## *Exercise 16.4*

**Practice in Combining.** Below are several model sentences that are formed by using the strategies just presented. Under each of these models are two sentences that can be combined to form one sentence with that structure. Produce that sentence. Then create a sentence of your own with a structure like that of the model sentence.

**1. *I did not know whether he was the best person for the job.***

> *The man did not know <u>something</u>.*
>
> *The house was priced too high.*
>
> *The man did not know whether the house was priced too high.*
>
> *The boy did not know whether his father would come to see him.*

**2. *Their chief goal was to make it through the semester.***

> *John's wish was <u>something</u>.*
>
> *John wanted to go to Disney World.*
>
> *John's wish was to go to Disney World.*
>
> *The man's continuing desire was to find his wife.*

**3. *I will abide by whatever the board members want to do.***

> *My friend wants to say <u>something</u>.*
>
> *I will support <u>something</u>.*
>
> *I will support whatever my friend says.*
>
> *I will believe whatever I am told.*

162  *The Longwood Guide to Writing* Instructor's Resource Manual

**4. It is unlucky that the team's best player was hurt before the tournament.**

<u>Something</u> *is likely.*

*The parts will arrive by this time tomorrow.*

*It is likely that the parts will arrive by this time tomorrow.*

*It is possible that Bill will be late for the game.*

**5. They were sure they could succeed by following the advice of their parents carefully.**

*The organizers improved attendance at the reunion by <u>something</u>.*

*The organizers chose a more central location for the event.*

*The organizers improved attendance at the reunion by choosing a more central location for the event.*

*The team improved its winning percentage by paying more attention to curfews.*

**6. The experts know the team has little chance of winning.**

*The teacher realizes <u>something</u>.*

*Mariana is trying hard to do her homework correctly.*

*The teacher realizes Mariana is trying hard to do her homework correctly.*

*The managers knew that the challenger intended to throw the match.*

**7. We will listen to what we want to.**

*They respect <u>something</u>.*

*The experts have <u>something</u> to say.*

*They respect what the experts have to say.*

*The men believe what their wives tell them.*

## *Exercise 16.5*

Examine paragraph 15 of Tan's essay, "Mother Tongue." Label the connections between sentences and clauses in this paragraph as we labeled the connections in Kozol's essay at the beginning of this chapter. How many of the tools presented above does Tan use in this paragraph?

*(1) I think my mother's English almost had an effect on limiting my possibilities in life as well.* ***CAUSE*** *(2) Sociologists and linguists probably will tell you that a person's developing language skills are more influenced by peers.* ***CONTRAST*** *(3) But I do think that the language spoken in the family, especially in immigrant families which are more insular, plays a large role in shaping the language of the child.* ***ASSOCIATION*** *(4) And I believe that it affected my results on achievement tests, IQ tests, and the SAT.* ***CAUSE*** *(5) While my English skills were never judged as poor,* ***CONTRAST*** *compared to math, English could not be considered my strong suit.* ***ASSOCIATION*** *(6) In grade school I did moderately well, getting perhaps B's, sometimes B-pluses, in English and scoring perhaps in the sixtieth or seventieth percentile on achievement tests.* ***CONTRAST*** *(7) But those scores were not good enough to override the opinion that my true abilities lay in math and science,* ***CAUSE*** *because in those areas I achieved A's and scored in the ninetieth percentile or higher.*

*Explanation. Although we don't talk about this in the text, there are times when one sentence has a relationship to a block of sentences that follows. That is what we find above. Sentence one has a <u>causal</u> relationship with the rest of the sentences in the paragraph, as is often the case when the first sentence in a paragraph is the topic sentence of that paragraph. Tan tells us that she thinks her mother's language had a limiting effect on her possibilities. The rest of the paragraph shows why she thinks this. The relationship between sentences two and three is clearly one of <u>contrast</u>, as signaled by the <u>but</u>. The relationship between sentences three and four is <u>association</u>, as shown by the <u>and</u>. In sentence three, Tan gives us a general statement, and in sentence four she shows how that general principle is related to what happened in her home. The relationship between sentences four and five is a bit hard to pin down. Overall, it seems best to call it <u>cause</u>, since in five we begin to see how the factors she is talking about in three and four result in the situation described in sentence five, namely, her language skills taking a back seat to her math skills. Note that we have labeled a <u>contrast</u> relationship between the clauses in sentence five. Actually, this is more aptly called a <u>concession</u>, but we are lumping these together with <u>contrast</u>. Sentence six is labeled <u>association</u> in its relationship to sentence five, since it continues with information on how she did in her English work. Sentence seven then shows that even though (<u>contrast</u>), she performed well in English, that work was overshadowed when seen against (<u>contrasted with</u>) her work in math. Note that there is a <u>cause</u> relationship between the clauses in sentence seven, where she tells why her math scores were so high.*

*One additional thing to note about this paragraph is that it is not nearly as tightly structured as the prose of Kozol (in the passage from "Distancing the Homeless"), in part because Tan tends to use few subordinating or coordinating conjunctions within sentences and to use shorter sentence structures. Thus, she has to rely on more connections between sentences.*

## Exercise 16.6

Examine the sample passages by Gates and Russell at the beginning of this section to determine how many examples of *ing/ed* phrases, appositives, and absolutes you can find there. Does one writer seem to use certain strategies more than the other writer does? If so, can you speculate as to why?

*Below are the passages. I've labeled appositives (**app**), present participles (**ing**), past participles (**ed**), and absolutes (**abslt**).*

*First, Gates's "Change of Life":*

*I noticed smaller changes. Mama, the fearless one, (**app**) suddenly became afraid of dogs. She started to alter physically, as well. Mama used to do exercises devoutly and weighed a trim ninety-eight pounds. At about this time, though, she gained fifty or sixty pounds. Then the clutter in our home started, because she would buy canned goods obsessively, as if to stock a bomb shelter we didn't have. She began to buy cloth too, bolts of material for some future occasion. (**app**) Before long, there were galvanized garbage cans filled with bolts of cloth.(**ed**) A sense of need, born of a childhood scarcity, (**ed**) now came upon her, spurring a pack rat's notion of providence (**ing**)–a contained panic about running short (**app**). Running out. (**ing**) Going without. (**ing**) Needing and not having.(**ing**) Even as the house became cluttered with her acquisitions, she became obsessed with cleanliness, spending a good part of each day vacuuming.(**ing**) Vacuuming and dusting.(**ing**) I liked trying to help her, and would cook, and clean, and even iron sometimes. I would read the pamphlets that started appearing all over our house, with titles such as "The Phases of Eve" and "The Change of Life," so that I might get a handle on this crazy, evil thing that had entered our lives.*

*Next is Sanders' passage:*

> *My father drank. He drank as a gut-punched boxer gasps for breath, as a starving dog gobbles food–compulsively, secretly, in pain and trembling. I use the past tense not because he ever quit drinking but because he quit living. That is how the story ends for my father; age sixty-four; heart bursting, body cooling and forsaken on the linoleum of my brother's trailer. (**ing** and **ed**) The story continues for my brother, my sister, my mother, and me, and will continue so long as memory holds.*
>
> *In the perennial present of memory, I slip into the garage or barn to see my father tipping back the flat green bottles of wine, (**ing**) the brown cylinders of whiskey, the cans of beer disguised in paper bags. His Adam's apple bobs, the liquid gurgles, he wipes the sandy-haired back of a hand over his lips, and then, his bloodshot gaze bumping into me, (**abslt**) he stashes the bottle or can inside his jacket, under the workbench, between two bales of hay, and we both pretend the moment has not occurred.*

**Comment..** *Obviously, both make quite a bit of use of these devices. Gates uses more in his passage, only because the passage by Sanders makes use of several compound subjects and verbs instead of verbals.*

## Exercise 16.7

**Practice in Combining**. Below are several model sentences formed by using the strategies just presented. Under each of these models is a series of sentences that can be combined to form a sentence with that structure. Produce that sentence. Then create a sentence of your own with a structure like the one in the model sentence.

*1. One of my favorite teachers, a choral director, died recently.*

> *The man ran to help the boy.*
>
> *The man was large.*
>
> *The man was a fireman.*
>
> *The fireman, a large man, ran to help the boy.*
>
> *The problem, a difficult one, was solved.*

*2. She moved quickly, darting through the field like a rabbit startled by a hunter.*

> *The speaker answered slowly.*
>
> *The speaker stared at the audience.*
>
> *The speaker was like an animal.*
>
> *The animal was frozen by fear.*
>
> *The speaker answered slowly, staring at the audience like an animal frozen by fear.*
>
> *The house burned quickly, blazing in the darkness like a lighthouse guiding sailors to safety.*

*3. Eyes darting, nostrils sniffling the air, the deer stood frozen in the clearing.*

> *His legs were pumping.*
>
> *His lungs were gasping for air.*
>
> *The cyclist seemed fixed in his determination.*

*Legs pumping, gasping for air, the cyclist seem fixed in his determination.*

*Students struggling, teachers frustrated, the school was not a particularly pleasant place that week.*

**4. My grandmother told her story, her hands gesturing gently in the air.**

>*The fire truck's siren was piercing the silence*
>
>*The fire truck rounded the corner.*

*The fire truck rounded the corner, its siren piercing the silence.*

*The master of ceremonies announced the winner, his face covered with perspiration.*

**5. The little boy sat down beside all the dental hygiene magazines, eased himself into what he hoped was a blind spot for the nurse as he awaited the inevitable.**

>*The little deer moved across the glen.*
>
>*The little deer glided softly across the glen as <u>something</u>*
>
>>*The boy watched in awe.*

*The little deer moved across the glen, glided softly as the boy watched in awe.*

*The man avoided the topic, eased his way toward something more pleasant, as he awaited her response.*

**6. They last saw him on Friday, swimming fearlessly in the high waves, and waving to them in utter glee.**

>*The mayor arrived at noon.*
>
>*The mayor was shaking hands with everyone in sight.*
>
>*The mayor was kissing every baby he could find.*

*The mayor arrived at noon, shaking hands with everyone in sight, and kissing every baby he could find.*

*The race car drivers rounded the corner, trading paint with each other, and looking for any advantage they could find.*

**7. Frank left the office quickly, dejected and hurt by the careless way corporate America treated those who had given so often at the office.**

>*The insurance adjustor arrived late*
>
>*The insurance adjustor was frustrated.*
>
>*<u>Something</u> angered the insurance adjustor.*
>
>>*Many delays hindered <u>someone</u>.*
>>
>>>*<u>Some people</u> try <u>something</u>*
>>>
>>>>*<u>Some people</u> perform their jobs well.*

*The insurance adjustor arrived late, frustrated and angered by the many delays that hinder people who try to perform their jobs well.*

*The teacher survived the interview, tired but pleased by the support fellow professionals give those who work so hard at their jobs.*

**8. Bill watched as Frank left, his hands folded protectively against his chest, his face guarded lest he give any offense to Frank or the company.**

*The woman glared as <u>something</u>.*

*Tom approached.*

*Tom's clothes were torn and tattered.*

*Tom's eyes were imploring <u>something</u>*

*She gives him some slight assistance.*

*The woman glared as Tom approached, his clothes torn and tattered, his eyes imploring that she give him some slight assistance.*

*The dog lowered its eyes as the man approached, its coat dirty and matted, its tail indicating that it expected more evil treatment.*

## Exercise 16.8

Not presented

## Exercise 16.9

Not presented

## Exercise 16.10

Not presented

## Exercise 16.11

**Practice in Combining.** Above, we saw examples showing how appositives could be very helpful in the production of cumulative sentences. There we defined the appositive as a noun that renames another noun in a sentence. By analogy, we can create free modifiers that rename other elements in a sentence. For example, let's examine the structure of this sentence: "She was walking, ambling rather aimlessly, down the road." In this sentence, the verb *walking* is renamed and elaborated on by the modifying phrase, *ambling aimlessly*. Below we offer sentences that can be combined to form structures with free modifiers that rename a verb (in the first case), an infinitive in the second, and a gerund in the third. Produce these combined sentences. We'll do the first one for you.

They swung futilely trying to hit that nemesis knuckle ball.

They flailed at it with rib racking fury.

They hacked at it in hurried aborted swings.

They missed it with all their might.

becomes

They **swung** futilely trying to hit that nemesis knuckle ball, ***flailed*** at it with rib racking fury, **hacked** at it in hurried, aborted swings, and ***missed*** it with all of their might.

1. They wanted to win the game.

*They wanted to prove they really belonged in the tournament.*

*They wanted to gain <u>something</u>*

   *The respect had been lost in last year's tournament.*

*They wanted to feel some pride again in themselves.*

   ***They wanted to win the game, to prove they really belonged in the tournament, to gain the respect lost in last year's tournament, to feel some pride again in themselves.***

2. *The judges managed to keep straight faces by <u>something</u>*

   *The judges were stifling incipient bursts of mirth.*

*The judges managed to keep straight faces by <u>something</u>*

   *The judges were actually thinking of the most boring parts of their own lives.*

*The judges managed to keep straight faces by <u>something</u>*

   *The judges were conjuring up intimations of their own mortality.*

   ***The judges managed to keep straight faces, by stifling incipient bursts of mirth, by actually thinking of the most boring parts of their own lives, by conjuring up intimations of their own mortality.***

*Exercise 16.12*

Not presented

*Exercise 16.13*

Not presented


Ron

# *Logology and The Longwood Guide to Writing: What We Owe to Kenneth Burke*

In a career spanning over half a century, Kenneth Burke produced a body of work that is astonishing for its sheer bulk alone. Yet not only does the volume of his writings overwhelm, Burke's individual works frequently intimidate the casual and serious reader alike, so much so that Burke has been and continues to be read but little by academicians. One very likely reason for this inattention to Burke is that there simply is little of his work readily available for use in the classroom. As Stanley Mullican states, "Before Burke can be of much use to teachers [ . . .] he must be translated into our language."

A fair amount of translation has been done concerning dramatism, Burke's system of examining human motivation. For Burke, ritual drama provided the best grounds for studying motive, hence, dramatism. And there's been much discussion of the pentad, Burke's five-term heuristic procedure–act, scene, agent, agency, and purpose–plus the ratios that obtain between them, e.g., act/scene, act/agent, and so on. So much attention has been paid to the pentad that scholars seem to have seized on it as the key to dramatism and so to Burke, at the expense of the rest of Burke's writings. But there's a great deal more to dramatism than the pentad, and there's a great deal more to Burke than dramatism. Specifically, I wish to outline the development of logology, indicate its place in Burke's canon, and then look at some of its implications for the teaching of writing.

"Logology" Burke defines as "words about words" (*The Rhetoric of Religion* 1). This is at once a simple yet complex definition, for Burke proposes to study our symbolicity, our use and misuse of language, its manipulative properties, ultimately how and why we think the way we do, all the while inviting us to turn our own language on itself to discern its power.

Central to Burke's thinking about logology is his essay "Definition of Man," in which Burke defines humankind, in part, as "[ . . .] the symbol-using (symbol-making, symbol-misusing) animal [. . .]" (16). Essentially, these symbols that we create, use, and abuse are words, and Burke proposes to explore how we are taken in by the "great deceptions of speech," "how [we] wander through 'forests of symbols'" ("Rhetoric Old and New," 202).

Consideration of this wandering became a major focal point for Burke, especially after about 1961. With the publication in that year of *The Rhetoric of Religion: Studies in Logology*, Burke gave primary attention to logology and its implications. It's not so much that Burke turned his back on his dramatism; it's more that logology supplanted dramatism as Burke's God term. William H. Rueckert explains the relationship of logology and dramatism this way: "[. . .] one can say that before 1961 there was Dramatism and logology and after 1961 there was dramatism and Logology" (1982: 242).

This shift in emphasis to logology was but a natural outgrowth of Burke's thinking about dramatism. Burke states that dramatism becomes a "philosophy of language" ("Definition" 16), a study of our linguistic action with all of human action seen in terms of verbal action. And that action is necessarily "language-ridden" (Rueckert 1963: 161). Our language shapes our view of reality, so much so that our language–the words we choose to represent situations to others and to ourselves–determines what we see. On this phenomenon, Burke cites Demetrius: "In fine, it is with language as with a lump of wax, out of which one man will mould a dog, another an ox, another a horse"(*On Style*, in Burke "Rhetoric–Old and New" 206 ).Burke would have us study our language and how we use it in the hope that we first would recognize the power inherent in it and that, after such recognition, we then would employ our language to effect unity rather than division.

At this point I need to backtrack just a bit to discuss *The Philosophy of Literary Form*, an often overlooked part of Burke's writings that actually stands as a watershed initially for dramatism and later for logology. In the title essay of this book, Burke foreshadows the theory and methods of analysis that inform his writings since 1941, discussing poetry as symbolic action and devising a method for analyzing it as such. By poetry, Burke means any critical or imaginative work, and he views poetry as strategic or stylized answers to situations, as "the adopting of various strategies for the encompassing of situations" (1). Burke holds that the poem, as symbolic action, is the "*dancing of an attitude*" (9. Italics Burke's), an attitude that becomes the poet's strategic answer to his situation. Poetry, then, records the drama of this response, and our goal, in analyzing it as such, is to discover how this response functions. In typical fashion, Burke expands the definition of a term–in this case, poetry–to encompass vast realms, every utterance, however long or short, vocalized or not, so long as that utterance forms a strategic response. Burke asks three questions to explore these stylized responses: "What is vs. what?"(69), "What goes with what?"(20), and "From what through what to what?"(70). Each contributes to the interpretive process, so that we may read a poem, derive some initial assessment of it, and then employ the questions to confirm, expand, or revise that assessment. By asking the first question–"What is vs. what?"–we may outline a work's "dramatic alignment"(69). That is, we may note what elements of a poem conflict with or oppose each other. The second question–"What goes with what?"–derives from Burke's view that a poem "contains a set of implicit equations"(20), and with this question we may discover images, acts, characters, or situations that "cluster" around the dramatically opposed elements, thereby providing a more complete description of those elements. The third question–"From what through what to what?"–enables us to trace the development of the poem as it progresses from one event or scene to the next; this question, which we may rephrase as "What follows or follows from what?," allows us to evaluate qualitatively the events with which the poet opens or closes his work or with which he surrounds its climax (70-71). The questions enable us to consider matters not only of content (poem as response) but also of form and structure (the stylized or strategic nature of the response).

This analytic sequence points toward the logological formula, which Burke presents in his essay "Terministic Screens," an essay in *Language as Symbolic Action*. This formula reads, "*Pick some particular nomenclature, some one terministic screen . . . [so] that you may proceed to track down the kinds of observations implicit in the terminology you have chosen, whether your choice of terms was deliberate or spontaneous*"("Screens" 47. Emphasis Burke's). Burke notes that essentially two types of terminologies exist: those that stress the principle of continuity and those that stress the principle of discontinuity ("Screens" 47). Those emphasizing continuity allow us to see two things (e.g., events, people, nations) as being substantially the same, while those emphasizing discontinuity allow for no such consubstantiality. (For example, U.S. political leaders of the Seventies who favored detente viewed the Soviet Union and the United States as embarking together on a mission aimed at achieving world peace, and so stressed the two nations' similarities, the principle of continuity in operation. Those leaders who opposed detente remembered that Russian Premier Nikita Kruschev promised to bury us.)

Central to this tracking down of implications is the concept of terministic screens. Essentially, these screens are "word filters" through which we perceive reality. Burke speaks of them as terminologies that cause us to focus on certain elements of situations we encounter rather than on others, a process he calls the directing of the attention ("Screens" 45).

These screens, while giving us an accurate picture of situations (accurate in the sense that they allow us to interpret situations, or reality, as we must see them), are potentially harmful, for as Burke notes, "Even if any given terminology is a reflection of reality, by its very nature as a terminology it must be a selection of reality; and to this extent it must function also as a deflection of reality" ("Screens"45). And here an example is in order.

Joe B. Wyatt opens an essay with this anecdote:

> Many years ago, a now-unknown Congressman sent the following response to a constituent who had asked, "Where do you stand on whiskey?"
>
> "If you mean the Devil's brew, the poison scourge, the bloody monster that defies innocence, dethrones reason, and topples men and women from the pinnacles of righteous, gracious living into the bottomless pit of degradation and despair, then certainly I am against it with all my power," the politician wrote.
>
> "But," he continued, "if you mean the drink that enables a man to magnify his joy and happiness and to forget life's heartbreaks and sorrows; if you mean the drink that pours into our treasuries untold millions of dollars, which are used to care for our little crippled children, our aged and infirm, to build highways and schools, then certainly I am in favor of it." (A56)

Clearly, this politician understood terministic screens, taking at once a negative and a positive stance on the same issue; he understood how to direct his constituent's attention through the smokescreen of his language.

Advertisers also understand how to use language to direct attention. On the evening of June 7, 1999, I was paying scant attention to a baseball game on the television, when this sign just to the right of home plate caught my attention: "Tobacco. Tumor causing, teeth staining, smelly, puking habit." This language clearly directs our attention to some less than desirable aspects of tobacco use, to say the least. Wanting to find a quick comparison, I leafed through a copy of *Sports Illustrated*, looking for a cigarette advertisement and its required statement of the U.S. Surgeon General's warning. The warning I found, "Cigarette Smoke Contains Carbon Monoxide," also directs our attention to a less than desirable aspect of tobacco use, but it's less direct in its message than the ballpark sign; it deflects more than that sign. The sign's language directs our attention clearly to the disease–cancer–often associated with tobacco use. But in the Surgeon General's warning, the significance of carbon monoxide in cigarette smoke isn't clearly spelled out, so we may gloss over the danger. While we may know that carbon monoxide is dangerous, just how dangerous is it in cigarette smoke? We relate immediately to the horrors of cancer as implied by the ballpark sign ("tumor causing"), but we're probably less informed about those of carbon monoxide. The advertiser's use of the simple declarative statement softens the message, deflects the reality of the dangers of carbon monoxide.

Terministic screens, by deflecting reality, by directing attention, allow us to wage holy wars or to justify the rightness of any causes we support. With his concern for our nature as the symbol-making, -using, and -misusing animal, Burke would have us analyze such screens to understand better how they manipulate. The logological formula, stressing the examination of continuity and discontinuity, provides a system for such analysis.

Continuity and discontinuity are the generating principles of investigation into terms: they require us to examine not only what is consistent or inconsistent with terms; they also require us to examine the implications of those terms, the kinds of observations implicit in them. Burke suggests in *The Rhetoric of Religion* (39) that we may adapt the three questions he presents in *The Philosophy of Literary Form* to form a means for analyzing terminologies. To discover what is continuous or consistent with a term, we may ask, "What goes with what?" For example, if we examine "democracy" as a terministic screen, we may find such entities as the freedoms listed in the Bill of Rights as being consistent with the term. To discover what is discontinuous or inconsistent with a term, we may ask, "What vs. or opposes what?" Continuing our example of "democracy" as term, we may find other systems of government or economics as being inconsistent with the term. And to discover the implications of a term, we may ask, "From what, through what, to what?" or, better yet, "What follows or follows from what?" Examination of "democracy" from this perspective leads to a consideration of the quality of life under a democratic system of government.

So far, this abbreviated consideration of logology reveals that this system is indeed a human-centered philosophy that takes linguistic action as a point of departure for the study of human action. Burke views language both as our damnation and salvation. All people are substantially the same; that is, as symbol-making animals, all of us create, use, and misuse symbols, and the symbol constructs we build tend to separate us, giving rise to faulty terminologies that lead to conflict. In this sense, language is damning. But language potentially holds our salvation, for if we use language to build faulty terminologies, we can also use it to repair them or erect new constructs that would not allow "absurd ambitions" to arise as readily as they might otherwise. Thus, one of Burke's catch phrases is "By and through language, beyond language" (Rueckert, 1963:161). And it is precisely this concern with the power of language that may inform today's composition class.

For too long, the essence of the composition course has been formats, grammar, and mechanics, with the rhetorician's role that of arbiter of taste, a grammarian first, a writing teacher last. But in the last thirty years or so, we have seen a strong demand for better developed content in student writing, so that more and more composition teachers are concerned with helping students to generate significance, that is, to find things to say that matter and ways to say them. This shift from correctness to content has been a profound one, because with it has come the paradigm shift from product to process. Accompanying that shift is a broadening of our understanding of what rhetoric means.

## *Rhetoric, Identification, and the Power of Language*

Rhetoric has held an honored place in letters from the time of the ancient Greeks. Aristotle's *Rhetoric* defines rhetoric as the art of finding all the available means of persuasion in a given situation (in Cooper 7). With its heavy emphasis on persuasion, Aristotelian rhetoric focused on the ways the rhetor could use it to successfully argue a case. This rhetor struggled against another rhetor, whose task was to argue the opposite side of the case. Thus, an adversarial relationship obtained between them, with both arguing a preconceived position, e.g., the innocence or guilt of someone, before an Athenian court. Both hoped to convince the court of the rightness of their respective position and worked various devices of invention, style, and delivery to do so. Such use of rhetoric is similar in nature to our court system, with a defense attorney arguing in favor of her client and a prosecuting attorney arguing against.

The definition of rhetoric today is broader than Aristotle's. One aspect of this definition takes rhetoric to mean a skillful, positive use of language, but another takes it to mean a skillful but insincere or bombastic use of language. All we need do is listen to the bandying back and forth of the term "rhetoric" as used by politicians to understand this second meaning. For our purposes, we'll define rhetoric as the art of effective communication, which will let us range far in our discussion of identification.

In "Rhetoric–Old and New," Burke defines the primary difference he sees between the old rhetoric (that of Aristotle) and a new rhetoric (one that Burke sees as emerging in this century):

> The key term for the old rhetoric was "persuasion" and its stress was upon deliberate design. The key term for the "new" rhetoric would be "identification," which can include a partially "unconscious" factor in appeal. "Identification" at its simplest is also a deliberate device, as when the politician seeks to identify himself with his audience. In this respect, its equivalents are plentiful in Aristotle's *Rhetoric*. But identification can also be an end, as when people earnestly yearn to identify themselves with some group or other. Here they are not necessarily being acted upon by a conscious external agent, but may be acting upon themselves to this end. In such identification there is a partially dreamlike, idealistic motive, somewhat compensatory to real differences or divisions, which the rhetoric of identification would transcend. (203)

Why did Burke see this change in rhetoric's key term–from persuasion to identification–as not just desirable but necessary? An answer to this question lies in the "compensatory" nature of Burke's "rhetoric of identification." Burke decried division between people and nations, seeing language as the primary culprit in creating and maintaining it. Writing through periods of intense worldwide unrest–e.g.,World War II in the 1940's and the Cold War beginning with the end of that war–Burke wanted nothing more than to reconcile the whole of mankind. His writings became "a humanist's counter-statement offered to the public at large as a reaffirmation of *human* purpose and as a means of 'purifying war' ([our] greatest rational lunacy, so that each person [. . .] may *peacefully* and intelligently pursue the better life" (Rueckert 1963: 161).

Truly a noble ambition. And how was this to occur? Burke says:

> A rhetorician, I take it, is like one voice in a dialogue. Put several such voices together, with each voicing its own special assertion, let them act upon one another in co-operative competition, and you get a dialectic that, properly developed, can lead to views transcending the limitations of each. ("Rhetoric Old and New" 203)

One of Burke's primary concerns is with creating unity rather than division through language. Alluding to the story from Genesis about the Tower of Babel, Burke says, "Rhetoric is concerned with the state of Babel after the Fall" (*A Rhetoric of Motives* 23). You'll remember that in Genesis 11, Nimrod decides to build a mighty tower. Genesis 11:1 tells us that "the whole earth was of one language, and of one speech." Nimrod, out of pride or vanity, decides to build a tower that would reach "*unto heaven*"(11:4), which doesn't please the Lord:

> And the Lord said, Behold, the people *is* one, and they have all one language; and this they begin to do: and now nothing will be restrained from them, which they have imagined to do.
>
> Go to, let us go down, and there confound their language, that they may not understand one another's speech.
>
> So the Lord scattered them abroad from thence upon the face of all the earth: and they left off to build the city.
>
> Therefore is the name of it called Babel; because the Lord did there confound the language of all the earth; and from thence did the Lord scatter them abroad upon the face of all the earth.(11:6-9)

Note that in 11:6, there is the implication that through unity of language, the people could do whatever their imaginations led them to, even to the point of approaching the Lord on their own terms. This arrogance led the Lord to "confound their language" (11:7), so that the people were separated solely on the basis of language. Rather than having a common language that each understood, every person came away from Babel with a different language. No one understood anyone else. When Burke says that "rhetoric is concerned with the state of Babel after the Fall," he clearly means that the role of rhetoric is to effect understanding despite differences in language. If we take a logical, Burkean extension of this notion, everyone who uses language is a rhetorician whom Burke would charge with creating unity. And the best way to achieve this goal is through language, with each of us learning to use our language to effect unity rather than division, so that we use language to transcend our individual and thus more narrow viewpoints through dialectic, through the give and take of presenting our views, hearing those of others, and then modifying, no, refining, those views, ours as well as others'.

Attempting to achieve this goal becomes paramount for all of us. Burke notes that *"[rhetoric] is rooted in an essential function of language itself, a function that is wholly realistic, and is continually born anew; the use of language as a symbolic means of inducing cooperation in beings that by nature respond to symbols"* (*A Rhetoric of Motives* 43. Italics Burke's.). Because of our nature as symbol-makers, -users, and –misusers, we can't not study the power of our language to "induce cooperation" through "co-operative competition." And this leads us to the concept of identification. Burke states, "You persuade a man only insofar as you can talk his language by speech, gesture, tonality, order, image, attitude, idea, *identifying* your ways with his" (*A Rhetoric of Motives* 55. Italics Burke's).

In *The Longwood Guide to Writing,* we rely heavily on identification. First, we invite students to consider their audience from the outset of their writing, not just to name a vague "reader out there somewhere" but to provide detail about their projected reader. This audience analysis figures in Chapters 2 and 3, Shaping an Essay and Revision, respectively. In Chapter 2, students are invited to make an initial statement about their reader; in Chapter 3, we discuss the reader as a necessary consideration for revision. Then, in Part 2 (Chapters 5-11), we ask students to consider the role that the reader plays in the various occasions for writing discussed there. The reader is one corner of the rhetorical triangle, and we base part of each of these chapters on that triangle. And in Chapters 15 and 16, we approach words and sentences in part through the rhetorical triangle.

Given Aristotle's definition of rhetoric as persuasion and Burke's definition of rhetoric as identification, we need to discuss the ways in which Burke informs our treatment of argument and persuasion in Chapters 9 and 10. In chapter 9, the Position Essay, we ask students to envision the reader, not as an evil or inept other, but rather as a rational and good person who happens to disagree with her on the issue in question. Rather than seeking to defeat the reader or to change him into someone who agrees with her, the writer sets herself the task of explaining calmly and rationally her position to a reader who dissents. The writer does not attempt to convince the reader to accept her position on this topic because in a Burkean framework, a writer cannot attempt to persuade someone with whom she cannot identify. In Chapter 10, the writer assumes an audience with whom she can identify; thus, she is in a position to persuade.

In a Burkean framework, however, the writer's overriding goal as defined in both these chapters, indeed, in all the other chapters in Part II, is to communicate. While Aristotle limited rhetoric to persuasion–finding the available means of persuasion in the particular case–Burke sees the study of rhetoric as the study of why and how we communicate, and we think the generating principle of rhetoric today should be the power of language in communicating with others and with self. The rhetorician's role in the classroom should focus on helping the student become aware of the power of her language, of the role it plays in shaping her thinking, her reactions to events, situations, people–in essence, her life. The composition classroom should become one in which the individual student has the opportunity to engage herself in dialectic and so use her language to come to know herself in the most comprehensive of senses.

Is all this view of the power of language strikingly unique and completely original with Burke? No, it isn't. But Burke has, in his own inimitable way, pushed, poked, prodded, and probed this view to the point that he provides an overarching theory, a rubric which allows an informed, theory-rich approach to composition.

## *Invention—Questions for Analysis*

Logology at once provides theory and methodology for invention (that is, generating ideas), with that method grounded in the logological formula and the three questions first outlined in *The Philosophy of Literary Form.* The Questions for Analysis, a heuristic procedure we present in Chapter 1, derive immediately from Burke's questions (see Figure 1 below). Here a definition is in order. A heuristic procedure is a set of steps to follow or questions to ask in investigating a topic. These procedures range from informal (e.g., the journalist's "who, what, when, where, why, and how?" set of questions) to more formal (e.g., the scientific method and Aristotle's *topoi*). The purpose of heuristic search is to make the investigator's task more systematic and so more manageable than it might be otherwise. When students begin a major writing assignment, they are often at a loss as to how to begin exactly. Having a heuristic procedure to rely on can be very helpful, for it can help bring some order to an otherwise daunting task.

# QUESTIONS FOR ANALYSIS

Note: In each of the following questions, the writer replaces *your topic* with a specific definition of her topic. E.g., if the topic is environmental protectionism, then the first question would read, "How do you define environmental protectionism?"

## *Association*

How do you define *your topic*? What is it?
What do you associate with *your topic*?
What are the physical elements or characteristics of *your topic*?
Where does *your topic* take place? In what context does it occur?
What has been written or said in favor of *your topic*?
How does *your topic* compare with other things like it?

## *Opposition*

Who or what opposes *your topic*? Why? What is the nature of this opposition?
What has been written or said against *your topic*?
How is *your topic* unlike other similar things? What sets it apart from those things?
How does *your topic* stand out against its context?
What about *your topic* seems odd, incongruous, or unusual?

## *Sequence*

What is the specific sequence in *your topic*? What comes or happens first, then second, then third, and so on?
How did *your topic* come to be?
What are the causes of *your topic*?
What steps, if any, are involved in *your topic*?

## *Consequence*

What did you learn from *your topic*?
What did you learn from your investigation of *your topic*?
What problems are inherent in *your topic*? What are their solutions?
What results from *your topic*?
What opportunities does *your topic* offer?
What are the implications of *your topic*?
What about *your topic* is good? Bad? Desirable? Undesirable? Necessary?
Should *your topic* be? Not be? Why or why not?

Figure 1. Questions for Analysis

Richard E. Young, Alton L. Becker, and Kenneth L. Pike offer these criteria for evaluating a heuristic procedure:

1. It aids the investigator in retrieving relevant information that he has stored up in his mind. (When we have a problem, we generally know more that is relevant to it than we think we do, but we often have difficulty in retrieving the relevant information and bringing it to bear on the problem.)

2. It draws attention to important information that the investigator does not possess but can acquire by direct observation, reading, experimentation, and so on.

3. It prepares the investigator's mind for the intuition of an ordering principle, or hypothesis. (120)

We think our heuristic procedure meets these three criteria. If a student writes a response to each question in turn, she will clearly generate information that she knows about her topic. And if she finds that she can't answer one or more of the questions, then the Questions will have met the second criterion, that of identifying gaps in the investigator's knowledge. But it especially meets the third criterion, that of leading the student writer to a realization of significance, because the last set of questions ask the writer to make a value judgment about her topic.

If you've looked at the Questions for Analysis carefully, you'll have noticed that we have divided the questions into four parts instead of Burke's original three. We think our division can actually help students grasp the nature of heuristic search more readily than Burke's original three, because his third actually takes two directions. Here are Burke's questions, with the guiding principle listed after each in parentheses:

What goes with what? (Association)

What opposes what? (Opposition)

What follows or follows from what? (Sequence and Consequence)

By dividing the third question into two—"What follows what?" and "What follows from what?"—we focus students on two related but substantively different principles of investigation. If we look at sequence as a generating principle of investigation, then we may note how one thing follows another in terms of time and space. But if we look through the lens of consequence, then we have to consider the effect of one thing on another, and that leads naturally to considering the quality of that effect. Splitting Burke's third question to form our third and fourth generating questions emphasizes the need of the student writer to judge the worth of her topic. And in that judgment lies significance, that elusive quality necessary for good writing.

## *Literature as Equipment for Living*

A third concept from Burke that we've used derives from *The Philosophy of Literary Form*. In the title essay of this collection of essays, Burke talks about the nature of works written for a purpose:

Critical and imaginative works are answers to questions posed by the situation in which they arose. They are not merely answers, they are *strategic* answers, *stylized* answers. For there is a difference in style or strategy, if one says "yes" in tonalities that imply "thank God" or in tonalities that imply "alas!" So I should propose an initial working distinction between "strategies" and "situations," whereby we think of poetry (I here use the term to include any work of critical or imaginative cast) as the adopting of various strategies for the encompassing of situations. These strategies size up the situations, name their structure and outstanding ingredients, and name them in a way that contains an attitude towards them. (1. Italics Burke's)

Later in this same essay, Burke writes of the purpose of poetry (and remember that he's defined poetry broadly): "poetry is produced for purposes of comfort, as part of the *consolatio philosophiae*. It is undertaken as *equipment for living*, as a ritualistic way of arming us to confront perplexities and risks. It would protect us" (61. Italics Burke's). These are important distinctions to bring to bear in a composition course, for they can help students understand that literature can be considered as something other than a piece of writing to be interpreted and written about solely in terms of its literary merit.

The idea of literature as equipment for living is one that figures in Chapter 8, Writing *About* and *From* Literature. While many students learn how to dissect a text in their high school literature classes, how to look for symbols and images and motifs and themes, they oftentimes don't know how to read a piece of literature for ways that it might become more to them than another story or poem to be interpreted. Our goal in incorporating a chapter on literature in a first-year composition textbook is to help make students aware that what an author says to them is at least as important as how that writer says it.

The term "writing *from* literature" evolved from Burke's "consoling philosophy" perspective. It means using literature as a springboard to writing, so that the student writer begins with a piece of literature and then moves beyond that story specifically to the more universal moments it embodies and their relation to his experience. This moving beyond may actually mean that the student writer will mention the specific story only briefly before exploring the connections he needs to make between the story and his experience. To some teachers, this may seem a curious way to proceed, because our instruction in literature has long focused on wresting meaning from a text by using a particular critical perspective and then writing an argument about that meaning. Being able to undertake this kind of literary exegesis is an important skill, especially for a student majoring in English or another of the humanities. It is essentially writing *about* literature, as we're defining it, and its focal point is clearly the text itself, with support for the argument being found in the text as well as in other works about the text or its author.

Writing *from* literature, on the other hand, takes the student writer as its focal point, so that an essay written from literature focuses more on the student than on the literary text as text. It may seem at first that writing *from* literature requires the writer to distance himself from the story, perhaps even to ignore it altogether. But this is not the case. Writing *from* literature does not mean closing your eyes to the text; instead, it's having the text saturate your thinking. The text becomes grounding for the writing, a scene out of which the writing grows. Writing *from* literature, then, requires that writer know the story perhaps even more completely than writing *about* it does, for the writer must not only understand the story as story but see how it moves beyond itself to become part of his own "equipment for living."

## *Where Are We Then?*

To ask one of Burke's favorite questions, "Where are we then?"(*The Philosophy of Literary Form* viii). Our discussion of Burke has been anything but exhaustive, but that wasn't our purpose at the outset. Instead, we've attempted to outline several of Burke's principles that inform *The Longwood Guide to Writing*, principles that derive from Burke's discussion of the power of language. If through our teaching we can help students come to understand the power inherent in their language and in their control over it, then we will have done them a service. And providing that service, it seems to us, is precisely what first-year composition courses should be about.

Bill

## Works Cited

Burke, Kenneth D. "Definition of Man." *Language as Symbolic Action*. Berkeley: U Cal Pr, 1966.

---. *A Grammar of Motives*. Berkeley: U Cal Pr, 1969.

---. *The Philosophy of Literary Form,* 3rd edition. Berkeley: U Cal Pr, 1973.

---. *The Rhetoric of Religion: Studies in Logology*. Berkeley: U Cal Pr, 1970.

---. "Rhetoric Old and New." *Journal of General Education*, V (April 1951). 202-209.

---. "Terministic Screens." *Language as Symbolic Action*. Berkeley: U Cal Pr, 1966.

Cooper, Lane. Trans. *The Rhetoric of Aristotle*. Englewood Cliffs: Prentice-Hall, 1932.

Mullican, Stanley. "Kenneth Burke's Rhetorical Theories: Implications for the Language Arts." Unpublished Ph.D. dissertation, Purdue University, 1968.

Rueckert, William H. *Kenneth Burke and the Drama of Human Relations*. Minneapolis: U Minnesota Pr, 1963.

Rueckert, William H. *Kenneth Burke and the Drama of Human Relations*, 2nd ed. Berkeley: U Cal Pr, 1982.

Wyatt, Joe B. "Our Moral Duty to Clean Up College Athletics." *The Chronicle of Higher Education* 13 Aug. 1999, A56.

Young, Richard E., Alton L. Becker, and Kenneth L. Pike. *Rhetoric: Discovery and Change*. New York: Harcourt, Brace, & World, Inc. 1970.

# Teaching Writing as Process

Nearly all writing teachers subscribe to a process approach to writing instruction. But there are important pedagogical differences in the practices of teachers who describe their approaches with the term *process*. Are all of these teachers really teaching writing as process? What exactly does process teaching entail?

## But First, What Process Instruction Isn't

Let's begin with an example of what process instruction isn't. As first-year writing students more years ago than either of us cares to count, we found ourselves taught by instructors who espoused a very linear approach to composing, an approach that has come to be labeled "think-outline-write." Bill's experience is typical of this method. Each week, he was assigned an in-class essay on Monday. By Wednesday, he had to have thought about the topic assigned (no freedom to choose any other topic) and to have prepared a sentence outline and a thesis sentence. Class discussion then focused on the correct outline and the correct thesis, which would result in the correct response to the assignment. Once the outline and thesis were approved by the instructor, nothing could be changed. Then on Friday, the essay was written. In that fifty-minute period, there was no time for a rough draft; students wrote the final copy, using their approved outlines as guides. At the end of class, Bill and his classmates submitted their papers (including outlines and thesis statements), received the reading assignment for the next essay, and left, relieved that that week's ordeal was over.

When we began teaching writing, we followed the examples of our teachers. Ron describes his initial teaching experiences thus:

> Some twenty-eight years ago, I structured my course around ten required essays. Of these ten essays, at least nine were written in class, in a fifty-minute class period. A typical sequence of class sessions would run something like this:
>
> | | |
> |---|---|
> | Meeting One | Introduce type of writing: for example, Comparison/Contrast |
> | Meeting Two | Write essay, in class |
> | Meeting Three | Go over "errors" in essays |
> | Meeting Four | Introduce next type of writing |

My students were doing a lot of writing, since there was a writing assignment given every three or four days. But I was doing little to help them develop their writing processes. As I've often said while reflecting on these early days, I gave my students a diagnostic essay at the beginning of the term to establish that they could not write very well and then proceeded to reconfirm that evaluation in a series of ten timed writings.

## A Writing Process of Stages

In a sense, there is an inherent contradiction in the term *process*. If something is a process, it is fluid; it flows where it will. That is the way it is with writing, when it goes well. The writer moves from one place to another naturally as her thoughts flow onto the page. She does not know what the writing process will produce or even entail before she begins writing. But where does teaching fit into such a process? How do we formalize this process without subverting it?

Writing teachers certainly talk about this process in formal terms. We often speak of writing as a three-step process involving prewriting, writing, and rewriting. A process approach to composing has become so widely employed that many of our students nod sagely as we talk about these three stages. Students most often understand these stages to mean:

> **prewriting**–what occurs before actual drafting. It may include brainstorming, listing, freewriting, applying the journalist's questions (who, what, when, where, why, and how), using a formal heuristic procedure (such as our Questions for Analysis in Chapter 1), and so on, as the writer works hard to discover exactly what she wants her essay to say. Once having found this main idea or focus and generated some information to support it, she's ready to engage the second stage of the process.
>
> **writing**–the actual writing out of the main idea, so that words simply flow all but effortlessly onto the page. As if by magic, the essay emerges. Once this draft appears on paper, the writer enters the third stage.
>
> **rewriting**–the correcting of grammar and mechanics. In this model, revision is reduced to surface editing. Student writers may change a word or two, maybe even rewrite a sentence or two, but they seldom make the kind of major changes that characterize revision in its most comprehensive sense.

This three-stage model captures the belief of many of our students that writing is linear, that it proceeds all but seamlessly from prewriting to writing to rewriting, with the final essay emerging at the end, ready to be handed in to the instructor. Clearly, such an understanding is actually a misunderstanding, for writing seldom if ever proceeds in such a straightforward fashion. Yes, there is a beginning that we can call prewriting, and students do write a draft, and they then have the opportunity to rewrite that draft to strengthen it. But ultimately, writing simply cannot be reduced to such a discreet three-step process. As we tell our students, speaking of writing in such terms is a convenient lie, a "useful fiction"–useful so long as we don't believe it.

Why do we call this lie a "useful fiction"? Writing is truly a complex enterprise that requires the writer to engage in a number of activities–generating material, considering her audience, selecting the right word, shifting the focus of her writing to reflect a modified purpose for the essay. Writing is, in fact, so complex that a number of our students fear it; they fear that they won't have anything to say and that they won't be able to say anything correctly. So anything we as teachers can do to decrease their anxiety has some merit. By dividing writing into a three-step process, by giving our students specific names for specific activities, we work to help them feel more at ease.

Still, we need to stress the non-linear nature of the writing process. At best, writing proceeds in fits and starts as the writer makes a start, writes a bit, decides to delete some of what he's written, or perhaps skips ahead to write a note or even a paragraph to use later in the essay. Writing is a recursive process, one that moves forwards and backwards. At times, it may even seem that these contradictory movements occur at the same time, as ideas emerge for, say, an introduction and a conclusion that must be dealt with immediately, else they'll be lost. It is no exaggeration to say that writing is chaotic. Our job as writing teachers is to help students learn how to manage that chaos, so that they make their writing and their writing processes as productive as possible.

Although we are mindful of the pitfalls of any attempt to capture something so complex as writing in a system, we have found it useful to ask students to pay attention to four elements crucial to all process instruction:

> Invention
> Drafting

Response
Revision

Each of these principles needs to be at work in every writing assignment we ask our students to complete; thus, we have to make time for each, even to the point of building in specific requirements in a given assignment that derive from each.

***Invention.*** Just as the term suggests, invention entails creating and discovering ideas. Writing begins in invention. As the writer considers the assignment and how best to respond to it, she invents ways of responding. That is, she speculates about a particular topic that would fit with the assignment, perhaps selecting one from several that occur to her. She engages in any of a number of prewriting activities available to her: freewriting, listing, clustering, visualizing, using a formal heuristic procedure (that is, responding to a specific set of steps or questions to generate ideas).

Students need initial instruction in various of these activities, and they need to be reminded that certain ones may be more helpful in completing a particular assignment. Part of a the writing teacher's job is to expose students to these activities through in- and out-of-class exercises and to offer suggestions about using them while completing a writing assignment. The prewriting strategies we offer in Chapter 1 are designed to help reduce the typical writing anxieties that students feel as they begin to write.

We must not, however, limit invention to what happens during the prewriting stage. Invention may occur any time the writer generates ideas. This may happen while he is drafting, when he reworks his draft to shape or structure his ideas for a particular audience–in short, at any stage of the writing process.

***Drafting.*** Your students may feel they need little instruction in drafting. After all, they have obviously had practice in drafting in every previous writing assignment they have completed. But drafting involves more than simply writing a rough draft. As we noted above, drafting involves inventing or discovering the best shape for an essay, one that works best to reveal the significance the writer wishes the essay to carry.

Many students begin writing before they are really ready to compose a draft of an essay. This may work well for them, because freewriting may be a very useful form of planning. In fact, our suggestion that students try writing a Discovery Draft (see Chapter 2) is intended to let them experiment with drafting as a form of extended freewriting. However, it is important for students to differentiate between that type of writing that is absolutely exploratory and writing that is guided by some sense of overriding purpose. In *The Longwood Guide to Writing*, the Discovery Draft is written with an eye to audience and purpose, though the writer gives herself enough freedom to keep invention in the forefront of her writing process while composing this draft.

Some writers tend to have difficulty with drafting because they cannot release themselves from concern with stylistic detail. Thus, they revise a sentence continually (and in the process lose the flow of their writing), or they get stuck for long periods of time trying to find a word that will not come to them. Such writers should be encouraged to leave some of these details for the revising stage and to see drafting as the stage at which they make a first attempt to get their thoughts into words.

Chapter 2 focuses on shaping ideas for audience and purpose, beginning with the writer's developing an initial Focus Statement for the paper, and then continuing with a Discovery Draft. From there, we offer various initial shaping strategies, including outlining, blocking, and drawing. Students who use such strategies to guide their drafting and subsequent revision frequently have an easier time in completing assignments than those who try to complete an entire essay in one sitting.

***Response.*** This is probably the least obvious ingredient in process instruction and the only one that doesn't have a parallel in the earlier *prewriting, writing, rewriting* model. In fact, a case could be made that writers could enact a writing process without any response to their writing. We would argue, however, that most inexperienced writers need assistance as they move into the revision stage, since they haven't developed their skills as readers of their own writing to the point where they can see what and how to revise. Thus, process teaching should build in some responses that will help students move to revision. We hasten to add that this response need not come exclusively from the teacher. As we will explain below, peer response can become a useful tool in developing writing skills and at the same time, can take some of the paper load off the writing teacher.

*Revision.* Revision may be the most obvious ingredient in process writing. Nearly all students know they are supposed to revise. However, as the old saying goes, far too many think that revising means "copying over in ink." Actually, today, they are more likely to see it as running a grammar and spell check on the computer and then printing out a final draft. A process approach requires that students see revision as a comprehensive step in writing in which they ensure that their words say what they mean.

To revise comprehensively means to consider both global and local matters. The writer engaged in global revision considers the larger issues of purpose, audience, and overall essay structure–does the essay reveal a purpose shaped for a particular audience and then structured to reveal that purpose effectively? The writer who engages in local revision attends to smaller (but still important) matters such as individual sentence structure and word choice–how effectively does each sentence work to develop the purpose; does each word convey the writer's intended meaning as effectively as possible? Chapter 3 offers a number of global and local revision strategies, providing a series of questions the writer may ask as she considers the effectiveness of her essay.

And here we need to say a word about editing. In *The Longwood Guide to Writing*, we make a distinction between revising and editing, focusing on editing as the last step in the process, one in which the writer runs the grammar and spell checks and corrects punctuation errors before printing a final draft. For too many students, editing passes for revision. But revision entails far more than correcting surface errors.

## Common Concerns in Process Teaching

Teachers unfamiliar with a process approach to composing sometimes have some concerns about teaching writing as process. Among the issues that must be dealt with before a process approach to writing can be successful are the following:

- managing the paper load,
- training students to read each others' writing,
- helping students to become independent writers, and
- fighting grade inflation.

*Managing the Paper Load.* A process approach necessarily entails a lot of writing. As we've said above, students should write every day, both in and out of class. But this produces a lot of writing from each student, and teachers are right to be concerned about managing the paper load. Of course the instructor need not grade all of this writing. Much of the prewriting and drafting that a student does in the process of producing an essay may be marked by means of a system of checks, with pluses and minuses.

Students may balk at having to submit work that won't directly receive either a grade or a teacher's comments. However, you should insist that students submit all stages in their writing processes in the folder with the final draft of the essay. Without evidence of prewriting, drafting, and revising, the paper should be considered incomplete. We count such evidence of process as a significant portion of the students' final grade; thus, if they don't submit an entire package, their overall grade will be significantly lowered.

As the sample syllabi in this guide make clear, we also envision a class in which students complete many exercises. Not all of these exercises, however, need to be read and responded to by the teacher. Instead, these pieces of writing can receive credit toward overall course requirements without being given specific response or grade. Here's one way that this can work: Require students to complete an exercise in, say, clustering, and make that exercise their "ticket" into the next class meeting. Bill has even made it a point to stand at the doorway to his classroom and check off those students who have the completed assignment with them, just to emphasize the importance of completing such assignments. Of course, Bill doesn't deny a student who hasn't completed the assignment admission to class, but that student knows that she now has an incomplete grade for that day's work. Assign a threshold percentage for completing such exercises: e.g., in order to receive an A in the course, a student must complete 90 percent of these exercises; a B, 80 percent; a C, 70 percent, and so on. Students then see that these assignments count. Of course, a certain number of these will have to be read to ensure that students take them seriously, but that number can be relatively small.

***Training Students to Read Each Others' Papers.*** Another way that teachers can manage the paper load is to enlist students as readers of each others' papers. But there is a much more important reason for having students undertake this task: they will make significant improvements in their own writing processes (and hence in their writing) as they develop the ability to analyze and judge writing.

Our students are quick to tell us that they don't know how to evaluate their peers' work. And for the most part, they're right. Just as they need instruction in writing effectively, they need instruction in responding effectively. We offer this instruction in two ways: we train them to take part in *Group Peer Reviews,* and we train them to perform individual *Peer Critiques.*

*Group Peer Reviews.* Training in peer group reviewing comes early in the semester. We begin with what Beverly Varnado (a teacher at Wando High School) calls a "Fish Bowl" session. This session is designed to help students prepare to work with one another in group critiquing situations. Here is Ron's description of the way he runs this session.

> Early in the semester, we dedicate a day to a practice critique of a student paper, usually one from my files. On that day, we ask for three or four volunteers to be in the "Fish Bowl." The volunteers come to the front of the room, or if possible, I arrange chairs so that the critique group sits surrounded by the class. One member of the group takes on the role of the writer of the paper, though she has never seen the paper before. She then reads the paper to the other members of the group. While she reads, the other members listen silently. Then, she slowly reads the paper a second time. This time, the members of the writing group may take notes about issues that catch their attention in the paper. [Note: they may or may not have copies of the paper themselves.] When the second reading is completed, the person playing the role of the writer allows some time (a couple of minutes) to pass while members of the group continue their thinking and note taking. Then the student playing the role of writer opens by saying what she likes best about the paper at this point. She then points to any issue in the paper that is particularly in need of work. [Note: it is very important to have an imaginative student playing the role of this writer. Be ready to help your "writer" if you need to.] After she makes these comments, other members of the group may speak. But the words of the first speaker must be words of encouragement. What works in the paper? What does this reviewer particularly like in the paper? Then the members of the group will continue to critique the paper, following the general rule that every comment must be intended to help the "writer" make her paper better and no comment may be intended to hurt or demean the writer.
>
> If you are fortunate, you will have to "muzzle" the rest of your class while this is going on. Watching from the sidelines, they will probably want very much to get in on the discussion. Hold them off until the critique session has run its course. Then, open the discussion up to the class with this

general question: what did you learn about critiquing from this exercise? You should find that they learn a great deal. At the end of the period, wrap up the discussion by drawing their attention to principal characteristics of successful group critique sessions.

Once students see this kind of group in action and have time to talk about critiquing, they are more ready to begin functioning as a member of such a group. The "Fish Bowl" usually happens just before a draft of the first essay is due. When that paper is submitted, peer groups are formed, and peer group reviews are undertaken. These occur throughout the semester. (For more information on Group Peer Reviews, see the sample syllabi in this manual.)

*Peer Critiques.* A second method of peer review is the peer critique. In this system, students exchange papers and critique each other's work In preparation for this process, students are given practice in using peer critique sheets that focus their attention on certain aspects of an essay. A critique sheet carries instructions for reviewers to follow for reading their peers' essays. Here's an example that Bill uses in his writing classes:

> Follow these instructions in reviewing the essays from your group members: (1) Before you read any essays, read the questions below. (2) Read each essay through once without marking anything. (3) Read the essay again, this time marking places in the paper that you think are strong and that you think need work. (4) Using the markings from #3 as a guide, respond in writing to the questions below. (5) Talk about your reading of the essay with its author.
>
> Above all else, remember the Golden Rule of Peer Review: Nobody says or does anything willfully mean.

The Golden Rule is crucial if peer critiques are to work. In learning to follow it, students must hone their ability to differentiate constructive from potentially damaging criticism. Students can handle constructive criticism; in fact, one of the common complaints from students engaged in peer review early in the semester is that their group members are "too nice" or "too easy" in their reading. This problem, we have learned, decreases over the course of the semester; just as student writing improves with practice, so does student response. What students should not have to handle is the occasional snide or churlish comment. If you find that such comments are at work in a given group and that the students themselves haven't been able to eliminate them, you'll need to confront the student who's making such remarks and tell him these comments are inappropriate.

In *The Longwood Guide to Writing*, a critique sheet or set of questions for review appears at the end of each of the writing occasion chapters (5-11) and at the end of Chapter 12, Researching and Writing. In addition, Chapter 3, Revision, contains a number of questions that you may use as part of a critique sheet for your students, and it offers some discussion of group procedures. (For additional information on using critiques, see "Planned Spontaneity and a Passel of Other Paradoxes" in this manual.)

***Helping Students to Become Independent Writers.*** Anyone who has used peer groups is aware that the same paper may receive advice that is absolutely contradictory from two different readers. Now, such advice isn't necessarily the problem that it may seem, for at least two reasons. First, receiving contradictory advice should suggest to the writer that different readers read differently, and that she will have to consider her audience carefully as she attempts to fit her topic and her language to her reader. Second, contradictory advice provides you the opportunity to talk about ownership of a piece of writing. Final responsibility for every aspect of a piece of writing lies with the writer, not her review group. On receiving contradictory pieces of advice, the writer must make a decision whether to follow one piece of advice or the other, or perhaps neither. Learning to make these decisions requires the writer to consider whether the section of the paper in question truly represents her understanding of her topic and of her reader. As they gain more experience in making these decisions, students tend to become more confident writers.

Some teachers may think that use of peer groups can cause students to become too dependent on peer advice to shape, and especially to edit, their writing. Teachers sometimes wonder how much credit for a finished product is due the student and how much is due the members of the writing group. Our response here is that we've found that peer groups tend not to assume ownership of a given group member's writing. The reviewers in the group will comment in response to critique sheets, and they'll make specific suggestions for strengthening the writing, but they won't write the paper for another student. They have only a limited amount of time for in-class review, and they have their own writing to revise following a review session. Further, we've found that the more experience students have in reading each other's papers, the better they become at reading their own, and the better their writing tends to be. Obviously, peer review will not solve all problems students have with their writing. However, it can help them become more independent by providing them a relatively safe environment in which to share their writing with a real audience.

*Fighting Grade Inflation.* This last concern is connected to the previous one, but the two are not exactly the same. Even when teachers feel that students are composing their own work, they often feel that a process approach traps them into a situation in which most students revise their work to the A or at least the B level. Further, writing teachers need to offer their students as much encouragement as possible, so that they don't become frustrated and assume that they can't write. Grades have been used to encourage students, and we've heard it said that good grades serve as a carrot and thus bolster student confidence, while bad grades reinforce the student's belief that he can't write.

One way to begin dealing with this issue is to have a class discussion of how you'll evaluate their writing. Bill begins focusing his students on evaluation on the first day of class by having them write in response to this question: "What is good writing?" Either in a paragraph or in a list, students define good writing. After they've written, Bill asks his students to read from their response, and he lists their comments on the board, commenting frequently on those he thinks most important. At the end of this session, he has his students copy the notes on the board and place them in their writer's notebook (also called a learning log or journal). When students ask–and invariably they do ask–how he arrived at a particular evaluation, Bill reminds them of the group definition of good writing and turns the question back on the student by asking, "How does this essay fit with our definition of good writing?" Oftentimes, students see where their writing worked and where it didn't, but at other times, they don't. And here you'll have to hold your ground. Even though you have made a very clear case for your assessment that the essay is ineffective, the student may still not agree. She spent a lot of time on the paper, she'll say, and tried really hard, and just doesn't understand why you can't see that. This indicates a confusion on the part of the student between effort and performance, and it may be that she'll never accept your opinion. All we can say is that you'll have to stand on your experience and training and hold your ground.

It is unfair to the student to do otherwise. If a writer leaves our class with an inflated sense of his writing ability, he may well be disillusioned when his next writing teacher, or a teacher in another discipline, gives a more realistic appraisal of his work. Giving high grades simply to make student writers feel good about themselves as writers is an invitation to criticism from many sectors, from a university's administrators to the general public.

But just how can you devise a system that will allow for an accurate assessment of students' writing abilities? If one of the major goals of a process approach is to help students become independent writers–and we contend that it should be–then students need to demonstrate the degree to which they've achieved this independence. We offer students two opportunities to do so.

The first comes through the portfolio we require near the semester's end. As we explain in Chapter 14 of *The Longwood Guide to Writing*, we require students to write an in-depth self-assessment as a major part of their portfolio. Allowing students to build a portfolio in the course of the semester does much to help them see their writing as continually evolving. It is important, however, as you design the portfolio, that you guard against some possible pitfalls. If grading is an issue in your teaching, you will want to consider the effect of the portfolio on how you grade. You may find yourself in trouble, as we have, if you put too much of the semester's grade on the portfolio. There is a tendency to do so when you and the students think of the portfolio as the goal toward which you are working. If a disproportionate percentage of the grade is given to the portfolio, students will have a tendency to give less attention to earlier drafts and to other activities in the classroom. At present, both of us assign 25 percent of the student's overall grade to the portfolio, which leaves a good bit of the grade to be earned from other activities.

As we also explain in Chapter 14, an important element in our portfolio is the reflective essay. A major factor in our assessment of the student's portfolio is his own assessment of his writing. We want to see how well he can describe and illustrate (from his work) what his strengths and weaknesses as a writer were at the beginning of the semester and what his progress as a writer has been during the course. Since we grade portfolios holistically, there is work for all students to do at this stage of the course. Even those students who have written papers that received A's when they were turned in must revise these papers and use them as evidence in their reflective essays. We continually make the point that A does not mean perfect, that writing can always be improved. And even if these papers were perfect and the student did a half-hearted reflective essay, he would not receive an A on his portfolio. As a rule, one does not have to worry about such matters; students who write A papers generally perform well on the portfolio assignment, but we like the fact that this system leaves us latitude for dealing with the atypical situations.

Second, we require a final examination. Yes, that's right–a final examination in a writing class. This exam focuses on the student's abilities as a reader and reviewer of writing. As we suggested above, the better students become at reading someone else's writing, the better readers they become of their own writing, and the better their writing becomes. This exam is a natural outgrowth of the emphasis on reading and on peer reviews in our writing classes.

As we noted above, most students enter our classes with little ability to read and critique writing–their own, or that of others. Much of our teaching practice, and thus much of the material in *The Longwood Guide to Writing*, is designed to help students improve their reading skills. For example, consider Chapter 4, Responding to Readings, with its exercises designed to help students develop their reading skills. Or consider the readings included at the beginning of each of the chapters in part 2, *Writing Occasions*. Another important component in our reading instruction is peer review. Every final draft of a major essay must include a critique written by another member of the class. At first, many students insist that they are not capable of giving helpful advice to their classmates. We assure them that they will learn to do so, and we tell them that a major part of their grade for the course will be determined by the skill they develop in evaluating each other's writing. Our tactic is first to convince students that they should learn these skills and then to provide them with the tools they will need to do so.

Unfortunately, we have been forced to rely on the grade as stick to convince students to work on these skills. For many years, we encouraged students to refine their critiquing skills in an atmosphere in which all evaluation centered on their own writing. We found that some students came with the ability to critique (usually our better writers) but that most were inexperienced. With no overt incentives in the system, we didn't have much success in helping students develop their reviewing skills.

In our current system, students are told near the beginning of the class that there will be a final exam in which they will critique a piece of writing. We explain to our students that we are convinced that their development as writers is directly connected to their development as readers of writing. We then chart a course that will result in their developing these reading skills, a course that includes guidelines for reviewing and much practice in responding to each other's writing.

The guidelines for reviewing come in the form of critique sheets that ask students to respond to specific questions about the writing at hand and those questions are reflective of the overall purpose of the type of essay being written. We begin by modeling critiques using sample essays that we bring to class as the basis for critique sessions. One student may argue for her claim that there is an effective thesis in a paper, while another student argues for his claim that there isn't. The members of the class will usually work toward consensus on such issues without a great deal of input from us, but we offer guidance as necessary. After students have received such instruction, they then move on to critique their classmates' papers. This process begins with group critiques.

Ron describes his experience with critiques this way:

> Early in the term, I introduce students to group critiquing.[For more information on this process, see "Planning for Spontaneity in the Writing Classroom and a Passel of Other Paradoxes," below.] At the rough draft stage, students bring copies of their drafts to class and critique one another's papers in small groups. These group critiques occur at one of the drafting stages for most of the papers written in the class.
>
> By the time we get to the second formal paper in the course, students should be ready to undertake a written critique of a classmate's essay. The process works something like this. Students write a first rough draft of their paper, which receives feedback in a group critique session. The student then revises and brings a second draft, with a copy to be critiqued, to class. At that stage, the paper is given to a classmate for critiquing. The paper and the critique are returned to the student writer in the next class meeting, and the writer then revises her paper, using whatever she finds to be helpful in the critique–and disregarding the rest. When she submits the final draft of the essay, she also submits all other drafts of the paper, along with the critique she received from her classmate. As I read the paper, I also read and evaluate the critique of that paper. Critiques receive an S (for satisfactory) and S+ or an S-. An S does not affect a student's grade. An S+ raises the grade a student receives on his own paper by one step (e.g., a B+ becomes an A-), and an S- lowers the grade on his paper by one step (e.g., a B- becomes a C+).
>
> These critique grades are based on my sense of whether the student is interacting with the paper he has critiqued in productive ways. The question is not whether the advice offered is advice I might have offered, but whether it shows an ability to read and diagnose this paper, given the writer's overall purpose and audience, which should have been made clear to the reader. If readers receive S- on their critiques, I expect them to spend time working on their abilities in this area, just as they would work on their own writing if they were receiving low marks on their essays. I continually remind students that improvement in their own writing is tied to their improving abilities to diagnose the writing of their classmates. And if this goal is a bit too abstract for them, I remind them that the final examination, which usually counts 20 percent of their final grade in the class, will consist in large part of an essay that they must critique. [Note: these final critiques usually take the form of a letter to the writer. As we get more and more skill in critiquing, I move away from formal critique sheets and give students the freedom to write letters in which they discuss their essays with one another. By using the letter format on the exam, I am able to include the important element of tone; students must find a way to tell the writer how to improve his paper in a tone that will allow the writer to accept their advice.]
>
> I should also mention that my final exam includes a section from a paper that is to be edited. That is, the student must correct various surface errors in a text. I encourage students to develop their abilities to edit throughout the semester, and I let them know that a portion of the final exam will test this ability. I mention this here because far too many students (and some teachers, I fear) have misheard what many of us say about editing. We insist that students should not concern themselves with editing until very late in the writing process–for very good reasons. First, we can't edit words and

sentences until we arrive at the words and sentences we want to include in our paper. Second, attention to editing in the early stages can get in the way of more global issues such as development and organization. However, none of this should suggest that editing is unimportant. As one of my own teachers put it: editing is absolutely trivial and absolutely essential.

## *Making Process Work*

We began this essay by suggesting that not everyone who claims to be teaching writing as process is doing so. Our essay has been both an explanation of why we would make such an assertion and an exhortation that we should all return to the basic principles of process instruction.

What exactly are those principles? We have attempted to capture them in our discussion of invention, drafting, responding, and revising. As we indicated above, there is a sense in which our terms–invention, drafting, and revising–could be seen as different words for an old concept–the concept that the writing process can be divided into prewriting, writing, and rewriting. As we have explained, we mean something much more complex by our terms than what many people have come to take these terms to mean. But how do we actually bring this more complicated understanding to bear in writing instruction? For us, response is the key. We use various strategies to help students develop their abilities to respond to others' writing and learn how to use the responses they receive from others, with the goal of helping them develop more and more insight into writing as a process and, more importantly, into their own writing processes.

Ron and Bill

# Giving Feedback to Student Writers: Marking, Evaluating, and Responding

Marking, evaluating, responding–these terms are often used as though they're interchangeable, but they're not. It's important that you and your students understand which of these activities you're involved in at any given time, and why.

## Marking

This term probably dates us. When we were students and even beginning instructors of writing, we often heard teachers talk about marking student papers. At times, this word referred to grading; teachers assigned marks or grades to their students' papers. At other times, it was used to indicate the corrections that teachers made on student papers, e.g., the marking of such grammatical problems as comma splices and such mechanical problems as incorrect spelling and faulty punctuation.

While few teachers talk about marking these days, most of us still do it. That is, we still put marks on papers. Some teachers, however, have come to take the student's ownership of her paper so seriously and so literally that they will not put marks on student papers. These teachers often write comments to their students on separate paper, leaving student essays unmarked. Our own experience suggests that students do not mind having marks put on their texts; in fact, some do not feel that their writing has received proper attention if it lacks these marks. We have also found that many students react to word processed comments as too formal and somewhat off-putting. So both of us continue to place marks on our students' papers.

We do believe, however, that you should be very purposeful in putting marks on students' papers and that you should avoid falling into the habit of over-marking. We have all heard stories told by students who receive papers back with every error meticulously noted, most often in red ink, so many that they cannot see their own writing. Students often feel defeated by such over-marking. They might have attended to a smaller number of marks, had the teacher taken the time to decide which marks were most important. However, they cannot (or will not) trudge through all the marks they find on their papers, so they give up and disregard all of the teacher's advice.

Below we offer four general principles that we have found helpful in marking student essays:

**1. Limit the number of marks you place on student papers.**

At some point, the time and effort you put into marking a student's paper will produce diminishing returns. Many students are less-than-confident writers, and seeing a paper with absolutely every error marked can be very discouraging. And it isn't necessary. The student is much more likely to absorb what we say if we limit ourselves to one or two major errors at a time. If, for example, a student has problems with sentence boundaries and so creates comma splices, run on sentences, and sentence fragments, then concentrate only on this kind of error. In a given paper, the student may have fifteen or twenty instances of sentence boundary errors. It may be best, in a situation like this, to focus only on these errors and to help your student see them not as fifteen to twenty errors but as one error that's been repeated a number of times.

If you don't mark all of the possible errors in a given paper, you'll need a tracking system, so that you know which errors you've identified for the student to be working on. One way to do this is for your students to maintain a writing folder in which they place everything–all prewriting, drafting, reviewed drafts, final drafts, and revisions. Inside the front cover of the folder, have them keep a summary sheet on which they chart the particular error with which they're working, noting an example from their writing and a correction of it. In this way, they'll build a personal grammar or spelling log, and you'll have a record of their progress with grammar and mechanics. Be sure students understand your marking system and that they do not assume that anything not marked is necessarily correct.

**2. Be sure your students know what your marks mean and refer to.**

If you use fairly standard editing abbreviations such as "awk" (awkward) "frag" (sentence fragment), and "cs" (comma splice), be sure to explain to your students what they mean. Either prepare a handout or point to a printed chart for this explanation (see the inside back cover of *The Longwood Guide to Writing* for such a chart).

Be sure that students have the context necessary to understand your marks. Teachers all too often write such a comment as "interesting" or "vague" in the margins of a paper, leaving the student to wonder exactly which word or idea is interesting. It's more than a little ironic for a teacher to tell a student that something is vague and leave the student wondering just what the teacher is referring to. We often place brackets around a sentence and then write in the margins such a comment as: "This sentence confuses me." Other times we will underline a word and place a comment such as "Good word choice" in the margin beside it.

**3. Be sure students can read your handwriting.**

When students receive feedback on their writing and especially when they're receiving word that their writing needs work, there is enough tension in the situation without creating more by making the student struggle to decipher your handwriting. If your handwriting is just not readable, consider keyboarding your end comments. There are a good many word processing programs available now that will even allow you to write marginalia on a draft submitted. If you don't have one of these, consider using some type of numbering system so that your typewritten comments are matched with the appropriate places in the student's text.

**4. Lose the red pen**.

Teachers use red ink to draw immediate attention to errors, and it is highly visible. But we find that students have too many negative associations with the red pen for us to want to use it, so, long ago, we gave up our red pens. Ron uses a pencil since it allows him to readily edit his comments once he sees them on student papers. Bill uses his favorite black ink ballpoint pen, simply because it's more comfortable for him.

## *Evaluating*

Why is evaluation such an integral part of the teaching of writing? One answer lies in the tradition of composition instruction. Through many years of education, students have been conditioned to think that they need not take anything seriously that won't be evaluated. Many teachers and students, as well, have expressed the opinion that students just will not work without that all-important carrot of a grade to encourage them. Whether this rather negative incentive for evaluation is warranted or not, there is a more basic reason for evaluation: writing programs require it. In most teaching situations, we must play two very different roles: coach and judge. And it is the judging that can cause difficulty.

## Basic Issues in Evaluation

***Subjectivity in Grading.*** The subjective nature of grades seems to cause more problems in writing courses than in any others. Even though our judgments are clearly subjective, we as writing teachers should not accept the implication that subjectivity and arbitrariness are synonymous; they are not. All testing and grading involve subjectivity. As a case in point, consider mathematics courses. Most students believe the grading in mathematics courses to be objective, but where is the objectivity in the teacher's decision of how many problems a typical mathematics student should be asked to solve in a testing period? Where is the objectivity in the decision to give partial credit on problems and just how much credit to allow? Where is the objectivity in the mathematics teacher's decision either to adhere rigidly to a standard ten-point scale or to curve grades according to student performance? As another case in point, consider the large number of multiple choice history or social science tests that ask students to choose the best answer from four potentially correct choices. How can the "most correct" answer be decided objectively?

It should be obvious, then, that there is subjectivity in testing in any discipline. However, since math grades and scores on multiple choice tests are usually rendered in numbers that seem to result logically from the numbers assigned to the various parts of the tests, these grades take on an aura of objectivity. All teachers, including those of us who teach writing, should be willing to accept the burden of subjective grading. As writing teachers, we should not accept the implication that we are somehow different because of the subjectivity involved in our evaluation, and we should insist upon a distinction between subjectivity and arbitrariness. Good teachers are not arbitrary in the judgments they make. Just as the math teacher bases his decision about the number of problems to assign in a testing period on his expertise in teaching math, the composition teacher's evaluations of writing are based upon her expertise in teaching writing.

***Skill vs. Art.*** In evaluating writing, it is crucial that you determine when you are assessing skills and when you are judging art. There are many skills necessary in successful writing. The writer must know how to spell, how to punctuate, how to show relationships between sentences, how to order a paragraph around an idea, and so forth. However, there is more to good writing than mastery of such skills. Good writers know how to use these skills to shape an idea for a purpose and an audience. An essay may be grammatically and mechanically correct without being good. If the writer fails to develop significance in his writing or if he fails to present his thoughts with a sense of style appropriate for his purpose and audience, the essay's correctness cannot compensate for that essay's sterility. The art of writing simply cannot be reduced to rote mastery of a set of mechanical skills.

***Performance vs. Practice.*** A writing course requires that students do a great deal of practicing and a certain amount of performing. Another way of putting this is to say that your students will complete exercises in response to prompts in the textbook; they will do practice freewrites in and out of class; they will critique each others' papers in class; they will discuss elements of good writing, and so forth. These are all a part of the practice that is necessary if they are to improve their writing. But they will also write final drafts of their papers. These final drafts constitute their performances in your class. An analogy that comes to mind is the difference between the practice sessions and the games (the performances) for a member of a basketball team.

## Designing An Evaluation System

Once we have identified these basic issues, we are in position to explore three decisions you should make as you design your evaluation scheme.

**1. Decide what minimum skills are required in order for a student to pass your course.**

You may wish to stipulate that a student must demonstrate in performances a certain level of skill in matters of usage and mechanics. We recommend that you deal with these issues on a pass/fail basis. That is, if a student fails to meet any of these requirements, he is not eligible for a passing grade of any sort. If he meets these requirements, then he is eligible.

Depending on your teaching situation, you may have some students who come to your class lacking basic skills of writing. This has been the case for us at varying points, and we have always attempted to meet students where they are and offer them ways of achieving the standards set in our classes. In many cases that has involved meeting with students one on one, encouraging students to work with each other out of class in peer group sessions and to avail themselves of the resources available in our writing centers and learning centers.

## 2. Decide what portion of your evaluation will be based on performance and what portion on practice.

Your students will write a number of papers during the course of the semester. No doubt many of those assignments will include prewriting, focus statements, rough drafts, as well as final drafts. We consider the final draft a performance. The other parts of the writing process would be considered practice. And there are very many other types of practice in a writing course. For example, students will complete exercises in response to prompts in the text; they'll do in-class critiques of each others' writing; they'll take part in discussions of readings and of principles of writing. How will your overall evaluation take into account their performances and their practices? Finding the right balance here is difficult, but important. We want to reward students for the kind of practice that we know will pay off in the long run. But we do not want students receiving A's in our courses when their writing is clearly below average as reflected in their performances. Again, a sports analogy might help. If a coach were required to give grades to the members of her basketball team, she might establish the following grading criteria:

A = Attendance at 90% of practices
An outstanding rating on practice sessions
Playing in at least 50% of the games

B = Attendance at 90% of practices
A good rating on practice sessions
Playing in at least 25% of the games

C = Attendance at 90% of practices
A good rating on practice sessions

D = Attendance at 80% of practices
A satisfactory rating on practice sessions

Note that the coach is making attendance at 80 percent of the practices a requirement for receiving a passing grade. If a player wants a C or better, she must attend 90 percent of the practices. Note also that the coach is requiring some success in performance in order to receive above a C. If the player does not succeed in developing her abilities to a level at which she can receive minimal playing time, then she may not receive above a C, even though she may have perfect attendance at practices and even though she may have received an "outstanding" rating on her practice sessions.

The analogy with composition grades should be clear. We want our system to allow students to receive passing marks if they achieve a certain level of skill and if they perform the minimum amount of practice requirements. However, we are not comfortable assigning A's and B's to students who are unable to perform at a certain level. Thus, if the student wishes to earn an A or a B, he must achieve increasingly high marks on both practice and performance.

There are, to be sure, problems with this analogy. To begin with, our coach, with only so many minutes of playing time to give out, would immediately set up a competitive situation–players would vie with each other for a limited amount of playing time. But we do not have to bring that part of the equation to the writing classroom. Unlike playing time, there is an unlimited supply of high marks, so students would not compete against each other for them. But, it might be argued, some students are not going to be capable (given their inherent abilities) to achieve A's and B's in such a system. That's true. Not every student will be an A or even a B writer. We think it odd that students understand that no amount of practice and effort will allow them to excel in certain sports but expect that effort and practice will result in excellence in any academic area, or if not in excellence in high grades. (We are indebted to Ron's colleague Tony Jackson for this analogy.)

**3. Decide upon a set of grading criteria to use in evaluating student performances.**

As we have already established, evaluating writing (like evaluating any art) is subjective. Don't apologize for the subjective nature of your evaluation. However, you should attempt to give your students some insight into your process of evaluation. That means breaking what is essentially a holistic rating into its components. If you do not have a system already in place, we recommend the following components: Content, Organization, Style, Mechanics. You may even want to go so far as to estimate the percentage of your overall grade assigned to each element. A fairly common system is the following:

| | |
|---|---|
| Content | 30% |
| Organization | 30% |
| Style | 20% |
| Mechanics | 20% |

You can explain this system easily in terms of the rhetorical triangle used in *The Longwood Guide to Writing*. That is, in judging a piece of writing, begin by asking whether the content, organization, and style of that writing are appropriate for the aim the writer has chosen. Note also that this system factors a skill element (mechanics) into the overall evaluation. That does not prevent you from requiring a certain level of skill for a passing grade. Once you have determined that this basic requirement has been met, you can evaluate the degree to which the writing moves beyond the minimum standard and assign an appropriate grade for skill. Finally, it is worth noting that this system assumes a standard against which an individual student's performance is measured. This standard exists in the teacher's mind and has been formed by means of experience. If your experience is limited, you may want to consult with experienced teachers to refine your sense of what constitutes an excellent, average, or below average performance.

**Sample Evaluation Scheme**

Below is an excerpt from a syllabus that Ron used in a first-year writing course in the fall of 1997.

English 1103: Composition
Lunsford
Fall, 1997

***Requirements:***

**Formal Essays:** You will write six papers (of 1,000 to 1,250 words each). Assignments will be provided at a later date. (30% of grade)

**A Word About Correctness:** Correctness is at once absolutely trivial and absolutely essential. I do not want you to concern yourself with correctness in the early stages of your writing, where your ideas should be the focus of attention. However, at the final draft stage, it is essential that papers be essentially free of errors. This is not to say that some misspelling will not slip by you or that some comma may not get in the wrong place. But when that happens, it should stand out as a slip. If errors seem to be the rule rather than the exception, your paper (no matter how proficient otherwise) will receive a "U."

**Portfolio:** You will submit a portfolio at the end of the semester, with two revisions of the formal essays listed above. The portfolio will also include a reflective essay (1000 to 1500 words in length) in which you discuss your progress as a writer in this course. (25% of grade)

**Weekly Writing Assignments:** During most of our class meetings, you will write a brief essay response to one or more of the assigned readings for that class meeting. (Average grade of these writings will count as 15% of class grade.)

**Writer's Notebook:** Your writer's notebook will contain your reactions to our assigned readings, your reflections on each essay that you write (and on comments you receive from classmates and me), and any other incidental writing you do for this class. (15% of grade)

**Final Examination:** The final examination will be a writing assignment designed to allow you to draw together the various threads of this course. It will be done in class during our assigned examination period. (15% of grade)

*Policy Statements*

**Absences:** Since writing is a communal activity, it is essential that we all be a part of the community. I will expect you to attend all class meetings. Should you miss more than two class meetings without a compelling reason, your final grade will be lowered by one letter. Should you miss more than three meetings, you will not pass the course. Tardies will count as portions of an absence, according to the degree of tardiness.

**Due Dates:** Papers will be due at the beginning of the designated class period. Failure to have a rough draft at the appropriate time will result in a penalty of one letter grade on the final paper. Late papers will be penalized one letter grade for each day they are late (unless you have explained the problem to my satisfaction before the due date.) All assigned papers must be turned in to receive a passing grade for the course.

As suggested above, this syllabus, requires a student to demonstrate a minimum level of skill if he is to receive a passing grade. The statement on correctness is actually taken from a separate sheet on which Ron gives students basic information about his grading practices.

A certain amount of practice is also required. Ron doesn't mention on the syllabus the fact that each of the formal papers will be part of a process, but in class he instructs students on the various stages of the writing process that they will practice in arriving at the final papers.

Two other types of practice–weekly writing assignments and the Writer's Notebook–account for 30 percent of the course grade. Students make high grades on these assignments if they read the assignments and attend to the directions.

The Portfolio, which accounts for 25 percent of the grade, is divided fairly equally between practice and performance. Ron grades the portfolio holistically, but attempts to give equal weight to the quality of the writing in the reflective essay and the quality of work in the revised essays (performance) on the one hand and the insights the writer has gleaned about her progress as a writer (practice) on the other.

Finally, the formal essays and the final examination are chiefly performance grades–constituting 45 percent of the student's grade.

In sum then, Ron's system would be analyzable as follows: Nearly 40 percent of the total grade is based on practice and slightly less than 60 percent is based on performance.

Your system may surely differ, but it will be most helpful if you have articulated what you see as skill requirements and what percentages of your grade are dedicated to practice and performance.

**Evaluation–Final Thoughts**

Evaluation is necessary and important, but it should not assume center stage. We give as little time to evaluation in a writing class as possible, preferring to find other methods of feedback. However, when we do evaluate, we attempt to achieve several goals. First, we want to be honest with our students. We want to let them know how much of our evaluation is based on performance and how we rate their performances. A second goal in evaluation is to have a system for making judgments that we can explain to students. In conference, we attempt to help students see their papers' successes and shortcomings through the lens of the rhetorical triangle, to consider how effectively they have communicated with their chosen readers. And finally, we wish to separate evaluation from the other roles we play as teachers of writing. We want to avoid using the comments on student papers as justifications of grades. Once students understand that we aren't defending (or writing a thesis and support paper for) our grades in comments, they can read them differently. That is, they can understand many of our comments as our part of an ongoing conversation with them about their writing–as we will explain more fully in the final section of this essay.

# *Responding*

We are careful to separate *responding* from *marking* and *evaluating* because we want to emphasize the conversational nature of response. Not every piece of student writing should receive a grade or even be marked. But all student writing should receive a response of some sort. Sometimes that response can be verbal instead of written, and sometimes it can come from a classmate rather than a teacher, from a tutor in a writing center, or from a roommate. But it should come. To write without response is to write in a vacuum.

In thinking about your interactions with student writers as responses, you free yourself from some of the constraints that might otherwise be there. If you are responding (rather than, or in addition to, evaluating), you may well share an experience of your own with a student in a comment such as: "I remember when I took my kids to Disney World" (written in the margins of a student paper about a family vacation). Such comments serve to keep the channel open between teacher and student in something of the same fashion that an "uh huh" does on a telephone. These channel clearers are absolutely necessary in conversation. If you doubt this, try listening to a speaker in a telephone conversation without offering any encouragement by way of channel clearers. See how long the person will talk before doing something to determine whether you're still there or still interested. Our students need to know that there is someone on the other end of this written conversation.

We have long since seen response as an important element in teacher feedback. That commitment has been corroborated by a study conducted by Ron and his co-author, Richard E. Straub (Florida State University). In *12 Readers Reading: Responding to College Student Writing*, Ron and Rick examine the responding practices of twelve well-known composition teachers and researchers. After analyzing the very many ways in which these teachers differ in their responding practices, Ron and Rick write a summary chapter in which they highlight common features of their responding practices, which we discuss below.

Ron and Rick found that the most important characteristic of their readers' comments is this: the teachers in the study see their responses to student writers as part of an ongoing conversation with students. In fact, the principles that follow (taken from chapter 5 of *12 Readers Reading*) all flow from this "conversational" view of response.

**Principle One: Write comments that are well-developed and text-specific.**

You should attempt to write full, understandable comments, even if that means you have to deal with fewer issues. Note how three responders develop their ideas in comments made in the margins of an essay to a student writer named Nancy.

- Not sure how you are interpreting LeMoult here. Does he blame "society"? Does he say that "society" is corrupt? (Richard Larson)

- You're beginning to respond to LeMoult's argument. What if you saved evaluative comments until later? How would this choice affect your argument? (Glynda Hull)

- This is in his 4th paragraph. What's he doing in the first 3 paragraphs? (Jane Peterson)

Each of these writers takes at least two sentences to respond to points that Nancy is making. Compare such comments as these to the kinds of marks teachers often put on student papers:

tone?
logic?
Society or certain persons in society?
Confusing!
Good idea!

In reading such cryptic comments as these, students may be able to deduce what the teacher means by studying the connections between their own texts and the comments in the margins. However, the students who need the advice the most will be those who have the most trouble understanding it.

A frequent problem with teachers' comments is that they are not text-specific. That is, the teacher doesn't make it clear just what part of the student's text is confusing or where the teacher sees a good idea. If you use one or two-word comments, be sure to do something to make the student know what, in the text, you are referring to. You may want to underline or circle certain words and draw lines from the word indicated to the comments in the margins that explain them.

**Principle Two: Emphasize global rather than local concerns.**

By global concerns we refer to such matters as Ideas, Global Structure, and Development as opposed to local concerns such as Sentence Structure, Wording and Mechanics. (See Chapter 3: Revision, for more information on these terms.) Below are examples of both types of comments:

Global Focuses

You have done a very good job of explaining your experience of being a leukemia patient. (ideas)

This is the kind of elaboration that helps me follow what you are saying. (development)

You might explain a bit more fully what this program is. (development)

Local Focuses

Needs more exact referent (word choice)

Consider reconstructing sentence. Can you see how? (sentence structure)

Check spelling (mechanics)

We are not suggesting that you ignore such local matters as these, but rather that you be sure that a sufficient number of your comments ask students to attend to global issues. Local matters are easy to spot, and it's easy to write comments about them. Global comments take more time, but they are crucial if students are going to do the kind of revising we present in Chapter 3. Especially in early drafts, our comments should draw students' attention to these larger issues.

**Principle Three: Leave as much control as possible in the hands of student writers.**

It is very tempting to fall into the role of editor when responding to student writing. When we make such comments as the following, we are really writing the student's paper for her:

Move this paragraph to the beginning of your essay.

This is your thesis sentence here; structure the rest of the paper around it.

I don't see what this adds to your argument; leave it out.

Such directive comments as these leave the student little room for input and tend to make revising an exercise in deciding how to give the teacher what she wants. In an effort to move away from such directive comments, many teachers have begun to fashion their comments in the form of questions. But questions don't always give the student a great deal of choice. Consider the following responses:

Do you really need this?

Why do you include this information about your childhood?

What is the person's name you're talking about here?

Such closed questions really have the effect of telling the student to do things to the text–in the first two cases to delete something and in the third to add something (the person's name). Compare these closed questions with the following open-ended ones:

How do you distinguish between morals and prejudices?

How do you think readers will respond to this choice?

What other details might help the reader understand the frustration you're feeling here?

In each case, the reader asks a question that leaves some choice and control in the hands of the student. Don't misunderstand us–we are not suggesting that you be disingenuous, but where possible, your comments should open up opportunities for students to develop their thinking and take control of their essays, rather than to close down and circumscribe what they may say in revision.

**Principle Four: Be selective and purposeful in the comments you make.**

Many teachers take a "scattergun" approach to responding to student writing. Their logic may well be that if they put enough comments on the student's paper, surely he will read some of them. We suspect, however, that just the opposite is true. The fewer the number of comments, the more likely the student will be to attend to them. This is certainly the philosophy of the teachers in the Straub and Lunsford study. That becomes clear in their reflections on their responses. Below are some observations they made after responding to a paper entitled "Leukemia":

> - I have purposely avoided any detailed analysis of the organizational and stylistic flaws–because one can overpower a student like this with too much correction. Let him deal with the problem of responding fully to the assignment first. (Donald Stewart)
>
> - The paper is, of course, filled with errors of all sorts. But there is no point in marking them, because the paper should not be edited; the writer missed the assignment almost entirely, and must rewrite an essay that fulfills the task. (Ed White)
>
> - The "I can imagine" note at the bottom of the first page is there to help the student see that I am thinking about the content, not just surface problems [. . .]. [H]e had so many errors in that first paragraph that I felt I needed something on that page to reassure him that I was listening. (Jane Peterson)

These teachers are clearly very purposeful in their responses to this paper. Rather than marking all errors, they take into consideration where the student is in his writing process and what kinds of information he can benefit from at this time. They also limit the number of concerns to three or four major issues, though these issues may be referred to in several different places in the student's text.

**Principle Five: Tailor your comments to the individual student and your developing sense of her abilities and needs.**

When you are faced with a large number of composition students and far too many essays to read, it is tempting to take a "new critical" approach to student papers and to respond only to the words in student texts. However, you know much more about your students than what you learn from any text, and you should not limit your responses to those texts. The best writing teachers tailor their comments to the individual needs of their students. What they would write to one student about a text is not necessarily what they would write to another, even if the two students had written identical texts. It is crucial, then, for teachers to know for whom they are writing.

We see how important this concept of the student behind the text is in the responses that the twelve teachers make to the hypothetical students in the Straub and Lunsford study. Even though these students were hypothetical to the twelve readers–that is, they had only the student texts and a brief summary about each writer–the teachers went on to invent a rich context in which they assumed a great deal of knowledge about each student. For example, there was one student who was called Nancy in the study. Peter Elbow's response to Nancy was given in the context of a student he imagined whose writing had put him off. He goes on to say that he would like to be honest with her about his response, but because he and Nancy have drifted into an adversarial relationship, he will write a comment that is "a kind of holding action, cop-out" and wait for a conference with her. Elbow notes that an important principle he has come to understand is that "whenever there is a contest as to whether or not the course will "reach" someone, the student can always win–always has the trump card" (Straub and Lunsford 34).

Chris Anson, however, imagined Nancy as a very different student. According to Anson, he first thought that Nancy was "very sure of herself, perhaps even stand-offish and overconfident." Anson found himself trying to challenge Nancy and being overly critical of her work. But now (at the time of his response) he has come to "recognize that her criticisms of the early work in the course, her argument that she has always done well in high school, and an air of superiority she carried into the conference groups [ . . . ] were really a mask for a fundamental lack of confidence, perhaps even a feeling of fear that she wouldn't be able to do well." Given this view of Nancy, Anson has decided to support her as much as possible, "using her expressed (if not actually felt) confidence in her favor" (Straub and Lunsford 372).

As you would expect, Anson and Elbow write very different responses to the same text. Their responses are very much influenced by their concept of the student behind the text.

## *To Mark? To Evaluate? To Respond?*

Writers–whether students writing to develop their skills, amateurs writing to satisfy a personal drive, or professionals writing to make a living–must have feedback; they need something coming back to them to indicate how well they are accomplishing the goal of communicating with an audience. That feedback can come from various sources, of course, but the two primary sources in a writing classroom are other students and the teacher. We have said a good deal about the type of feedback that can come from other students elsewhere in this manual–see "Planned Spontaneity and a Passel of Other Paradoxes," and "Teaching Writing As Process." Here we have focused on the three primary types of feedback that teachers provide: marking, evaluating, and responding. Each has its place in the teaching of writing: marking allows you to give students feedback on matters of usage and mechanics; evaluation allows you to give students feedback on how their work measures up against some standard of communication effectiveness; response allows you to converse with students about their work. We think most teachers tend to overuse marking and evaluating and to under-appreciate the role that responding can play in encouraging and empowering students' writing. We encourage you to make judicious use of all three types of feedback in your teaching.


Ron and Bill


Work Cited


Straub, Richard, and Ronald F. Lunsford. *12 Readers Reading: Responding to College Student Writing*. Cresskill, New Jersey: Hampton Press, 1995.

# *Planning for Spontaneity in the Writing Classroom and a Passel of Other Paradoxes*

Last semester one of my students produced a rough draft of an essay which began with the following paragraph:

> I am now a first year college student and throughout all of my school years I have witnessed, like any teenager, every kind, shape, and form of teacher possible. Some were terrible, most were mediocre, and then there are always the outstanding few, one of whom this paper is devoted. She was my twelfth grade English teacher. Her name was Mrs. Knapp and the course she taught was "Great Books." The way she taught was like no way that I had ever been subjected too. It was fantastic. I learned more in that one year course than any other class that I had taken.

After this draft was read and reviewed by one of his classmates, the student produced a final draft of the essay, which began as follows:

> "Hey all you schnerts out there, listen up!" she blared, "we need to get class started, so form a circle." This was a typical beginning of one of my favorite classes of all times. The course was "Great Books," taught by the fantastic Mrs. Knapp. Her method of teaching was like nothing I had ever been subjected to, yet it was wonderful. I am now a firm believer in her style of teaching because I learned more in that one course than in any other course I have ever taken.

The paper which followed this introduction was far from perfect. But it stands out in my mind as one of the best revisions I have seen in a writing class, and I am convinced that the paper's success can be traced to the role that peer-group critiques play in my writing course. These critiques do not work magically; the teacher must plan carefully before using them if they are to work.

I recently began a workshop for writing teachers by asking them to list all the problems they might encounter should they decide to use group critiques in their writing classes:

- Students can plagiarize from each other.
- Students can be too hard on one another's writing.
- Students can be too easy on one another's writing.
- Students can take bad advice from peers.
- Students can fail to heed helpful advice from peers.
- Students can dominate group sessions.
- Students can refuse to contribute in the sessions.

Given all of the ways in which group critiques can fail, it is not hard to see why many teachers either have never tried them or have given up on them after an initial unsuccessful attempt to use them. This is especially true for teachers new to the classroom. But there are those of us who continue to use groups year after year despite these potential problems. Why? And how have we reduced the risks involved?

We use groups to help students begin to view writing as a process because group work emphasizes revision. Whether the members of groups see a paper only once before it is turned in to the instructor or see it at two or more stages of development, the critique process suggests that writers must revise their pieces. Even if peers do not see the writing a second time, the teacher will see the draft that was submitted to peers and will compare it to the final draft. Thus, he can determine whether the final draft represents revision or recopying.

All too often, students confuse these two activities. Students may be required to submit a rough draft, but if no one responds to that draft, they can easily fall into the trap of editing–correcting only grammatical and mechanical errors–when they should be revising–rewriting to make meaning become clear. The peer group critique ensures that writers will get responses to their drafts, and these responses make it harder for them to see their task in producing a final draft as nothing more than "copying over in ink."

In addition to enabling us to focus on the writing process, peer groups allow us to engage students in their own learning. Students teach themselves as they teach their peers. I am convinced that there is a close relationship between being able to analyze the strengths and weaknesses of a piece of writing and being able to produce good writing. This is not to say that one's ability to write will always match her ability to analyze, but if a student continues to sharpen her analytical skills, her writing will improve as well.

Peer groups also allow weaker students to see the writing of their more able classmates. It is one thing for a teacher to tell a weaker student that his writing lacks development or voice. It is another for that student to see writing from his peers with that development and voice.

These are at least some of the benefits that group work can afford us–if the groups work. But the list of the potential problems above may well cause us to doubt that they will. They sound good in theory, but if the groups do not work in practice, we are right back where we started, or worse. The crucial question, then, is "How do we make them work?" As the title of this essay suggests, successful group work requires careful planning on the part of the teacher.

I suspect that many teachers miss this important principle because group work looks so effortless on the surface. When one first sees a successful peer group session, the process looks like magic. In one group, a student is telling another that a particular paragraph seems out of place. In another group, a student is asking a writer just how she wants to make her audience feel and then beginning to describe how he felt as he read the piece in question. In yet another group, a student is commenting that the connotation of a particular word does not seem appropriate and suggesting another word that the writer immediately recognizes as better. And the teacher observes, moving from group to group, serving as a consultant only when she is called upon.

In such a situation, an observer is likely to attribute the success of the groups to the excellence of the students rather than to any method employed by the teacher. Paradoxically, while all of this looks very spontaneous (and in one sense of the word, it is), the spontaneity is the result of the teacher's careful planning. Successful critique sessions do not just happen.

## *The All-Important Plan*

Below I will outline the method I use to prepare my students for group work. I would not expect anyone to follow my procedures slavishly; I have certainly adapted the critique plans of other teachers to suit my own style of teaching. Many different plans will work; the key is that there be a plan–that teachers spend time in preparing students for the task at hand.

Let me begin by giving an overview of my plan before discussing what I see as its most important elements. In a typical freshman course, I expect to receive seven or eight papers. One of these is usually a diagnostic paper, one is a final examination, and two or three are in-class writing assignments; thus, I have time for only three extended out-of-class writing assignments. In these assignments, students are required to follow a writing process that includes prewriting, a planning page, an audience analysis, a rough draft, and a final draft. Writing groups are used extensively throughout this process. Students meet in groups to discuss their topics while they are in the midst of prewriting for their papers; they also meet to discuss planning pages and audience analyses. When we reach the rough draft stage, however, the procedure changes somewhat.

The change at this stage is a recent development in my method. Before, I had assumed that as we worked our way through each assignment, every student had to present a draft of his paper to his writing group and receive feedback on it before producing a final draft. In order to complete these critiques, groups were limited to ten minutes per paper. This was simply not enough time for students to respond to one another's papers, but the only alternative involved spending what seemed an inordinate amount of time in the critiquing process.

I was struggling with this problem when I heard another writing teacher suggest that students did not have to receive group feedback on all of their papers. I immediately saw a solution to my problem. Since I require three long assignments, I divided each of my writing groups into thirds. A third of the group (usually two students) submits a draft of the paper in question to the group for review; a third submits a draft to me; and a third is given no formal review of that draft. This is not to suggest that members of this latter group cannot seek assistance if they want to, but the assumption is that they will benefit from the process of reviewing the papers of their peers. After all, if they cannot begin to apply the principles at work in groups to their own papers, the entire group process is questionable. The effect of this plan, then, is to provide students with a formal review at the draft stage of two of the three out-of-class assignments in the course.

Students are familiar with the procedures of this method, and they know well in advance what kinds of help they will receive in writing each paper. When a student is to receive a group critique of her paper, she brings a copy of her draft for each member of the group to the class. During the critique session, each paper is discussed for approximately thirty minutes. The writer begins by reading her paper aloud to the group. Then other group members offer suggestions for revision. They then take time to capture some of their thoughts on paper in response to questions on the critique sheet I provide for that purpose. (See the appendix for a sample critique sheet.) The writer then produces her final draft and submits to me all materials generated in the writing process, including the reviews she has received from group members.

This, then, is the procedure in rough form. As I mentioned above, certain key features warrant further discussion. Perhaps I should begin by commenting on the size of groups. An average-sized composition class of twenty-three to twenty-five students will consist of four groups of approximately six members each. These groups are larger than the ones I used when I assumed that all students had to receive critiques for each assignment. But the smaller groups were often ineffective. In a group of only three members, two of the three must be able to work effectively in group sessions if the group is to succeed, but in a group of six, two or even three weaker students do not necessarily prevent the group from functioning.

Once the groups are formed, students must be trained to critique papers. The training takes two forms in my class: one short-term and the other longer. Early on in the semester, I introduce students to peer critiques by having a selected group perform for the class in what we call a "Fish Bowl" experience. (I took both the term and the idea from Beverly Varnado, a teacher at Wando High School in Mt. Pleasant, South Carolina.) Before this session, I talk about the group-critique process with the students who are going to perform. We decide what paper will be reviewed. If one of them is working on an essay which he would like to use in the session, we critique that paper; if not, I will provide a paper from a previous class and ask one of the students to play the role of writer. In the "Fish Bowl" experience, the students in a featured group demonstrate the critiquing process for the rest of the class. The writer (or person playing the role of writer) reads the paper in question. Afterward, members of the group begin by pointing to the particular strengths of the paper. Then they offer suggestions as to how the paper might be made better. They point to passages that are unclear and/or to sentences that might be improved. They may even focus on individual word choices which could be better. After the group has completed its review of the paper, we discuss the critique process as a class, dealing with some of the problems that may arise.

The long-term training involves critique sheets I devise for each essay (see Appendix). In the class before a group critique, I introduce students to a critique sheet designed for that assignment by asking them to critique a draft that has been turned in to me. Remember that approximately a third of the students in the class will submit a draft of each out-of-class essay to me for review. Since these drafts are due at the class meeting before I introduce the critique sheet, I am able to read them and choose one that should prove particularly instructive to the class as a whole. At the beginning of this class meeting, I give all students a copy of the essay and the critique sheet we will use for this assignment. They spend half the period analyzing this sample essay as practice for the critiques they will do of papers by members of their writing groups. We then spend the second half of the class discussing this sample essay, paying particular attention to the kinds of comments that should prove most helpful to the writer in her revising process.

In directing this discussion, I attempt a difficult balancing act. I obviously know more about what makes for successful writing than the students do, but it is important for the students themselves to respond to the drafts we are examining. Therefore, I am as open as possible to the comments individual students make in response to this draft. If a student offers what I see as bad advice, I wait for other students to counter it. In the event that good advice is not forthcoming, however, I do offer my opinion and explain my reasons as best I can.

One final element of these sessions merits some explanation. I mentioned above that students begin critique sessions by reading their papers aloud. For a good many years, I used group critiques without insisting upon this practice. It might seem a small thing, but when I began to stipulate that papers be read aloud, the quality of critique sessions seemed to improve dramatically. I am convinced the improvement was at least in part due to this change. In part, I believe this is because writers develop a stronger sense of responsibility by reading aloud. Their papers cannot be dashed off, turned in to a teacher, and forgotten; students have to listen to their own papers as they read them. It is common for a student to stop in midsentence to exclaim: "This sentence is terrible!"

## *Results*

At the beginning of this essay, I offered a brief example of what can be accomplished in group critiques. Below I would like to offer a second example. The final draft is not particularly impressive, but the writer's process in producing it draft is. My point in presenting such an essay is to show the kinds of improvement even an average writer can make following peer review. The essay was written as a final examination for a freshman writing course. The writer was responding to a prompt that asked her to choose the best teacher she had ever had and to "show" why that teacher was excellent. She wrote a draft of her essay before coming to the final. During the first hour of the exam, she exchanged drafts with a class member, and they critiqued each other's work. Then, she produced her final draft in the remaining two hours of the examination period.

Draft (untitled)

The major purpose of teaching is to have the students learn. There are few teachers who have what it takes to be an effective teacher and can accomplish the goal of having students learn.

The teacher must first of all convince the students that he knows the material he is teaching, and earn their respect.

The bell rang for my 9:30 Physics class to begin. As Mr. Wilson walked in, a blanket of silence covered the room. The only noise to be heard was that of his heavy footsteps moving toward his desk. He spoke to that class and then began to lecture. This went on for about one week. It was his way of letting us know that he knew what he was doing and earning our respect.

Then he expressed what his objectives for the class were. They were to understand the basic principles (concepts) of physics, to develop an understanding of problem solving, to do our best and keep up. We accepted his goals and tried to work toward achieving them. He always made sure that he was getting his message across to us. One day class started as usual and Mr. Wilson decided to check everyone's homework. This was fine, but not very many people had theirs.

This got him slightly upset. He wrote these grades in his book. About a week later he checked homework again and everyone had it so the people who didn't have it the first time received credit and those who did received extra credit. This was his way of knowing that he had gotten his message across.

Also when lecturing, Mr. Wilson would use examples that were funny and related to our lives to communicate effectively with us.

Another one of his concerns was that all of his students had a reasonable understanding of the material. If he felt that your grades were not as high as they should be, he'd ask you to stay after school, otherwise, it was optional whether you stayed or not. Also, everyday, he'd review the previous days work and answer any questions we had.

To make Physics fun was a difficult task, I'm sure, but some days Mr. Wilson would have experiments set up for us to observe, participate in, and enjoy. Also, some days he would tell us about his adventures hiking in the mountains and caring for his honey bees.

Mr. Wilson was respected by his students and made them really want to learn. Although many students were intimidated by him, Mr. Wilson was an effective teacher to me. He kept me on my toes, provided me with the extra help I sometimes needed, and made physics interesting and fun to learn.

The author received the following response to her draft:

Dear [writer's first name]:

It seems that you have a good start on this paper, but you need to develop your ideas more. There are places that this paper has potential if the ideas were more detailed. I really like paragraph 3. The detail about the blanket of silence and the sounds of the heavy footsteps is great. It makes me feel as if I'm there.

I feel that the thesis is clear because you tell about Mr. Wilson throughout the paper, but again you need to give more detail. For your introduction, you need to catch the reader's attention more. As the introduction is now, the reader has a difficult time getting involved in the paper. Maybe if you gave a personal experience first, the reader could get more involved. I feel the same way about the conclusion. You need something that stands out, and something that the reader will remember.

Your paragraphing does not seem effective, and you also need better transition between paragraphs. It seems that paragraphs 3 and 4 could be combined because I don't see why you started a new paragraph at the point you started it. Why did you start a new paragraph after paragraph 4? At the end of paragraph 4 you tell about the homework incident, and at the beginning of paragraph 5 you are still talking about the homework incident. You don't need to begin a new paragraph there. These are places where I have trouble with your paragraphing. Either you need to combine some of these paragraphs or make them more detailed. If you keep them separate, you need to use transition.

There are also several places where I have questions about what you have written. In paragraph 2, your sentence, "the teacher must convince . . . their respect" is misleading. Aren't there other ways that the teacher can gain respect other than knowing the material? In paragraph 3, your sentence "This went on for about a week" is misleading. Did he teach for a week without stopping? In paragraph 4, what do you mean by this was fine, or who was it fine for? In paragraph 5, the 3rd sentence, I seem to get lost in the long sentence. You need to make it into 2 sentences. Also in paragraph 3, how did the students know that he knew what he was doing? In paragraph 1, it seems that you could say "what it takes" in a different way. Maybe you could say, few teachers have these qualities.

[name of writer], you need to give more detail and develop your ideas more. Paragraph more effectively and use better transition.

Sincerely,

[name of reviewer]

P.S. You picked a good audience.

When the writer received her review, she produced the following final draft:

## An Effective Teacher

The main purpose of teaching is to have students learn. There are few teachers who have all of the qualities necessary to be an effective teacher and achieve the goal of having students learn. A good, effective teacher is one to whom students can relate, trust in, and respect. Mr. Wilson is an ideal example of an effective teacher.

The bell rang for my 9:30 Physics class to begin. As Mr. Wilson entered, a blanket of silence covered the room. The only noise to be heard was that of his heavy footsteps moving towards his desk. This being the first day, he explained what the course was going to be about and what was expected to be accomplished in the course. With a smile on his face, he asked, "Can we do it people?" We responded positively and had free time the rest of the period to glance over the book.

Mr. Wilson taught only "high" students and served as an example of what college was going to be like by the way he dressed and conducted his classes. He always wore nice slacks and a shirt and tie. This was unusual because most other teachers dressed in a more casual way. He didn't assign any "busy work," he made assignments which helped us learn and understand, not feel as if we were wasting time. He made sure that we understood the material when we came to class the following day by welcoming questions on the assignment, at first, then giving a quiz on that material. This helped us learn, just as his lectures did.

Mr. Wilson's lectures were most interesting and informative. He really impressed us because he rarely referred to his book or notes. He always welcomed questions. If he didn't know the answer; which happened very rarely, he would find out by the next day. Also, he used examples in his lectures that related to our daily lives or added a touch of humor.

One of his major concerns was that of making sure that all of the students had developed a reasonable understanding of the material. If he felt that your grades or progress were below the average considerably or if you didn't feel comfortable with your work, he would stay after school to provide extra help.

> Mr. Wilson realized that his love for physics was not shared by everyone, therefore, he set up experiments and arranged for speakers to come and talk about various science-related topics. He even arranged tours to Oakridge Nuclear Station. Occasionally, he would share his adventures of hiking through the mountains and keeping up his honeybee farm.
>
> Aside from teaching physics, Mr. Wilson served somewhat as the school's electrician. Every time a teacher had a problem with an overhead or filmstrip projector; tape recorder or television, he'd call Mr. Wilson to fix it.
>
> Mr. Wilson was also the sponsor of the photography club. He trained members of the newspaper staff to take and develop their own pictures instead of hiring a photographer. He also learned to operate the computers so that his senior students could at least have the opportunity to gain a general idea of how to work them since a computer course was not offered in the regular curriculum.
>
> Mr. Wilson is an effective teacher because he has earned the respect of the students and other teachers of Gaffney Senior High. He makes his classes interesting and informative and doesn't overemphasize grades. Most importantly he achieves the goal of being an effective teacher, having students learn.

I think this example illustrates that group work can yield impressive results. Obviously, it is an indirect illustration of the benefits of group work, but I would contend that this student reviewer demonstrates critical abilities developed by the group process. I chose this example because in it we see an average writer offering help to another average writer. I could have chosen drafts written by excellent writers. I have such examples, and, as one might expect, the changes from rough draft to final draft are often dramatic. But it is my experience that excellent writers come to our writing classes with the ability to revise. They often do produce remarkable revisions, but one often wonders just what role advice in the reviewing process plays in those revisions.

It is much more important for us to see what kinds of help average writers can give and receive. Here an average writer has offered some very good advice. As an experienced teacher of writing, I could hardly offer better advice than the reviewer's suggestion that the writer develop her ideas more fully and provide the reader with more detail. Of course, one could argue that this advice is applicable in most situations and that the reviewer is simply parroting back what she has heard teachers say many times before. I do not think this is the case, however, because of the specific comments she makes about the writer's paragraphing. It is clear to me that the reviewer intuits a connection between these underdeveloped paragraphs and the overall lack of detail in this paper. In almost every case, her advice concerning weak paragraphing is right on target.

In addition, I am impressed by the questions the reviewer asks the writer. She goes beyond stylistic and mechanical matters to ask the writer just what she intends to say. I too wonder just why one needs to lecture on a topic to get students' respect. I also wonder how the students in this physics class were able to recognize that this teacher knew what he was doing.

These are certainly not earthshattering insights into this paper, but they surely helped the writer make the paper better. I am particularly impressed by the fact that these comments come from a student who began the course writing paragraphs marked by a lack of development and by a tendency toward vague statements like the ones she is questioning in this draft. By the end of this course, she had not completely solved these problems, but she was beginning to develop the critical eye which will help her write better.

One other factor in this student analysis is worth mentioning. The student reviewer was given no critique sheet in the process of producing this analysis. She was simply asked to write a letter showing how the essay could be improved. Her letter demonstrates that she has understood many of the principles introduced by critique sheets earlier.

But the final measure of success is the product at the end of the process, right? While I would not agree with this statement entirely, I do think that we can see important improvements from the rough draft to the final draft of this essay. The reviewer suggested that paragraphs three, four, and five in the rough draft were problematic. In looking back at paragraph three in that draft, we can see that the writer moves from a description of Mr. Wilson's entrance into the classroom to a general statement concerning what he did for the first week. As the reviewer suggests, there is also a problem in the connection between paragraphs three and four. The writer moves from a statement of what Mr. Wilson would do for the first week (at the end of paragraph three) back to the first day's class, in which Mr. Wilson expressed his objectives for the course (at the beginning of paragraph four). In the revised paper, paragraph two is given to a description of Mr. Wilson's behavior on the first day and of his method of stating course objectives and establishing rapport with the students. In the next paragraph, the writer moves to a general discussion of the students that Mr. Wilson taught and of the manner in which he conducted himself.

In general, the paragraphing is much improved in the final draft of this essay. But arc all of the changes in the final draft good? Probably not. There are places where detail in the first draft is omitted in the second; for example, information concerning the way Mr. Wilson dealt with students who had not done their homework disappears. And does the writer remedy all of the problems her reviewer noted? Clearly, she does not. The reviewer suggests, for example, that the introduction is in need of some work; she asks for "something to catch the reader's attention more." One still feels this need after reading the introduction to the final draft.

This example, then, shows that peer review does not always produce perfect revisions. And, as noted early in this essay; there are many other potential problems for the teacher who would use peer critiques in her class. I have certainly not offered solutions to all of these problems here. Such solutions do not exist. But should that cause us to abandon group work?

## *Problems versus Benefits*

Perhaps we can best answer this question by once again looking at the problems teachers fear and balancing them with the potential benefits of peer critiques. The following chart reveals some interesting relationships.

| *Fears* | *Potential Benefits* |
| --- | --- |
| Students may plagiarize. | Students may share ideas. |
| Students may be overly harsh on the work of peers. | Students may develop the ability to see problems in peers' papers and their own. |
| Students may become domineering. | Students may develop leadership abilities. |
| Students may become lax. | Students may enjoy a non-threatening environment in which to write. |
| Students may be intimidated by the excellent work of their peers. | Students may benefit from seeing excellent work by their peers. |
| Students may become dependent upon help from peers. | Students may become more confident writers with help from peers. |

Each of the fears of group work is balanced by a corresponding potential benefit that might arise in the critiquing process. We should not allow such fears to cause us to avoid group work. To do so is to make our goal avoiding failure rather than achieving success.

Any teacher can make sure that nothing goes wrong. If he wants to make sure that there is no plagiarism, he can see to it that there is no sharing of ideas whatsoever and that all writing is done in class. If she wants to ensure that students do not dominate conversations, she can plan the class so that there is no student talk. If he fears that some students may take advantage of editing help from peers, he can strictly forbid students to share what they know with one another.

The teacher who uses peer critiques, on the other hand, cannot be motivated by fear of failure. Group critiques are not for teachers who spend a lot of time worrying about what might go wrong in the writing class: they are open invitations for things to go wrong. Paradoxically, they are also invitations for students to engage in real learning. For learning can take place only in those situations in which teachers and students do not know beforehand exactly what will take place in the classroom. Learning is always spontaneous; we never know exactly how it will happen or what shape it will assume.

From semester to semester, I never know exactly how group critiques will work; I never know what personalities will be in each group. I continue to use groups, however, because they allow me to teach writing as a process and because they allow students to become learners and teachers simultaneously.

The basic premise of group work seems contradictory to students and, I suspect, to many teachers. Students come to us to learn something about writing, but rather than offering them sage advice that will make them better writers, we ask them to become advisors to others who wish to become better writers and to learn from these same learners.

But this seeming contradiction becomes a paradox when we look more closely. All writers need to know how readers will react to what they have written–group work allows student writers to experience these reactions. However; one does not become a writer until she learns to trust her own instincts, to know that ultimately she, and she alone, is responsible for what is on the page. Group work helps the student writer move toward this responsibility; for it provides a reader whose role is to nudge, like an alter ego, rather than to negate, like a dictator.

Ron


This essay first appeared in *Training the New Teacher of College Composition* (Urbana, IL: National Council of Teachers of English, 1986), ed. Charles W. Bridges, with the assistance of Ronald F. Lunsford and Toni a. Lopez. We wish to thank NCTE for granting us permission to reprint it here.

# APPENDIX

## *Critique Sheet for Expository Essay*

1. Is there one single point this paper is trying to make? Write a sentence which captures that point if there is. If there isn't, explain, as best you can, the confusion you feel.

2. Is the overall organization of this paper effective? What is the primary organizing device? Point to any places where the organization breaks down.

3. Does the paper contain information that will be interesting and/or useful to its intended audience? Point out any passages which contain information that might insult the reader's intelligence.

4. Does the introduction give the reader a clear idea of what the paper is about? Does it capture the reader's attention? Does it avoid trite generalizations and stage directions? Does it contain a thesis or center of gravity? Try to think of one other way in which the writer could have begun this paper.

5. Does the conclusion work? Is it basically a summary? Does it suggest a plan of action? Does it do something else? What? Try to offer the writer one other way to conclude the essay.

6. Paragraph checklist:

    a. Give the number of any paragraph that lacks unity or coherence. Explain.

    b. Give the number of any paragraph that lacks development. What is missing?

    c. Give the number of any paragraph that seems to be out of place in the essay. Where should it go? Why?

    d. Give the number of any paragraph that lacks transitions.

7. Word choice checklist:

    a. List any trite or cliched words.

    b. List any words that sound pompous or overly formal.

# Newcomers in First-Year Composition: Teaching Writing to ESL Students

Nancy Pfingstang
University of North Carolina–Charlotte

*The telling has not been easy. One has to convey in a language that is not one's own the spirit that is one's own. One has to convey various shades and omissions of a certain thought-movement that looks maltreated in an alien language. [ . . .] We cannot write like the English*–Indian writer Raja Rao, lamenting the problems of writing in English as a second language. (McCrum, Cran, & MacNeil)

The 1980s began the greatest wave of immigrants to the U.S. since the turn of the century. These newcomers, arriving at a rate of more than 1 million a year, will by 2025 make up nearly a third of the nation's population, with Hispanics and Asians in the lead, and because a college education is still part of the American dream, they are flocking to U.S. academic institutions in record numbers, surpassing, in some states, the native-born student population. New York, New Jersey, Illinois, Mississippi, New Mexico, California, and Texas have already felt the tremendous impact of these new students on their campuses, with Florida expecting newcomers to comprise over half of its college-age population by the year 2010.

In addition to new immigrant students, the numbers of international students enrolling in U.S. colleges and universities has jumped markedly. These students, who are studying under the guidelines of U.S. student visas and who will return to their home countries after graduation, now number almost 500,000, with the largest groups coming from Japan, China, and the Republic of Korea.

## ESL Students in First-Year Composition

As our classes continue to grow more multicultural and linguistically diverse, many first-year writing teachers find ourselves in uncharted waters. To complicate matters further, some of our students who speak English as a second language (ESL) are fluent in three, four, even five languages, while others do not have basic literacy in their parents' language even though it is the language spoken in the home and, technically, the students' first language. Many of these students are admitted to our colleges and universities as "at risk" students because of low scores on the SAT, a test which has been shown to be culturally and linguistically biased against newcomers, although they may have superb academic backgrounds from institutions in their home country. Others, who have had their education interrupted due to political or social turmoil in their countries, may enter with sketchy academic backgrounds. International students on U.S. visas are generally admitted with scores from the Test of English as a Foreign Language (TOEFL), which tests language proficiency but not academic readiness. All of these ESL students, however, will enter our classes with the challenge of learning how to navigate the academy in English.

The research findings from studies that looked at the factors determining academic success for ESL students are daunting. It may take an ESL student 5 to 8 (some researchers say 10) years to acquire the academic language proficiency necessary to compete with students who are native speakers (NS) of English. While students generally enter the academy with a written vocabulary of 10,000 to 100,000 words, ESL students enter with only 2,000 to 7,000 English words. If you add the demands of learning the cultural cues and rules governing class discussions, conferencing, peer work, and teacher expectations, you understand the considerable constraints facing ESL students. Yet the attrition rate of these students is comparable to that of NS students, and among some newcomer groups, it is lower.

## *Influence of Culture and First Language*

Although many of the finer points of contrastive rhetoric are still being debated, researchers do agree on the following:

- Different cultures exhibit different composing conventions.
- These conventions influence the way we write in a second or other language.
- The ability to write in one language does not guarantee the ability to write in others.

With regard to specific discourse patterns of different cultures, researchers are hesitant to make generalizations, yet studies show that the ways we, as writers, present ideas and our expectations when we, as readers, are presented with ideas are heavily influenced by our culture.

Speakers of Asian languages, for example, often choose to be indirect in their writing, suggesting their ideas and the relationships among them rather than stating the ideas directly. It is not uncommon to see a thesis statement weakened with "perhaps" or "maybe" because it is considered rude to present a strong and confident opinion. These writers may also choose to support their ideas with honored traditional knowledge, which carries more weight than expert knowledge.

Speakers of Arabic come from cultures with rich histories of oral discourse, often memorizing as children long passages from the Qur'an or intricate folk tales. As a result, these writers often equate writing with written-down formal speech, focusing on the beauty of the language and the power of analogies and parables. For support of their ideas, they may choose teachings from religious texts or personal experiences.

Writings in Spanish are often described as elaborate. Unlike NS writers of English, especially academic English, Spanish writers tend to develop ideas through generalization and extended digressions of minor but related points, trusting that their readers' intelligence will allow them to follow layered discussions and form their own opinions. Elegant language, especially the well-turned phrase, acknowledges the educational background of the writers, thus giving added support to their credibility.

Each of these rhetorically distinct patterns assumes active participation on the part of the audience by assigning a great deal of responsibility for the comprehension of the text to the readers. English, on the other hand, charges the writer with the task of making the text coherent and credible.

In order to work successfully with our ESL student writers, we need to understand how these contrasting cultural and linguistic conventions influence their writing in English. This does not mean that we need to have extensive knowledge of their languages and cultures, only that we need to be aware of and sensitive to the ways our students conceptualize and represent discourse concerns, such as voice, audience, topic, and rhetorical logic in their writing.

## *Discourse Concerns of ESL Writers*

Developing an authentic voice in English is very difficult for ESL students. Because voice is interwoven with our sense of self, which is initially defined through our first language, the act of representing that identity in another language often requires language manipulation beyond our students' abilities. Many are distressed when they find that their voices–their identities–are distorted, even destroyed, when filtered through the rhetorical conventions of English discourse. As one of my Japanese students resignedly observed, "Since writing often reflects the writer's personality, I must kill my personality in order to write in American culture, or I need to find a compromise which works in both cultures." This feeling of surrendering identity when writing in English is a well-documented concern of many ESL writers.

In addition to preserving their identities, ESL students may also struggle to preserve their privacy. A number of ESL students come from cultures that not only respect but may even demand very little personal disclosure. Because these students have no experience with introspective writing in their own cultures, they are at a loss as to ways to satisfy an assignment which asks them to take a personal position on a particular issue or belief, especially one that is in conflict with the teachings of their home culture. Thus, the self-discovery essay that NS students enjoy writing because it allows them an opportunity to express their opinions becomes an uncomfortable experience for some ESL students.

Understanding the needs of the U. S. audience is yet another challenge for ESL writers. Those of us who teach writing often assign "the other students in the class" or "the general public" as the audience our students must consider, yet ESL students are at a disadvantage when trying to assess the needs and expectations of these readers who are foreign to them. Unable to see from the eyes of the assigned readers, ESL writers often fail at establishing the loop of shared information so critical to the successful exchange of meaning in writing. Instead, these writers fall back on choosing themselves or others from their home culture as their audience, thereby avoiding the problem of writing to the unknown.

For many writing teachers, the most striking feature of an ESL composition is the organization within the text. Sometimes we are confused as to how the writer got from point A to point B or why the student introduced a seemingly unrelated topic in the middle of the paper. Rhetorical logic, researchers tell us, is socially constructed; this means that our English system of organizing information is just that–*our system*. Much has been written on the discourse patterns of other languages and the ways that ESL writers transfer those patterns to other writing situations. For example, our ESL students may not share our assumptions regarding what constitutes proof of an assertion. While we value authority and statistics, writers from other cultures may value personal experience or teachings from religious texts. At a contrastive rhetoric conference in Egypt recently, I heard a respected language scholar, a native speaker of Arabic, argue eloquently and convincingly that the best way to learn to write in English is to read English, giving his own experiences as the only support for his claim. Had the scholar been a native speaker of English, I probably would have heard the argument developed in a different manner, one supported with studies and data.

## *Teaching ESL Writers*

Although there are many important similarities between the composing processes of NS writers and ESL writers, the differences are significant enough that we can no longer depend on first language writing theory and pedagogy as our sole guide in teaching our ESL students. The two *caveats* that writing teachers hear most concerning the needs of ESL student writers have to do with *more* and *less*, with *less* being the reason for *more*.

Overall, the composing processes of ESL writers are less effective than those of NS writers. When writing in English, ESL students engage in less planning and goal setting, use time less successfully, reread and review their texts less often, write less, and revise less. On essay exams, ESL writers are less able to comprehend the exam questions, less aware of the appropriate forms for the answer, and less able to paraphrase important ideas. In their research papers, they are less effective in working from sources and avoiding plagiarism. Their sentences contain fewer subordinating clauses, modifiers, articles, prepositions, prepositional phrases, and passive structures, and their vocabulary is less sophisticated and varied, with less clear terms and fewer synonyms.

The second *caveat* is that ESL students may need "more of everything"–more attention to each concept taught in the writing class, more time to complete assignments, and more exposure to U.S. audiences and rhetorical conventions through extensive reading. They often require more help in generating ideas, text structuring, revision strategies, and vocabulary development. In the classroom, they need guidance in group work and peer editing. Finally, ESL writers benefit from more one-on-one conferencing with both their teachers and tutors in writing centers.

It is not surprising that first-year composition teachers feel discouraged, even defeated, after learning that ESL writing students need more of everything from us. Already stretched to our limits with large classes and often little administrative support, we rightly question how the extra time and attention will materialize in our teaching day. Fortunately, ESL writing researchers have also identified instructional strategies which appear to be most effective with these writers and which can be incorporated into our existing teaching repertoire.

## Modeling

ESL writers benefit from observing their teachers model good writing behaviors. Writing teachers who model such composing strategies as prewriting, planning, or identifying the needs of an audience pass on to their ESL students important cultural information about the rhetorical conventions of English. Called *think-alouds* in ESL pedagogy, modeling is particularly effective in showing both the rhetorical logic of writing in English and its recursive nature–the hesitant starts, exploratory side steps, and tentative stops which propel us back to more hesitant starts.

In modeling, the composition teacher "thinks out loud" in order to demonstrate to students the strategies of a skilled writer. Researchers have found that ESL students are better able to appreciate the complexity of the writing task when they observe the teacher puzzle out important parts of assignments, give attention to directives, form hypotheses about how best to respond, make choices about language, organize and support information, rough out drafts, and, finally, write and edit finished documents.

The following assignment, taken from a first-year composition class, illustrates the problems that ESL writers experience when given a complex writing prompt.

> Write a paper that analyzes a current problem in American society. In this paper, your audience includes members of the general public who are very concerned about this problem. You will need to define the problem carefully, describe its causes, and explore its consequences. You will also need to present and evaluate at least one solution recommended by social scientists (or other experts) who have studied the problem. Include information from at least five published sources to support the focus of your paper and the major points that you choose to include.

Because English is their second language, our ESL writers, for the most part, have *learned* English rather than *acquired* English. This means that they do not have native intuitiveness regarding its structures but, rather, have had to learn them through formal study. For a second-language learner, this prompt is structurally complex, conveying its most important information through five relative clauses, two uses of the modal "will," and one passive structure, made more complicated by being part of a reduced relative clause. Furthermore, the prompt contains six directives: analyze, define, describe, explore, present, and evaluate. If we then add the necessity of understanding the U.S. American public as audience, the ability to include and document information from published sources, and the knowledge of how to organize and support a thesis, we can begin to appreciate the formidable task facing our ESL writers.

By saying aloud what goes on in our heads when we read a writing prompt, we allow our ESL students to listen and watch as we note that the audience for the prompt above is not the general public at large but, rather, only those members who are concerned and that the tasks of defining, describing, and exploring refer to the problem, while presenting and evaluating refer to the solution. As we think through the demands of the assignment, we have opportunities to show ways that we might satisfy these tasks, trying out different approaches, forms of organization, and methods of support in order to determine which would be most effective.

After the students have had opportunities to observe us and discuss the think-alouds with us, we need to give them repeated opportunities to practice responding to writing prompts on their own, first by asking them to respond to guided assignments–shorter, more manageable prompts–and finally to apply their new strategies to longer, more complex assignments.

## Conferences

One-on-one conferences are particularly valuable to ESL writers because they provide opportunities for students to learn the needs of the U.S. academic audience–their teachers–and they allow teachers opportunities to learn the writing backgrounds of their students. Conferences, however, can be culturally-loaded encounters. The cues to begin and end, the various ways to navigate and negotiate, and the paralinguistic behaviors, such as body language and eye contact, are all culturally determined. For many ESL students, entering into the very specific culture of the U.S. academic conference is an intimidating experience.

Students from Asian countries may be reluctant to make eye contact or directly request help, while students from Latin America or the Middle East may feel they are required to begin the conference with polite small talk, asking about our health, families, or vacation plans, topics which we feel waste our time or even invade our privacy. During the conference, teachers and students frequently find themselves dancing through a minefield of possible misunderstanding. One ESL student may confuse us by nodding her head to indicate that she hears us, not that she understands or agrees with us, while another may make us feel uncomfortable by sitting very close and staring intently at us to show that he is paying attention.

Since ESL students may not know how to prepare for a conference, it is helpful to tell them in advance what to expect, saying for example, "We're going to talk about your revision tomorrow and work on a plan to support your main idea more." Then give the students a set of questions about the paper, perhaps the ones used in class for peer groups, to answer before the conference. During the conference, ESL students have a better chance of grasping what they need to consider in a piece of writing if we give them explicit explanations. For example, telling an ESL writer that a passage is incoherent assumes she has native-like intuition of what a coherent passage is. This writer would benefit more from knowing precisely what it is that confuses an English-speaking reader, why it is confusing, and what the reader would require to make the passage more comprehensible. At the end of the conference, the student should have clearly specified writing tasks to work on in the revision, such as using examples to support an idea. It is in the conference, working directly with our ESL writers on their papers, that we can best help them develop successful writing strategies.

## Responding to ESL Writing

The teacher's process of responding works in tandem with the student's process of writing. As student writers go through the stages of idea generation, writing, and revision, writing teachers serve as guides at each stage, giving suggestions, directions, and, in some cases, red alerts. Much has been written about this tandem process for NS writers, but it has only been recently that researchers have begun looking at the most effective ways to respond to ESL writers.

Writing teachers frequently feel overwhelmed when first confronted by an ESL writer's initial draft, not knowing whether to address rhetorical or grammatical concerns first. This indecision is often made worse by ESL students' common belief that if we correct their grammar, their writing will improve. Second language studies, however, indicate that this practice is as fruitless with ESL writers as it is with NS writers. Although we may need, at some point in the process, to give instruction in sentence-level concerns, our responses are most effective when we attend to our ESL students' rhetorical needs first.

As in conferences, ESL student writers benefit more when our responses are explicit and specific. Many of our ESL students have never formally studied writing in their native languages; therefore, their repertoire of revision strategies may be quite limited. Advising students to give additional information or examples to support and clarify a point is more effective than asking, "Can you support this more?" However, demonstrating for our students the strategies that good writers use when they question, rethink, try on different perspectives, and take risks is most effective of all. ESL writing teachers frequently recommend that their students keep learning logs, a type of metacognition journal, to note the different strategies they have tried and their effectiveness. This allows the writing students to build a repertoire of strategies while developing a vocabulary with which to discuss their writing process.

## Using Portfolios to Assess ESL Writing

At many schools, writing teachers debate whether ESL writers should be evaluated differently from NS writers or whether all students should be measured against a single standard. There are compelling arguments for both views. Those who believe in one standard hold that a different standard means a lowered standard, a substandard, while those who believe in separate standards argue that most second language (L2) writers will always write with an accent–sometimes labeled interference–from their native language and should not be evaluated negatively for this quality. In fact, with the explosive growth of World Englishes around the globe, even a U.S. American speaker of English is thought to have an accent these days. Mindful of this debate, ESL writing teachers often choose to take the best from both perspectives by requiring writing portfolios, which allow them to assess both a student's individual development through the writing process and her finished product as measured by a class or department rubric.

Rather than just a collection of finished papers in a folder, a writing portfolio is a collection of student work which allows the writing teacher the opportunity to see the full range of what an individual student is capable of producing. These writings (e.g., journal entries, in-class drafts, essays, and research papers) along with revisions, if appropriate, convey not only a student's growth as a writer but also her mastery of what has been studied. More importantly, however, portfolios benefit ESL writers by encouraging sustained effort.

As noted above, ESL writers frequently work under the constraints of *more* and *less*–needing more time and attention, while being less able to understand assignments, plan, write for an academic audience, or revise. Portfolio assessment, with its emphasis on interaction between teacher and student, on revision, and on student reflection, provides the needed time and attention. Moreover, because portfolio assessment encourages students to engage in dialogue about their writing and their writing process with their teachers, writing center tutors, and peer groups, there are many built-in opportunities for ESL writers to continue to develop as writers of English.

## *Learning from Newcomers*

Newcomers are valuable resources on our campuses because they bring important cultural diversity to the classrooms. But beyond teaching us about their rich traditions and beliefs, newcomers encourage our NS students to examine their own culture and to rethink what it means to be part of it yet belong to the global village as well. No longer can we be satisfied with the tourist view of culture, content to focus primarily on foods, major festivals, and monuments. The writing class today is able to study and write about issues of gender, age, race, religious and political beliefs, and sexual orientation through different cultural perspectives, thereby encouraging students to listen to and learn to respect the views of others.

## Bibliography

Althen, G. (1994). Cultural differences on campus. In G. Althen (Ed.), *Learning across cultures* (pp. 57-71). New York: NAFSA.

Conrad, S., & Goldstein, L. (1999). ESL student revision after teacher-written comments: Text, contexts, and individuals. *Journal of Second Language Writing*, 8, 147-180.

Davis, T. (1999). *Open doors: What the new numbers mean.* New York: NAFSA.

Elllis, P., & Stebbins, C. (1996). Providing access to linguistically diverse students. *Community College Review*, 24, 3-20.

Grabe, W., & Kaplan, R. (1989). Writing in a second language: Contrastive rhetoric. In D. Johnson & D. Roen (Eds.), *Richness in writing* (pp. 263-283). New York: Longman.

Hamp-Lyons, L. (1993). *Assessing second language writing in academic contexts.* Norwood, N.J.: Ablex.

Harklau, L. (1998). Newcomers in U.S. higher education: Questions of access and equity. *Educational Policy,* 12, 634-659.

Harris, M., & Silva, T. (1993). Tutoring ESL students: Issues and options. *College Composition and Communication*, 44, 525-537.

Leeds, B. (1996). *Writing in a second language.* London: Longman.

Leki, I. (1992). *Understanding ESL writers.* Portsmouth, N.H.: Boynton/Cook.

Leki, I., & Carson, J. (1994). Students' perceptions of EAP writing instruction and writing needs across the disciplines. *TESOL Quarterly*, 28, 81-101.

Matsuda, P. (1999). Composition studies and ESL writing: A disciplinary division of labor. *College Composition and Communication*, 50, 699-721.

Matsuda, P. (1998). Situating ESL writing in a cross-disciplinary context. *Written Communication*, 15, 99-122.

McCrum, R., Cran, W., & MacNeil, R. (1986). The New Englishes. *The story of English* (pp. 307-341). New York: Viking.

Paulus, T. (1999). The effect of peer and teacher feedback on student writing. *Journal of Second Language Writing*, 8, 265-289.

Reid, J. (1993). *Teaching ESL writing.* Englewood Cliffs, N.J.: Regents/Prentice Hall.

Santos, T. (1988). Professors' reactions to the academic writing of nonnative-speaking students. *TESOL Quarterly*, 22, 69-90.

Silva, T. (1993). Toward an understanding of the distinct nature of L2 writing: The ESL research and its implications. *TESOL Quarterly*, 27, 657-677.

Vandrick, S., & Messerschmitt, D. (1996). ESL in the academy today. *Education,* 116, 403-410.

Ward, M. (1998). Myths about college English as a second language. *Education Digest,* 63, 65-68.

Zamel, V. (1995). Strangers in academia: The experiences of faculty and ESL students across the curriculum. *College Composition and Communication*, 46, 506-521.